Teaching and Evaluating Writing in the Age of Computers and High-Stakes Testing

Teaching and Evaluating Writing in the Age of Computers and High-Stakes Testing

Carl Whithaus
Old Dominion University

LEA LAWRENCE ERLBAUM ASSOCIATES, PUBLISHERS
2005   Mahwah, New Jersey   London

Lawrence Erlbaum Associates, Inc., Publishers
10 Industrial Avenue
Mahwah, New Jersey 07430
www.erlbaum.com

Cover design by Kathryn Houghtaling Lacey

Library of Congress Cataloging-in-Publication Data

Teaching and Evaluating Writing in the Age of Computer and High-Stakes Testing,
by Carl Whithaus.

ISBN 0-8058-4799-5 (cloth : alk. paper).
ISBN 0-8058-4800-2 (pbk.: alk paper).

Includes bibliographical references and index.

Copyright information for this volume can be obtained by contacting the Library of Congress.

Books published by Lawrence Erlbaum Associates are printed on acid-free paper,
and their bindings are chosen for strength and durability.

Printed in the United States of America
10 9 8 7 6 5 4 3 2 1

Contents

Illustrations

Preface

In what may be a rather strange move for an academic book, I have tried to put *Teaching and Evaluating Writing in the Age of Computers and High-Stakes Testing* together with a sense of play and a sense of intense academic inquiry. Although you are holding a printed book in your hands,[1] the text reflects the techniques of collage, sampling, and visual design that are so important in many of the multimedia student projects I have had the privilege to read and to evaluate.[2]

OVERVIEW

The Introduction locates this study in relation to the works of Paulo Freire (1970), Jacques Lacan (1978), Marjorie Goodwin (1975, 1990), and Eva Baker (1998). It shows how these ideas connect with samples of student "multimedia" compositions, and ends with a discussion of the interdisciplinary Work and Professional Studies Electronic Portfolio Project at Old Dominion University. Chapter 1 takes a broader sweep by looking at reports from the College Board, Educational Testing Service, the New London Group, and the Bertelsman and AOL Time Warner Foundations on educational policies, writing assessment, and information

---

[1]I realize that a good number of you may be reading this through Net.Library, and hence may not be holding a printed book in your hand at all. Well, so be it.

[2]In ways that are hard to acknowledge explicitly throughout the text, David Shapiro's art criticism (1984) and his poetry, particularly *After a Lost Original* (1994), and Dave Egger's (2000) *A Heartbreaking Work of Staggering Genius* and *McSweeney's* have had an influence.

technologies. Chapter 1 also maps out developments in Automatic Essay Scoring (AES) and electronic portfolios.

Chapters 2 and 3 turn to the work of Gregory Ulmer (2003, 1989, 1985), Geoff Sirc (2002, 2000, 1998, 1997, 1995, 1993), Jeff Rice (2003), Ernest Morrell, and J. Duncan-Andrade (2002) in order to explore the emergence of new genres in print-based as well as screen-based composing. I am particularly concerned with considering how genres and pedagogies influenced by hip-hop, gangsta, and punk do and do not work in today's schools. Understanding these compositions requires considering the *situation* in which the works were created; however, situated assessment does not simply open up the possibility of creating student-pleasing avante garde composing techniques. Chapter 3's discussion of situated assessment shows how a teacher might fairly grade three very different projects created in response to a single assignment: a letter to the vice president for Action at NOW, a Web site intended to inform the public about selective serotonin reuptake inhibitors (SSRIs) and addiction, and e-mails to doctors and medical researchers to express concerns about the increasing numbers of prescriptions of antidepressants.

Chapters 4 and 5 report on my experiences teaching at an engineering college, Stevens Institute of Technology, in New Jersey. Chapter 4 extends the concept of learning contracts (Shor, 1996) into a dialogic format for negotiating assessment criteria. This process reveals the ways in which students bring expectations about the types of writing valued by English teachers into class with them. Their expectations suggest that standardized exams have a marked influence on the qualities first-year composition students associate with good writing. Chapter 5 asks how a teacher's experience as a reader and a student's experience as a writer change when an essay is presented in html format and the feedback process takes place through Instant Messenger (IM) or another synchronous discussion space (e.g., Blackboard's Virtual Classroom) rather than pen-and-paper commentary. Drawing on the works of Freire, Shor, and hooks, the concept of dialogue as risk is contrasted with traditional school dialogue for control. I argue that students develop into effective communicators when they have something to say and someone to say it to.

Chapter 6 pushes forward the idea of distributive evaluation—having multiple readers provide feedback on student compositions. Grounded within classical hypertext pedagogical theories (Joyce, 1988; Landow, 1989, 1992; Lanham, 1989, 1993; Moulthrop & Kaplan, 1994), this chapter traces the ways in which descriptive student responses to two Web site projects facilitate student understanding of multiple audiences. By looking at writing instruction at the City University of New York (CUNY), chapter 7 returns to the battleground of high-stakes testing and its impact on writing instruction. It explores the difficulties of teaching in a system that insists on using print-based tests as entrance and graduation requirements while at the same time trying to develop students' literacy skills with new media composing.

Drawing on Deborah Brandt's (1995) concept of "piling up" literacies, chapter 8 asks how the treatment of information and communication technologies (ICT) as tools for correction and media for communication could be synthesized. By looking at blogs (web logs) and automatic essay scoring (AES) software, the argument is made that the either/or formula often imposed on thinking about ICT and writing instruction is a mistake. Software will correct student writing on the sentence-level, and it will provide feedback in generalized ways to text-based compositions, but those forms of correction and feedback do not represent the scope of communication skills needed to succeed in computer-mediated communication environments. In addition to using software agents to provide feedback, students must be taught how to use these tools rather than being used by the tools. But beyond that move, both teaching and assessment techniques must be developed that acknowledge ICT as media. Sketching the impact of blogs and AES software suggests the distance that must be transversed by groups that want to use computer technology as a tool for correction and those that want to use computer technology to build communication opportunities for students.

Chapter 9 closes the book by examining three compositions: a print-based essay, a revision of that print-based essay into html format, and an essay composed for reading through a web-browser. I discuss student learning in each case, and I argue that by working on multimodal and multimedia compositions from the beginning of the writing process students will learn more about the challenges of using 21st-century literacies. Mutlimodal and multimedia projects encourage students to use software as both a tool and a medium; further, these projects have students creating the types of communications they will need to employ in the future. Writing skills used to be tested by using multiple-choice tests. The release of the SAT W-component demonstrates a movement forward by using actual writing samples to measure students' writing abilities. The next step is to acknowledge that writing is only one mode of communication, one form of composing that students must master to be successful. Because writing is being tested by having students actually write, students' skills in multimodal and multimedia forms of discourse should also be assessed by having them produce those types of communication.

Throughout the book, I advocate for the incorporation of distributive, interactive, descriptive, and situated assessment techniques. These concepts do not emerge only from within *Teaching and Evaluating Writing in the Age of Computers and High-Stakes Testing*, but also assimilate pedagogical strategies and evaluative techniques developed by teacher-researchers working on critical pedagogy, AES, and electronic portfolios. This project makes explicit the connections among writing instruction, writing assessment, and information technologies through classroom narratives and systemic analyses. Further, it invites readers to see classroom experiences as important areas for creating—and reshaping—assessment tools to better reflect the interactive methods of communication used by today's students.

ACKNOWLEDGMENTS

A book is never written alone. George Otte, Ira Shor, David Greetham, Leo Parascondola, Mark McBeth, Tim McCormack, and Wendy Ryden read and commented on early versions of chapters 4, 5, 6, and 7. In the process of composing this book, I have benefited from conversations with Sondra Perl, Deborah Sinnreich-Levi, Sophie Hales, Margaret Tabb, Janice Peritz, Stuart Cochran, Ian Marshall, and Beth Counihan. In addition to having many good conversations with David Metzger, I found the issue of *Pre/Text* that he guest edited particularly useful for my thinking about Lacan and pedagogy. Joyce Neff's dedication to teaching and writing research has helped me make this work far stronger than it would have been if she were not a colleague and a collaborator on other research projects. Dawn Hayden read an entire earlier draft of this book; I greatly appreciate her feedback. Much of my thinking about computers and writing has been influenced by conversations and e-mails with Grant Jenkins, Rice Rich, and Anthony Atkins. Although he may not agree with all of my conclusions in chapter 2, Jeff Rice kindly read and responded to that material; the final version is far better because of his comments. I also need to thank the external reviewers commissioned by Lawrence Erlbaum Associates: Bertram Bruce of the University of Illinois at Urbana-Champaign, Bill Condon of Washington State University, Alister Cummins of the University of Toronto, Jim Cumming of the University of Toronto, and Steven D. Krause of Eastern Michigan University. In addition, I need to thank the many students at CUNY, Stevens Institute of Technology, and Old Dominion University who have shared their thoughts and compositions with me over the last 10 years.

At Old Dominion University, the Work and Professional Studies eportfolio team has suffered through all sorts of technical and programmatic issues with me; they have always brought good cheer and a willingness to work on mundane practical issues as well as larger theoretical concerns. I owe all of them a great "thank you": Mary Beth Lakin, Michele Spires, Lou Lombardo, Virginia Tucker, Nabil Akdouche, and Hari Siripuram. Within the administration, Charles E. Wilson Jr., Janet Katz, and Chandra DeSilva have been constant in their support of my interdisciplinary teaching and research projects; in addition, their support for the study of writing and information technologies has been unwavering. Knowledge is sometimes produced directly, and sometimes it takes a round about way into existence; studying with Ephraim Schwartz has had strange and subtle echoes in the composition of this book.

As a book editor, Naomi Silverman has helped me shape this project in many ways; her friendship and her dedication to publishing works that challenge the status quo continue to amaze me. Acknowledgments are never complete without the bow toward one's family. If at times my parents may have wondered about my obsessions with reading, writing, and computers, their support has never wavered. I am lucky to have learned from them that the building of boats as well as books is a task without end. Thanks. I know it is also customary to thank one's spouse and children for giving one the space to finish a scholarly work. However, I need to thank Shannah, Lillian, and Hannah for *not* giving me space, but rather for making sure that their lives were twined around this book in more ways than I can recall. Shannah has created a home where books and ideas, reading, and studying always have a place. Lillian and Hannah have colored on discarded drafts and listened to me think out loud. All together they have made my life happier than I ever imagined it could be.

Introduction

The emergence of information technologies is changing how students write. E-mail, Instant Messenger (IM), chat room dialogues, and Web sites with graphics and sounds are all compositions that a literate citizen will need to compose as well as read in the 21st century. Today's writing assessment systems evaluate print-based writing, not the multimodal compositions students already produce in their classrooms and in their lives. This book asks two apparently contradictory questions:

1. What can the developers of assessment systems learn from the multimodal, and often multimedia, compositions students and teachers are already producing?
2. What can writing teachers and program administrators learn from recent advances made in automatic essay scoring (AES) and electronic portfolio systems?

The answer to these different questions moves, surprisingly, toward a synthesized response: If it is acknowledged that writing is becoming a more complex, multimodal task—really, if textual and linguistic writing is changing into opportunities for multimedia composing—then the inadequacies of large-scale assessment systems and methods of teaching writing must be confronted. The synthesized answer to these troubling questions—to the changed environments for composing—lies not with the development of one-size-fits-all testing regimes and teaching methods, but with a careful and detailed examination of student compositions as *situated* communication activities.

The development of teaching and assessment techniques that honor the situated variables of student compositions, however, does not equate with a rejection of high academic standards or with the rejection of all forms of standardized writing assessment. Rather, acknowledging that student compositions, the teaching of writing, and the assessment of writing are situated activities calls for an increased integration of software tools (e.g., grammar checkers and AES feedback agents) into the techniques for teaching composition. Timed, standardized writing exams, such as the W-component of the new SAT and many statewide proficiency tests, do have a place in the teaching of writing. But, if they are treated as the only goal, then the higher order thinking skills and the risk taking associated with bold, powerful compositions will not develop. This book is about how to acknowledge the importance of high-stakes writing exams, how to teach students to pass the narrowly focused writing components on those exams, and how to advocate for changes in large-scale assessment systems so that these systems better reflect both traditionally defined writing competencies as well as the higher order, multimodal skills students employ when they have multiple windows open on their computers and they are exchanging IMs, surfing the web, writing e-mails, and using Illustrator to create a graphic for a Web site due tomorrow in English class.

In the last 10 years, I have seen many teachers react in despair to the implementation of statewide testing regimes. However, teaching with technology provides one way around, or perhaps through, the roadblocks to good writing instruction created by standards-based testing. When talking with other writing teachers about high-stakes tests, I argue that we should have neither a blind faith in testing nor a knee-jerk reaction against testing. Rather, we should proceed to have careful and detailed discussions with people in power (i.e., school board members, principals, and state legislators) about the relations between testing and teaching. We need to know the work of assessment experts and computational linguists. We also need to grapple with how to teach effectively in an educational environment where high stakes writing tests are a reality *and* where students need to learn computer-mediated communication skills.

Measurement and assessment experts such as Eva Baker and Carl Bereiter acknowledged the difficulties test designers face when accounting for students' abilities as communicators in new media. In her discussion of K–12 testing, Baker (1998) noted that current systems and theories of assessment do "not meet our expectations for guiding practice and improving learning" (p. 15). She made it clear that her complaints about testing do not emerge from the usual ideological positions that resist "the capital letters TESTING INDUSTRY" (p. 15).[1] Baker argued

---

[1]Baker (1998) argues that her

thesis, that there is something wrong with our system of K–12 testing, does not flow from the same impulse as many such analyses. It is not developed as a critique of the factory model of education, the one that sees children as outputs and that is a vestige of the industrial age. It does not attack tests and their results as reductionist oddities. It does not compete with the findings of tests developed by the capital letters TESTING INDUSTRY against a sometimes more romantic view of the wisdom and accuracy of classroom teachers' judgments of their students' that current methods of assessment are failing to meet the needs of students, teachers, communities, and policymakers because they center on measurements of discrete skills. System validity and multipurpose testing are "heretical" ideas for the assessment community (p. 16). Research (Blythe, 2001; Bolter, 1991; Bromley & Apple, 1998; Cooper & Selfe, 1990; Hawisher & Selfe, 1999; Mayo, 2001; Salvo, 2001; Sirc, 1995; Winkelmann, 1995) in computer-mediated composition suggests that students draw on a variety of communication skills and interact with other writers and audience members in multifaceted ways. For the evaluations—either classroom-based or large-scale—of computer-mediated compositions to be valid and authentic, then, the assessment tools must take effective communication as their benchmark instead of discrete skill-based standards.

But what is effective communication? How can it be defined? And what does it look like in classroom settings where students write compositions using new media tools? This chapter sketches a quick definition of effective communication, and the rest of the book is dedicated to exploring this definition in relation to multimodal and multimedia works students are already producing. Effective communication is not simply the transfer of bits of information from one person or container to another. Rather, these bits transform, blend, and bleed over into the containers that are "carrying" them. Written from the perspectives of education, psychoanalysis, and anthropology, the works of Paulo Freire (1970), Jacques Lacan (1981), and Marjorie Goodwin (1990) are critiques of any simple container/contained notion of transference in communication and learning. Freire's view that "education is suffering from narration sickness" speaks directly to the ways in which words when treated as part of a system of transferring information "are emptied of their concreteness and become a hallow, alienated, and alienating verbosity" (p. 52). When assessment is used to measure a student's learning about writing in terms of the transference of an already known chuck of information from teacher to student and then student to exam paper, the words are emptied of their meaning. The opportunity to use assessment as a means of measuring how a student is creating new knowledge about composing and about language is missed.

To define effective communication, and to think about how it might be measured, the discussion draws on the works of Freire, Lacan, and Goodwin. Building on a critique of education as simple transference, Ellie Ragland (1994) claimed that "a Lacanian pedagogy would seek to avoid identifying with either myth or story—that is, seek to avoid identification with a body of knowledge taken as content. But the explicitly Lacanian part comes into play in the use of analytic strategies, in how the teacher deals with questions asked, with doubts, and with the reaction of the student *qua* other" (p. 68). Applied to the teaching of writing and composition, the works of Freire and Lacan argue that the most important ques-

---

performance. Last, it will not deny that policymakers have the right and responsibility to demand testing programs that shed light on school progress and real policy options, and that such programs be developed on a schedule shorter than the Pleistocene era. (p. 15)

tions are not about the teacher and teaching but rather about learning. How do students learn? How do people learn to compose? How do they learn to compose texts? How do they learn to compose themselves? For that matter, how do they learn to compose multimedia works that analyze the world?

Freire and Lacan urged asking questions not necessarily about media or about whether it is "better" for students to learn to compose in traditional print documents first and then compose in electronic media. Rather, the complexities suggested by Freire's and Lacan's work take on the possibilities of transferring knowledge from one person to another, from one medium to another, and urge asking complicated questions about the processes of schooling and the goals of students being able to write "better." In other words, the question should not be: Is the knowledge of composing in electronic environments transferable to print-based writing situations? Instead, the questions should be: What is the point of teaching writing or composing skills? What knowledge or skills do educators aim to produce? What ideas do they want students to come into contact with in language arts, English, and composition courses? And why do they want them to engage with these ideas?

In *He-Said-She-Said*, Goodwin (1990) demonstrated the importance of participation frameworks for creating an interpretative framework for a speech act. She showed how children living in southwest Philadelphia both respond to and build their social world through complex communicative actions. Their talk is structured in such a way that it "creates *participation frameworks*: an entire field of action including both interrelated occasion-specific identities and forms of talk; a speaker may transform the social order of the moment by invoking a different speech activity" (p. 286, Goodwin's emphasis). According to Goodwin, a child's speech does not only respond to the world but constitutes that world through specific speech acts that draw forth reactions from others. For instance, "by switching from a contest of verbal contention to a story, a participant may dramatically reshape a dyadic form of interaction into a multiparty one; this may permit an opponent to recruit others to visibly confirm his/her position" (p. 286). In this case, the child's communicative activities are situated in an immediate verbal context, a dyadic verbal contention—a "he-said–she-said" argument. By changing the form of discourse from an argument to a story, the child signals that other children can participate in the exchange, and this action changes not only the discourse, but the social setting by inviting other children to participate. Given Freire's, Lacan's, and Goodwin's work, effective communication is a dialogic process situated within a social context.

How can effective communication be judged and evaluated? It is a far more difficult task than the already difficult and challenging task of assessment in print-based writing. Goodwin's concept of participatory frameworks provides a means of thinking about how to develop writing assessment systems that acknowledge and account for composing as a dialogic activity situated within a social context and distributed among multiple "reading" agents.

While the testing community needs to adapt their instruments to include so-cially situated variables in the assessment of computer-mediated compositions, writing teachers and researchers need to move away from the theoretical and hu-manist rejection of technology that has dominated responses from Ken Macrorie's (1970) and Patrick Finn's (1977) attacks on Ellis Page's (Page & Paulus, 1968) *The Analysis of Essay by Computer* through Anne Herrington and Charles Moran's (2001) and Tim McGee and Patti Ericsson's (2002) latest critiques of computer-graded essays. Software, such as Microsoft Word, is already reading and responding to students' writing (Whithaus, 2002), and as Cizok and B. A. Page (2003) noted "automated scoring of extended responses to test items is a *fait accompli*" (p. 125) for test developers and computational linguists. Software will read, respond to, and assess our students' writing, but it will not replace human readers in evaluative systems where compositions are acknowledged to be com-plex, multimodal, and interactive. The development of these systems requires a dialogue between those interested in the computer as a tool for the testing and quick processing of many essays (i.e., as a tool for large-scale assessments and easing the burden of grading essays), and the computer as a medium through which individuals interact in ever new and changing modes of discourse.

IT IS CHANGING HOW STUDENTS WRITE

The idea that emerging information technologies are changing the way students write can be seen in the following three examples.

In a first-year writing course, a group of students write separate essays about women in Asian society (Fig. I.1). They then return to those papers and repurpose them for a Web site. In the process of editing down the size of the documents, they add a navigational system, graphics, and some sound files to the project.

Another group of four students in a college-level Introduction to Scientific and Technical Writing course research the Small Aircraft Transportation Sys-tem (SATS) being developed at NASA. They write a 32-page research report, but they also compose a PowerPoint presentation and a digital video about the project (Fig. I.2).

Also, a high school student writes a letter to his congressperson asking that copyright laws be changed and objecting to the shutting down of Napster. This letter is one of the end products of a series of writing projects about music that in-cluded a Web site review of an album by Nine Inch Nails, a series of exchanges in an Internet chat room and on a discussion board about intellectual property, and the leading of a class discussion about Napster (Fig. I.3). Before leading the class discussion, the student wrote a meeting agenda, which he handed out to the class.[2]

---

[2]The screen shots of the discussion board and the review are recreated samples; to keep the stu-dent's pseudonym in place, they are not direct reproductions of the student's work.

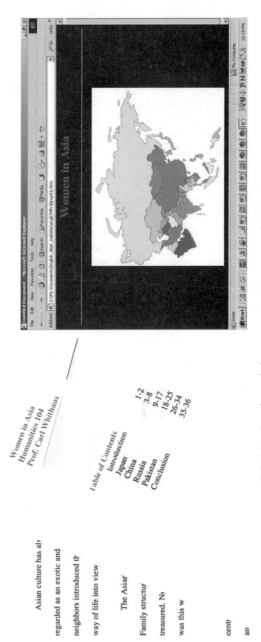

FIG. I.1. Sample work for women in Asia paper and Web site.

Women in Asia
Humanities 104
Prof. Carl Whithaus

Asian culture has al...

regarded as an exotic and

neighbors introduced th

way of life into view

The Asiar

Family structur

treasured. N¡

was this w

cent

an

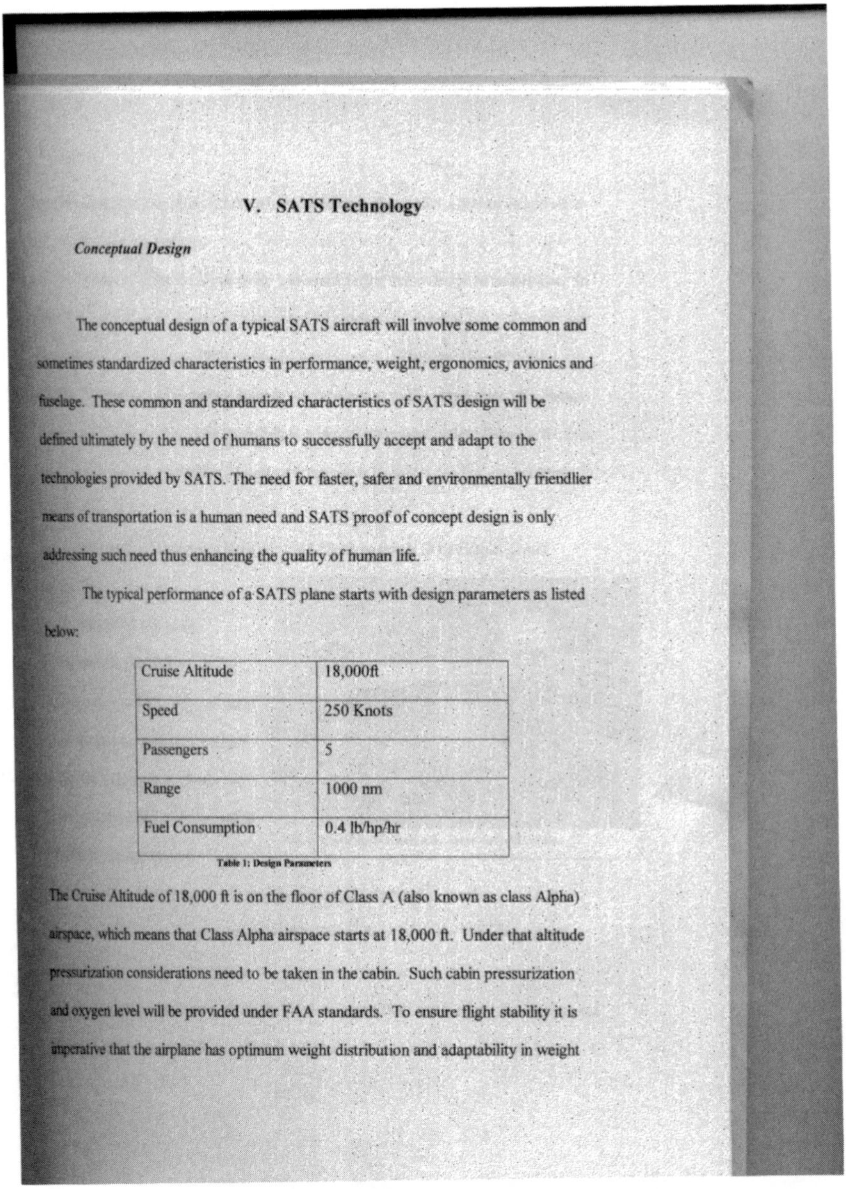

V. SATS Technology

Conceptual Design

The conceptual design of a typical SATS aircraft will involve some common and sometimes standardized characteristics in performance, weight, ergonomics, avionics and fuselage. These common and standardized characteristics of SATS design will be defined ultimately by the need of humans to successfully accept and adapt to the technologies provided by SATS. The need for faster, safer and environmentally friendlier means of transportation is a human need and SATS proof of concept design is only addressing such need thus enhancing the quality of human life.

The typical performance of a SATS plane starts with design parameters as listed below:

Cruise Altitude	18,000ft
Speed	250 Knots
Passengers	5
Range	1000 nm
Fuel Consumption	0.4 lb/hp/hr

Table 1: Design Parameters

The Cruise Altitude of 18,000 ft is on the floor of Class A (also known as class Alpha) airspace, which means that Class Alpha airspace starts at 18,000 ft. Under that altitude pressurization considerations need to be taken in the cabin. Such cabin pressurization and oxygen level will be provided under FAA standards. To ensure flight stability it is imperative that the airplane has optimum weight distribution and adaptability in weight

FIG. I.2.   *(Continued)*

FIG. I.2. SATs essay, PowerPoint and digital video.

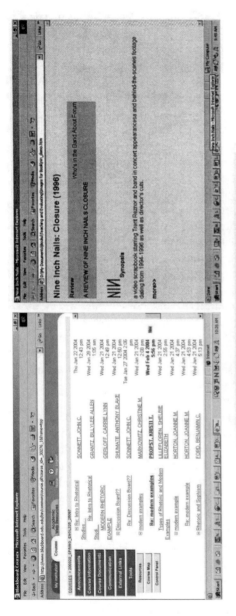

FIG. I.3. Nine Inch Nails and Napster: Discussion board, Web site review, and meeting agenda.

Each of these projects demonstrates the ways in which writing is becoming an increasingly multimodal and multimedia activity. A multimodal composition draws on graphic, textual, and oral communication formats, and multimedia composition uses IT to present these various formats. The college students in the humanities writing course produced a traditional essay and then repurposed the content of that essay for the medium of the Web. They proceeded through a process in which they demonstrated their proficiency in the "basics" of print-based literacy, and then adapted their written products for another medium (as the College Board recommends). In this case, their composing processes primarily engaged them in tasks traditionally associated with writing and English courses and then they built on these skills by extending and revising their product.

The science and technical writing students also created a traditional printed report, but their research and writing processes made them compose two other products: a PowerPoint presentation and a digital video as they were working on the written report. In fact, the PowerPoint presentation and the digital video were shown to the class a week before the written report was turned in, and the written report reflected comments and feedback that the students had received in response to their earlier presentations. Each of these "secondary" projects required the students to consider their audience, organize their information for that audience, and adapt—or design—the presentation of that information within the confines of a particular medium and a particular social context. All of these activities were *situated*. Composing—the generating of ideas, the organizing of those ideas for an audience, and then designing and editing of multiple products within multiple media—is no longer only about the written word but extends the graphical and oral into students' writing processes. These students are discovering, refining, and presenting complex ideas through digital video editing, designing a PowerPoint presentation, and writing a research report.

The high school student who wrote and mailed a printed letter to his congressperson was concluding his assignment sequence with what looks like a traditional writing assignment—write a letter. But his means of arriving at this product engaged him in modes of composing that would not have been possible a decade ago. His review of Nine Inch Nails' album included two html files and three graphics, his use of an Internet chat room and online discussion board had him writing to others outside of his immediate peers, and his leadership of a class discussion made him think about how a meeting is organized and the ways in which a text (i.e., the meeting agenda) can be crucial for organizing a talk and interacting with an audience. Writing continued to play a vital part in this student's thinking, but the web review and the synchronous discussion made him use language in ways that did anything but adhere to the conventions of standard written English. His success in these environments was tied to his ability to write beyond the standard and to employ a form of English often thought of as unable to handle sophisticated ideas. However, the student was also able to recognize the need to switch registers when writing to a member of Congress. Composing multimodal and multimedia texts then requires that students learn how to code switch. Because of advances in Information and Communication Technology, proficiency as a communicator can no longer be measured as discrete skills used in a single environment. Students must be taught to compose in these multimodal formats, which means figuring out how to evaluate the complex compositions they produce.

WHERE DOES THAT LEAVE THE TEACHER-READER?

An authentic evaluation should be able to assess student compositions, both multimedia and print, by including as many situational elements as possible. Because communication always happens in a context, the most accurate representations of students' writing and composing are not gained from assessments that attempt to capture decontextualized skills. The most valid assessments of students' general skills as writers and communicators draw on multiple samples of student work. They show strengths and weaknesses across disciplines and across writing environments.

Up until this moment in time, writing assessment has relied on the human technology of multiple readers, and psychometricians have been fascinated with interrater reliability. New developments in the apparently opposed "disciplines" of automatic essay scoring (AES) and electronic portfolios move things beyond a need to rely on human-to-human interrater reliability. Developed by computational linguists, AES systems—e-rater, Project Essay Grade (PEG), and Intelligent Essay Assessor (IEA)—promise that the reading and scoring of large-scale writing assessments will change once the technology is accepted more widely.[3] On the other hand, electronic portfolios, often developed by researchers in computers and writing studies and computer science, promise the ability to see multiple samples of student writing and multimedia compositions. These electronic portfolios will include processes for collection, selection, and reflection, as well as emphasizing visual design elements in communication processes. They will not only make assessments more authentic and increase their validity, but also have impacts on pedagogy.

Italo Calvino's novel, *If on a Winter's Night, a Traveler,* reflected on the reading process. Calvino recounted the difficulty of fits and starts, the interruptions a reader experiences when trying to "get into" a novel. His book is full of lost novels—started and incomplete. Calvino's work is a series of frustrations, perhaps perversely enjoyed, by the determined literary reader. In describing reading experiences, Calvino's paean to the novel relies on a reader's love of the printed word to overcome many obstacles. Reading itself becomes a quest, a journey, a goal.

---

[3]E-rater is the software developed by ETS, PEG was developed by Ellis Page; and IEA was developed by Knowledge Analysis Technologies and is now owned by Pearson Education. Each of these systems "reads" and evaluates student writing. See Shermis and Burstein (2003) and Haswell and Ericcson (forthcoming) for more details on these AES systems.

But what happens when the reader is a teacher? What happens when what is being read is a student paper? What happens when all of these processes move onto the computer screen? That interface was not designed for comfortable reading. As Neal Gershenfeld (1999) said, it is as if a flashlight is being held behind the page of a book, and the reader's eyes become tired and strained from focusing for extended periods on these backlit letters.

Can this be called reading? Is there an obsessive passion that drives the teacher-reader-grader onward, or is the screen merely a screen, the paper more drudgery to be bypassed, checked off, graded, and finished with? Most teachers, especially teachers of writing, do seem to have a passion for their subject. But the computer deadens that passion for some. Coupled with the rise in state-mandated exams in middle schools and high schools and departmental or universitywide exams in colleges, it is no wonder that many English teachers lament their career choice. It feels as if teaching English is no longer about words, about writing, about creativity, or about a love of reading. Rather, English, language arts, and composition have become about checking off the required categories on scoring rubrics.

This book cannot change all of that, but it can provide a careful look at the invigorating alternatives to the one-size-fits-all, McDonaldized approaches to teaching and assessing writing that have been proliferating in middle schools, high schools, and colleges. Amazingly, even in an age where schools and policymakers are increasingly relying on high-stakes testing to improve writing proficiency, classroom teachers, scholars of assessment, and information technology experts are at work developing pedagogies and assessment techniques that leverage the flexibility and individualized learning potential of increasingly sophisticated information technologies.

The teachers, students, and researchers discussed in this book are not opposed to high standards, but they do question the potential for students to become proficient composers within digital communication technologies when the tests they take emphasize pen-and-paper modes of composing, thinking, and arguing. If students are to become ready for the multimodal literacies that education researchers (e.g., the New London Group, 1996; Cope, Kalantzis, & New London Group, 2000), business groups (e.g., Bertelsmann Foundation and AOL Time Warner Foundation 2002), and consortiums (e.g., the College Board's National Commission on Writing, 2003) have identified as the next wave of literacy, then student compositions must be assessed in these multimodal, digital environments. There must be study of how computer-mediated pedagogies and flexible, often portfolio-based, evaluative systems challenge the idea that the best way to develop student competencies in writing is through mastering composing strategies designed to pass standardized, paper-based exams.

Groups such as the New London Group, Bertelsmann, AOL Time Warner, even ETS (2001) and the College Board (2003), know that the future of literacy and writing is screen-based. The job of English and writing faculty may be to make these

21st-century literacies as engaging, fun, and challenging as Calvino's *If on a Winters Night, a Traveler*. There may also be a need to learn how to break away from bureaucratic testing regimes without sacrificing the high academic standards of the classrooms. Techniques, as advocated for by Celestine and Elise Freinet (1990), not rigid methods or predefined criteria for building assessment systems, are needed to distribute the functions of reading and evaluating among multiple audiences.

WORK AND PROFESSIONAL STUDIES ELECTRONIC PORTFOLIOS

Moving forward with the premise that writing projects that engage students, make them reach beyond the walls of the academy, and involve them in writing for real audiences are worthwhile, then ways of assessing these works that are valid, reliable, and fair must be developed. As a process for assessing student work, descriptive evaluation provides a methodology for responding to diverse texts in ways that document the student's work, observe the rhetorical effects of linguistic and visual features within the different texts, and create a collection of data to be reviewed by the grader before a final judgment on the value of a piece is made. In these ways, keeping descriptive records of one's response to a variety of multimedia compositions enables a teacher to document the interactions with others that occurred as the students composed. Taken together, considerations of interactive composing processes and descriptive evaluations, enable a capturing of the situational elements that are part of a multimedia composition's participatory framework.

The challenge, then, is to develop systems for assessing multiple, multimodal compositions that incorporate the strengths of both database-driven and design-driven electronic portfolios. The narrowly focused writing assignments promoted by statewide writing exams and the new SAT can be an important part of students' work, and they can lead to valid assessments of narrowly defined competencies in print-based writing. Because it is possible to score these focused writing activities and offer feedback to students via software, a truly effective system for multimodal writing assessment would incorporate AES. This multipurpose testing system would have a system validity not found in the discrete standards-based forms of writing assessment that dominate large-scale assessment systems today. It would also acknowledge the limits of software-based feedback and evaluation. AES software can score text-based compositions, but works that incorporate images use a variety of fonts for design purposes, draw on discourse forms used in IMs and chat rooms, construct bulleted lists for slideware, or make use of digital videos require a situated evaluation by multiple agents (humans and software).

What would such a system look like? It would ask students to reach beyond the walls of the academy so that they were writing for real audiences. In addition, it would incorporate an assessment technique such as narrative or descriptive evaluation, where graders first document what they and others see in the composition before making a final assessment. Providing a real-world purpose for the student writer and using techniques to observe what the piece does, rather than what it fails to do, would allow an assessment system to reflect the participatory framework that was part of the compositions. Instead of excluding context (making the grader a universal grader), this system would insist that each one of the multiple readers (human and software agents) be situated in relation to the composition. In acknowledging the situatedness of these readers and the multimodal compositions, these systems combine the database-driven and the design-driven forms of student portfolios.

Viewing a series of electronic compositions from multiple perspectives creates the need to look at discrete elements of the composition, say a short 15-minute writing exam, a digital video clip, or an annotated synchronous discussion log. Some viewers will need to see parts of the student's electronic portfolio in a standardized template to make their interaction with the composition easier. Other viewers will want to experience the students' own designed metaphor or organizing idea, because they will be evaluating the ways students make connections between different electronic compositions. In a multimedia portfolio, these connections are not made simply by linking from one text to another but by the ways in which the designer prepares the reader to move through her metaphor. These situated electronic portfolios would allow some readers to use a template-driven mode of viewing the students' compositions and others to use a metaphoric mode of viewing the compositions.

The Work and Professional Studies (WPS) Electronic Portfolio Project at Old Dominion University is developing a system that incorporates these flexible approaches to interacting with student compositions. Based on the Open Source Portfolio (OSP) software, WPS Eportfolios provides an option for viewing a collection of a student's work as a work-in-progress template, a finished template, or a student-designed interface (Figs. I.4, I.5, and I.6).

As an interdisciplinary studies program, WPS gives students and faculty opportunities to focus their attention on specific issues that affect people everyday. All students in the program take three core courses. In these courses, the students explore John Gardner's (2001) writing on excellence and ethics, Robert Reich's (2000) theories about success in the workplace, Ellen Galinksy's (1999) interviews with parents and children about work and family, and Studs Terkel's (1997) interviews with workers in Chicago. The students and faculty use these courses to build students' electronic portfolios by refining their professional resumes and writing reflectively about external interviews of mentors, models, and colleagues. Further, they examine electronic archives of their work from on the job and in the academy. These multiple, multimodal compositions, which can include PowerPoint slides, Word documents, or graphic files, are the central ground on which the students build their final presentation portfolios.

Multiple agents assess the work within these electronic portfolios from a variety of perspectives. Some readers are faculty evaluators of experiential learning;

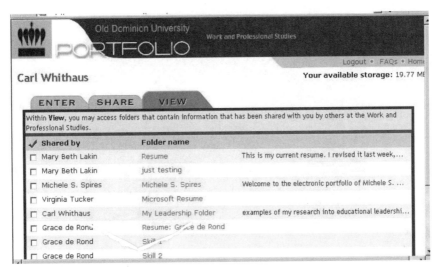

FIG. I.4   Work and professional studies electronic portfolio, working template version.

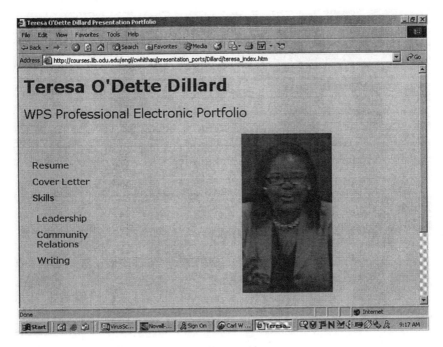

FIG. I.5.   Work and professional studies electronic portfolio, finished template version.

FIG. I.6. Work and professional studies electronic portfolio, student-designed interface.

these readers look at a discrete project and decide whether or not that work-based project and the student's additional reflection on that project merits course credit. Some readers are the teachers of the interdisciplinary seminars the students take; these teachers look at work students produce in the core courses, but they may also turn to some of the other works included in the archives. Students may also provide future employers with access to parts of their electronic portfolios, and by doing so create another audience.

This system values assessment techniques that include:

- *interacting* with students as communicators using synchronous and asynchronous environments;

- *describing* the processes and products of student learning rather than enumerating deficits;

- *situating* pedagogy and evaluation within systems that incorporate rather than exclude local variables; and

- *distributing* assessment among diverse audiences.

The WPS electronic portfolio system realizes the possibility—perhaps even the necessity—of creating methods of evaluation that reflect the risks and complexities of student-generated, computer-mediated compositions. Each of these techniques for assessment reflects a growing understanding of evaluation as a process of communication.

1

Educational Policy, Testing Writing, and Developing Multimedia Composing Skills

The challenge of composing in multimedia environments has not escaped American's education community. In September 2002, the College Board—the nonprofit organization of over 4,300 schools and colleges—created the National Commission on Writing to respond to the board's plan to add a writing component to the SAT exam and to analyze the state of writing instruction in U.S. schools. Among its many findings, the National Commission on Writing (2003) argued that "just as [computers] have transformed schools, offices, and homes, [they] have introduced entirely new ways of generating, organizing, and editing text" (p. 22). Because of these changes,

> teachers have to reconsider their inherent attitudes about the value of writing grounded in new technologies. Far from undermining libraries, the Web puts the world at students' fingertips. Letters and notes are still appropriate in many circumstances, but e-mail, instant messaging, and electronic conferencing provide writers with an immediate and much larger audience. Educators need to tap into students' inherent interest in these methods of creating and sharing writing. (p. 22)

In other words, teachers should not reject the types of prose that students create in chat rooms, in Instant Messages (IMs), on web pages, or in text messages out of hand. Although these forms of writing appear less rigorous than traditional academic prose, they are the adaptations of language to new modes and new media. Like water filling up a newly dug hole at the beach, language adapts and shapes itself to new containers. Still, the creation of new forms of acceptable language (R u cRus?—i.e., "Are you serious?"—in text messaging) does not mean that the conventions of written English are discarded in all environments. Rather, students need to know how to "code switch," or how to move from one mode of writing and talking to another.

1

MULTIMODAL MULTILITERACIES

Preceding the College Board's *The Neglected "R"* report by nearly a decade, a group of international educational researchers, called the New London Group (so named because their first meeting was held in New London, NH), met and began discussing the future of literacy teaching. Whereas the group continued meeting throughout the 1990s, their first statement on the changes to literacy was published in the spring 1996 edition of the *Harvard Educational Review*. This piece, "A Pedagogy of Multiliteracies: Designing Social Futures" (New London Group, 1996), laid the groundwork for the group's collection of essays called *Multiliteracies* (Cope, Kalantzis, & New London Group, 2000). In both of these works, the New London Group extended the notion of "literacy and literacy teaching and learning to include negotiating a multiplicity of discourses" (2000, p. 9). Practically speaking, this statement means that educators should account for the contexts of communication when teaching and evaluating student work. It also means that they need to account "for the burgeoning variety of text forms associated with information and multimedia technologies" (p. 9). How do teachers and test designers account for students' competencies as writers and communicators when the compositions students are producing include a complex interplay between visual images and the written word? How do teachers and test designers evaluate the linking of a sound file to a web page? How much do they count off for a broken hyperlink? How ineffective is a broken link to an image file if the writing on a particular web page is effective? The gap on the page can appear devastating, but the error can be a single capital letter (see Fig. 1.1). For instance, if in a student's html code, the directory and file name that she is linking to is "week3/One.htm" and the student's code is "week3/one.htm," the result is an HTTP 404 error. Is this error equivalent to a sentence fragment? Is it more serious? Or, is it less serious? The disruption an error causes should be judged in terms of its effects on a situated reader. A teacher who has recently explained the importance of capital and lowercase letters for web design would judge the error in Fig. 1.1 as a serious error, whereas a teacher who had not yet discussed this issue should access the correct file and explain the error. If the student adjusts the composition for the next draft, then that student has shown an important adaptive skill. If the student does not, then the teacher evaluates the work based on the student's situated failure, that is, the failure to adjust as an aspect of the composition based on direct reader feedback.

To answer these types of questions, the New London Group began developing its theory of multiliteracies. Gunther Kress, a University of London writer and researcher, explained the need for this new semiotic theory as growing out of the "multimodal texts/messages" already in use. The theory, and the methods of teaching and assessing learning that would grow out of it, would have to deal with "the processes of integration/composition [in] various modes in these texts" by acknowledging changes in "production/making and in consumption/reading" (New London Group, 2000, p. 153). The concept of multimodal and multimedia compositions as important within educational environments did not remain the

:rsace dresses. Overall, we can conclude that styles are changing
of what everyone else is wearing, designing, and modeling.
.ich <a href="week3/One.htm">variety, assortment and selection?</a>
there are multiple scores of different people with different

rc="photo-33.jpg" align="right"><b>Have you ever seen anyone wear
interesting? Well if you find it attractive, isn?t it only logical
ou have the money? In society most people would, and do. If so,
if you increase the amount of people in a certain area, then you
:r peoples clothing, through the multiplied interactions the

at people have in cities comes the obvious influences their styles

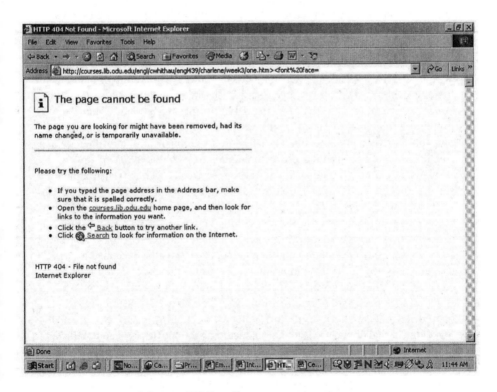

FIG. 1.1.   HTML coding error as grammar error.

3

property of educational institutions such as the College Board and groups of educational researchers such as the New London Group. In 2002, the Bertelsmann Foundation, the philanthropic arm of the publishing giant Bertelsmann-Holtzenbrink, and the AOL Time Warner Foundation, the philanthropic arm of the new and old media giant, sponsored a conference in Berlin on 21st-century literacy. The participants at the summit worked to define the use value of the emerging literacies created by IT and analyzed by the New London Group.

Not insignificantly, the white paper produced from the summit maintains the singularity of literacy by calling itself the *21st Century Literacy Summit*. However, within the document, the multiple skills that make up this new type of literacy are clearly acknowledged. The report noted that "in this new century, information and knowledge matter more than ever, and the ability to use them effectively rests on a set of abilities that extend beyond the traditional base of reading, writing, math and science" (2002, p. 4). As a result, "teachers, students, and employees" must incorporate technology literacy, information literacy, media creativity, and social competence and responsibility into our approaches to learning and into our daily lives. The 21st Century Literacy Summit is significant because it shows large corporations and government agencies developing policy statements in response to the changes wrought by new forms of communication. Whereas the New London Group cut its teeth exploring the future of literacy and literacy teaching, the 21st Century Literacy Summit saw those ideas moving beyond the academy into business and government. Interestingly, and perhaps troublingly, the possibilities of multiliteracies, their multimodal and multimedia potentials, are contained within a much more traditional formula of literacy as a singular noun—as a useful tool for maintaining the status quo.

In January 2001, the Educational Testing Service (ETS) convened a panel to study the relation of emerging Information and Communication Technologies (ICT) to literacy. The panel's goals were to examine the need to measure ICT literacy and to develop a framework for designing large-scale assessment instruments as policy tools and as diagnostic measures of individuals' skills. Among the panel's findings were: (a) "The notion of a literate populace must be expanded to include technology-based skills and abilities that will enable citizens to function in an increasingly technological world." (b) ICT literacy is not just a mastery of technical skills but includes critical cognitive skills as well. And (c) ICT literacy is a continuum of skills not an either–or for the individual or in terms of society (i.e., the notion of the digital divide needs to be exploded/transformed) (p. 1). The panel's definition of ICT literacy was "using digital technology, communications tools, and/or networks to access, manage, integrate, evaluate, and create information in order to function in a knowledge society" (p. 2). Each of the terms in this list become key points for ETS researchers and test developers to think about in terms of assessing competency in ICT. Students should understand how to access, or find, information resources, and they should be able to manage what can often be an abundance of sources. Students need to be able to take the ideas that they encounter through IT channels, which can include chat rooms, blogs, and discussion boards, as well as Web sites and online library resources, and fit those concepts within their own work in meaningful ways. In addition, students need to be able to evaluate the authority and agenda behind a source; and finally, new assessment systems should not only measure students' ability to interact with existing sources of information, but they should also be able to assess the products that students create using ICT.

Although the ETS study creates a valuable framework within which to view the broader concepts of multimodal multiliteracies (New London Group) and useful applications of 21st-century literacy tools (21st Century Literacy Summit) applied to assessment theory, the study does not examine the fine points of how these concepts would apply to writing assessment. To gain a fuller understanding of how to assess compositions written for electronic environments differently, as compared to essays created for print, consider the work of experts in online design and information architecture. For example, the structure for a Web site is associative and linked to ease of navigation. Writing for www.sun.com, Jakob Nielsen, PJ Schemenaur, and Jonathan Fox (1999) pointed to two usability studies from Sun's Science Center as evidence for using different criteria to construct Web sites. They claimed,

> Writing for the Web is very **different from writing for print**:
> - 79% of users **scan the page** instead of reading word-for-word
> - Reading from computer screens is 25% slower than from paper
> - Web content should have **50% of the word count** of its paper equivalent
>
> (¶ 1, emphasis in the original)

On a linked page, they expanded on these claims: "In print, your document forms a whole and the user is focused on the entire set of information. On the Web, you need to **split each document** into multiple hyperlinked pages since users are not willing to read long pages." They stressed that "users can **enter a site at any page**" and that navigation tools and links must point to background information. In addition, they suggested that the online version of a document should contain "**half the word count** used when writing for print" because "users find it painful to read too much text on screens, and they **read about 25 percent more slowly**." In addition, "users don't like to scroll through masses of text," so writers should "write in the 'news you can use' style to allow users to quickly find the information they want." Finally, "**credibility** is important on the Web where users connect to unknown servers at remote locations. You have to work to **earn the user's trust**, which is rapidly lost if you use exaggerated claims or overly boastful language; avoid 'marketese' in favor of a more objective style" (¶ 2–4, emphasis in the original). These differences in how information is organized are tied to how readers and users interact with the information on the screen. For instance, even the use of bold in the online documents helps the reader get faster access to the writer's main point while scanning the work. In print (as in the previous quotations), the bold appears heavier than necessary, partly because people have learned the convention that emphasis in print is in italics and partly because of the physical differences in reading the page and reading the screen. It can be theorized that some measure of a designer's skills is knowing that key terms need to be bold for emphasis and that emphasis needs to be used more often online than in print, and should be part of what is assessed in students' electronic compositions.

There is also the more complicated issue of assessing the parts of the web page that are in bold. Can a student use bold for the wrong part of a sentence? Yes. For instance, placing emphasis on "**You have to work**" rather than on "to earn the user's trust" in the aforementioned example would constitute a weaker web page. Given multiple examples of this type of "error," it could be concluded that the writer who emphasized "you have to work" would have less proficiency with composing in electronic environments than the authors who emphasized "to earn the user's trust."

But the judging of students' composing skills in digital compositions is not simply a matter of applying new rubrics based on the structural qualities of web pages and sites. Composing and cognition in electronic environments are affected by the differences in what types of evidence is presented as well as how the delivery of that evidence is shaped. In a chat room: "u r crazeeee" would be a fine sentence; in a paper, the same point might require the following sentence: "Jessica Ginzburg's point about school vouchers does not make sense." Evidence online can be a simple paraphrase like "Foucault says that power is like a mobius strip—both inside and outside of us" or a direct link to the evidence itself "Go see http://www.theory.org.uk/f-essay1.htm." But evidence in print is a quotation followed by an MLA or APA in-text citation: "We should admit rather that power produces knowledge (and not simply by encouraging it because it serves power or by applying it because it is useful); that power and knowledge directly imply one another; that there is no power relation without the correlative constitution of a field of knowledge" (Foucault, 1979, p. 27). These different forms of citation reveal a different structure and valence to evidence as the students shift media. This change is not surprising. When conversing with friends about health conditions, people accept a different level of evidence than when they are reading a report in the *New England Journal of Medicine*. The same subject in different situations and in different media varies in the types of evidence required. Recognizing that the type and depth of evidence required varies by situation and that situation is affected by the medium in which the composition is written is a crucial step to becoming a skilled composer and communicator.

Students' composing processes are becoming multimodal. As they write traditional essays, they are producing "side products" that include IMs and chat room discussions, Web sites, blogs, and digital videos. What is fascinating is that these "side products" no longer appear to be side products, but rather are examples of the types of literacy activities valued by the College Board, the New London

Group, the 21st-Century Literacy white paper, and the Educational Testing Service. The challenge for teachers and test developers then is to compare the texts valued by existing assessment systems with the compositions produced in IMs, on Web sites, and in digital videos. Value is not only the final product (e.g., the letter to a congressperson), but rather the processes and products created on the way to that destination. The difference between this change and the shift from product to process is that the whole concept of destination and final product that informs high-stakes programs is challenged. The side products are no longer "sidelined," but of equal or greater value compared with the "final product."

WHAT WRITING ASSESSMENT SYSTEMS ARE LOOKING AT NOW

Despite the recommendations of the National Writing Commission and ETS's ICT panel, large-scale writing exams at the high school and college level continue to test a rather narrow band of writing proficiency. Quick looks at the expectations in place for high school students in Texas and New York, as well as on the writing component of the "new SAT," demonstrate the ways in which writing tests continue to look for rhetorical structures associated with effective writing in print and continue to validate the importance of the surface features in students' language.

Two of the most prominent rhetorical structures in print-based school writing are cohesion and evidence. Although the mechanisms for testing these two rhetorical structures vary from assessment to assessment, they are both valued on the exams used in Texas, New York, and Virginia, as well as on the "new SAT." In addition to looking at rhetorical moves associated with printed essays, all four of these exams value the surface features of language associated with standard written English. Unfortunately, the standards that are applied to cohesion, evidence, and the surface features of language in print do not correspond directly with the forms of English used in online synchronous or asynchronous discussions. They also do not include ways to value the visual elements or the adding of emphasis to places within the linguistic and textual parts of a student's composition. Understanding how the "new SAT" and the writing exams in Texas, New York, and Virginia value cohesion, evidence, and the conventions of standard written English will help with the decision concerning how these assessment tools need to be modified to include the wider range of skills that the College Board, the New London Group, Bertelsmann and AOL Time Warner Foundations, and even ETS see as the future of literacy.

Texas TAAS

The designers of the Texas Assessment of Academic Skills, Exit Level Writing Exam, would seem to agree with Nielsen, Schemenaur, and Fox's view that "in print, your document forms a whole and the user is focused on the entire set of information," because they have devised a scoring system that uses "focused holistic scoring . . . to evaluate each TAAS written composition. This scoring system is 'holistic' because the piece of writing is considered as a whole" (*Texas Assessment of Academic Skills, Exit Level Scoring Guide for Persuasive Writing*, 2001, p. 2). In their discussion of the test's objectives, the test designers acknowledged that writing is a situated activity. In outlining the test's objectives, the designers said,

- The student will respond appropriately in a written composition to the purpose/audience specified in a given topic.
- The student will organize ideas in a written composition on a given topic.
- The student will demonstrate control of the English language in a written composition on a given topic.
- The student will generate a written composition that develops/supports/elaborates the central idea stated in a given topic. (p. 2)

The TAAS objectives stress: purpose/audience, organizing ideas, control of the English language, and development/support/elaboration of a central idea. Given the emphasis placed on organizing ideas to support a central thought, the TAAS development team valued coherence and evidence. The essay should be organized around a central idea, and the readers should also examine how the writer uses particular pieces of evidence to support that idea. In addition, components of correct usage, mechanics, spelling, and syntax are addressed under the point of "control of the English language."

New York State Regents Exam

The writing components of the New York State Regents Exam also value essay structure and cohesion. Across the various exams, the use of evidence is an important evaluation criteria. For instance, on the Task Reading and Writing for Literary Response on the New York State Regents Exam, the grading criteria for the development mention evidence repeatedly. A Level 6 paper, the highest possible score, will "develop ideas clearly and fully, making effective use of a wide range of relevant and specific evidence and appropriate literary elements from both texts [that the student has been given]," whereas a Level 2 paper, the second lowest possible score, is "largely undeveloped, hinting at ideas, but references to the text are vague, irrelevant, repetitive, or unjustified." The value placed on evidence is further developed in the sample benchmark essays provided with the scoring rubric. One of the greatest contrasts is between a Level 5 essay and a Level 4 essay. The Level 5 essay quotes directly from the sample text and paraphrases many times. Within individual paragraphs, the direct quotations and the paraphrases all support the topic sentence of that paragraph. On the Level 4 essay, in contrast, the direct quotations are minimal and the writer relies more on brief summaries and references to the text. The sample papers for scores of 1–3 contain no direct quotations from the text. In the New York Regents, then, evidence is an important component of the exam, but the exam is constructed to value the types of direct quotation and paraphrase used in print-based literacy.

SAT Writing Component W-Section of the New SAT

By adding a writing component to the new SAT, the College Board aims to promote writing in schools and improve the predictive validity of the SAT. Students will have 50 minutes to complete two sections, which will both be scored under the W-portion of the SAT. One section will be multiple-choice questions and will test students' abilities to improve sentences and paragraphs, and to identify errors in diction, grammar, sentence construction, subject–verb agreement, proper word usage, and wordiness. The other section will be an essay written in response to a controlled prompt; the essay section will be scored holistically and it should demonstrate students' abilities to organize ideas, express those ideas clearly, support an organizing idea, and use standard conventions of written English. The essay section of the exam will be scored holistically by two readers on a scale from 1–6. If the two readers' scores differ by more than two points, then the exam will be read by a third reader.

A closer look at the break between a 3 and a 4 score on the current SAT II reveals how the SAT values evidence, surface features, and correctness. A 4 essay uses "examples to support ideas," whereas a 3 has "inappropriate or insufficient details to support ideas."

Score of 4

A paper in this category demonstrates adequate competence with occasional errors and lapses in quality. Such a paper:

- Addresses the writing task
- Is organized and adequately developed, using examples to support ideas
- Displays adequate but inconsistent facility in the use of language, presenting some errors in grammar or diction
- Presents minimal sentence variety

Score of 3

A paper in this category demonstrates developing competence. Such a paper may contain one or more of the following weaknesses:

- Inadequate organization or development
- Inappropriate or insufficient details to support ideas
- An accumulation of errors in grammar, diction, or sentence structure

The correctness and surface features are valued when readers look for "facility in the use of language" read through the criteria of grammar or diction. An interesting contrast between an essay scored with a 4 and a 3 has to do with "sentence variety" in a 4 and "errors in sentence structure" in a 3. Although the other criteria are parallel between the scores, these criteria are slightly askew. A student may write an essay with no errors in sentence structure, but also with little sentence variety. In fact, when students push themselves and use a wider variety of sentences they are more likely to have errors in sentence structure.

In conjunction with the multiple-choice usage section, the SAT's 25-minute essay values correct surface features and a single, coherent theme. By judging students' abilities to organize ideas, express those ideas clearly, support a main idea, and use standard conventions of written English, the exam promotes writing that supports a unified theme with clear supporting evidence. Furthermore, the conventions associated with standard English will be judged according to usage, syntax, and diction. These are not faulty methods of judging student writing, but they are limited. They judge writing according to the standard, print-based categories of cohesion, supporting evidence, and correct usage. As the norm that students will learn to write toward as teachers prepare them for college entrance exams, these criteria will lead toward an overemphasis on a narrow form of print-based writing.

More complex writing, writing that carries multiple and conflicting ideas, what Keats (1817) called negative capability and what psychological literature calls a tolerance for ambiguity is not valued in the SAT's scoring rubric. Although the writing sections in the ACT and SAT may reach the level of synthesis in Benjamin Bloom's (1956) taxonomy, they do not push writers into evaluative activities. Even if these writing components are requiring students to employ more critical thinking skills than the multiple-choice sections of these tests, they are not reaching the higher level of evaluation as described by Bloom. The clean, concise 25-minute essay based on cohesion, support, and correctness can be a useful tool within its limitations. However, when those limitations become the yardstick by which a student's proficiency as a writer is measured and their likely success in college writing predicated, something important is lost for the future. This produces student writers whose cognitive and critical skills are shaped to meet narrow criteria, and it neglects the multimodal skills that are needed by students in the 21st century.

CRITIQUES OF HIGH-STAKES WRITING ASSESSMENT

Recently, critiques of large-scale writing assessment systems have not focused on the failure of these exams to adapt to changes in literacy driven by advances in IT. Critiques have concentrated, however, on the ways in which these exams claim to increase learning (Amrein & Berliner, 2002) and the ways in which these exams ask students to produce simplistic forms of writing within the options of print-based literacy (Hillocks, 2002). Proposed solutions to the dilemmas of assessing student compositions in electronic environments need to account for these existing critiques.

In "High-Stakes Testing, Uncertainty, and Student Learning," Audrey L. Amrein and David C. Berliner (2002) examined the effects of high-stakes testing programs on student learning in 18 states. They did not use scores on the state exams, but looked at student scores in the tested domains on the ACT, SAT, NAEP, and AP exams. In 17 of 18 states, student learning as measured by these external tests was indeterminate or decreased following the implementation of the statewide exams. Progressive educators long ago began to critique the sorting and ranking functions of large-scale assessments.

Focusing on the implementation of statewide writing exams, George Hillocks (2002) examined the effects of the increase in large-scale writing assessment programs during the 1980s and 1990s on teachers and students. He defined "the central problem of testing" as "knowing whether a test does what its proponents claim it does or not." He noted that "in most states, students are given prompts of various kinds and asked to write in response to them" (p. 5). His work attempted "to determine what such tests actually test" (p. 5). Hillocks concluded that many writing assessments do not improve the quality of student writing. However, "there is little question that the assessments have made the teaching of writing a more common and extensive activity than Applebee found in 1981" (p. 205). In the states that Hillocks examined, with the exception of Kentucky and Oregon where portfolio systems are used, students are writing more, but the quality and types of writing they are being asked to produce are narrow and do not provide a rich array of writing situations.

In these cases, writing is less about thinking through a problem and more about shaping whatever material is placed in front of the student into a predetermined form (i.e., often the five-paragraph essay). Test reliability, the fact that two scorers are likely to agree on the assigned score rather than validity often became the "gold standard" by which these testing regimes evaluated themselves. Ironically, automatic essay scoring systems have a higher interrater reliability than well-trained human readers. The reason is simple: Different human readers read differently. Or, put another way, the value any given reader assigns to a text is a situated value. Norming readers, the training that any grader of a mass exam receives, attempts to pull them out of that situation into a universal one, but it is a difficult task. In fact, it is a task that is better accomplished by software.

AES SYSTEMS AND GRAMMAR CHECKERS
AS SOFTWARE RESPONSE/FEEDBACK AGENTS

For all the objections that have been raised about software reading and evaluating student writing, this is an age in which software does exactly that. Microsoft Word's grammar checking function is a default response agent for many students. They trust the authority of that grammar checker more than they trust the authority of their own teachers. The development of automated essay scoring systems has been a dream of test designers and computational linguists reaching back to Ellis Page's work (1966, 1968). Understanding the ways in which Page's Project Essay Grade (PEG), Thomas Landauer's Intelligent Essay Assessor (IEA), and Jill Burstein's e-rater read and respond to student work demonstrates the possibilities for using some of these software agents as teaching tools as well as assessment instruments.

Originally developed in Connecticut during the 1960s, PEG has maintained its fundamental principles for over 30 years. First, Page's system is based on the "assumption that the true quality of essays must be defined by human judges and that the use of more and more judges permits a better approximation to the 'true' average rating of an essay" (Page, 2003, p. 47). In addition, because the computer is able to identify approximations for the intrinsic characteristics that these multiple human judges would respond to, one computer can replace many human readers. That is, according to Page's research (Page & Petersen, 1995), the computer will have a higher reliability than a human scorer. Generally, PEG has looked mostly at surface features, although recently it has been combined with General Inquirer, a content analytic engine. Used to score the PRAXIS exam, PEG and General Inquirer supposedly can judge both subject knowledge and writing ability. The combination of subject matter vocabulary and the stylistic variables that PEG is famous for helped the program triangulate the value of an essay, and has led to claims about the construct validity of this software as a reader (Page et al., 1997). Because PEG examines surface features and combines this analysis with vocabulary terms, the system developers claim that different topics have not caused problems for the evaluation of essays. The basic software reads and evaluates the form of the essay, and General Inquirer examines the student's proficiency with the key terms in any discipline-based writing task.

While PEG relies on stylistic analysis coupled with vocabulary analysis, the Intelligent Essay Assessor (IEA) is driven by an entirely different software engine: Latent Semantic Analysis (LSA). LSA uses an algorithm that relies on the spatial separation of key terms within an essay to evaluate a student's content knowledge (Landauer & Dumais, 1997; Landauer, Foltz, & Lanham, 1998). Landauer describes this approach as concentrating "primarily on the conceptual content, the knowledge conveyed in an essay rather than its grammar, style or mechanics." As is a machine learning method, LSA acquires a mathematical representation of the semantic relations among words and passages by statistical computations. These computations are applied to a large corpus of text based on human subject knowledge experts' scoring (Wohlpart, 2003). In promoting his system over PEG and ETS's e-rater, Landauer (2003) claims that "we would not expect evaluation of knowledge content to be clearly separable from stylistic qualities, or even from sheer length in words, but we believe that making knowledge content primary has much more favorable consequences; it will have greater face validity, be harder to counterfeit, more amenable to use in diagnosis and advice, and be more likely to encourage valuable study and thinking activities" (p.

87). For writing instruction, LSA has been combined with software that assesses style and mechanics "for validation of the student essay as appropriate English prose, and as the basis for some tutorial feedback" (p. 89). Like PEG, then, IEA relies on a combination of content and form analysis. The old debate in composition studies about form and content shaping one another has become embodied in the development of these software applications. In fact, this embodiment is an important step in imagining how the development of software response agents will move beyond the formal concerns of grammar checking programs to more robust tools for responding to student-created compositions.

Some of the most exciting—or terrifying, depending on your perspective—work in computational linguistics has gone on in the development of e-rater at ETS. The algorithms embedded in the design of e-rater are intended to reflect the criteria used for scoring essays. Like PEG and IEA, the algorithm in e-rater attempts to capture elements of writing that are directly related to a generalized and abstract formulation of writing competency. Assessment studies have shown that the measures in e-rater are directly traceable to the construct of writing competency (Burstein, 2001; Burstein, Kukich, et al., 1998).

If a piece of writing is about reproducing known facts, then IEA has possibilities (as it is being used at Florida's Gulf Coast College in Art History). If a piece of writing is an act of discovery for the writer or if a piece of writing is intended to convey something new to the reader, PEG, IEA, and e-rater are not appropriate response agents. These software agents must know the ideal form and the ideal content to be found in a student's writing before the question is answered. Situated assessment asks about the context in which any given assessment tool is being used. If the situation is one that demands that students reproduce knowledge that has been given to them as a measure and a means of their learning, then IEA, as it does in Florida, can work effectively. If what is valued is the formal, standardized linguistic qualities of a student composition, then PEG and e-rater are valuable tools. If multimedia and multimodal compositions are valued, then PEG and e-rater provide only partial tools for responding to and assessing a student's composition. The possibility of an AES system providing some of the feedback and assessment a student receives should not be dismissed. Acknowledging student compositions as situated and complex should lead to the use of AES in conjunction with other responders and evaluators. Using AES within an electronic portfolio system that provides multiple samples of student compositions would create links between assessment and teaching systems, and this process could help shape future developments of AES systems into more useful tools for students and teachers.

ELECTRONIC PORTFOLIOS

While computational linguistics and assessment experts have been developing software programs capable of assessing student essays, composition specialists and other higher education professionals have been exploring the possibilities of electronic portfolios as tools for assessing communication skills and learning across the curriculum. Researchers such as Helen Barrett at the University of Alaska lead the way in the development of electronic portfolios for teachers and for middle school and secondary students. Work on electronic portfolio systems for representing student work over an extended period of time has been pioneered at Alverno College (2000), Kalamazoo College (2000), and the University of Minnesota's *Open Source Portfolio Initiative* (2003).

The development of student electronic portfolios has two major intellectual roots: portfolios in writing instruction and electronic portfolios as cross-disciplinary tools for assessment and advising. Pat Belanoff and Marcia Dickson (1991) pioneered the use of portfolios in writing instruction at SUNY-Stony Brook. The program they developed there in the early 1980s presented a practical turn away from the existing norms of the holistically scored, timed essay or multiple-choice exams. Although Belanoff and Dickson's work was exemplary in this area, one of the interesting things about the development of writing portfolios was that they occurred at a wide range of schools at almost the same time. As Belanoff and Dickson continued to develop theories at SUNY, many educators in the field were embracing this method of teaching and evaluating writing.

As a way of evaluating and judging students' writing abilities, portfolios provided a wider range of materials and involved a look at the development of students' abilities over time. They also foregrounded three techniques: collection, selection, and reflection. Collection meant that students were to gather all the materials they had written over a certain period of time. Selection created a process whereby students highlighted pieces of writing they found useful, engaging, or challenging. They were to look at samples of their writing and decide that these were either the best examples of their writing or that these pieces presented a certain unique perspective on the development of their writing abilities. By highlighting selected samples of their writing, students became part of the process of assessment—they were evaluating a corpus of their own work and then making a decision about which samples represented them best for a particular audience and a particular purpose. The final, and perhaps unique, technique in portfolio assessment was reflection. The students had to produce meta-commentary about their learning process; they had to reflect on the meaning and significance of their selections and locate those selections within the broader collection of writing. The students' reflections, then, became the window through which the graders would read the portfolio, but the process of reflection, a process tied in with evaluation, also became a tool for learning. No longer was writing assessment a decontextualized activity only marginally connected with course activity. Writing assessment became a process of learning. Although writing portfolios opened up a new stage in the development of writing assessment, cross-disciplinary electronic portfolios for assessment in a wide range of disciplines were also being developed. The technologies behind these early electronic portfolios can be divided roughly into two: database-driven and design-driven portfolios.

While Alverno College and Kalamazoo College led the way in the early development of electronic portfolios, the recent work at the University of Minnesota on the Open Source Portfolio and the work at the University of Texas on the Learning Record Online have created some of the most exciting possibilities for database-driven electronic portfolios. These robust systems allow developers to run customized versions of the electronic portfolio software as the front-end interface for students, while working with Oracle or MySQL as the backend. Individual colleges and programs can customize the electronic portfolios to meet their own needs (e.g., Work and Professional Studies at Old Dominion University).

In contrast to the database-driven models of electronic portfolios, design-driven portfolios put the students in the driver's seat in terms of design. In these cases, students are responsible for working out an organizing metaphor and navigational system that has a conceptual "fit" with the project. In "Composing the Intranet-Based Electronic Portfolio Using 'Common' Tools," Rich Rice (2002, pp. 38–39) argues that the production of these organizing metaphors and navigational systems are in fact an integral part of the reflective process in a computer-mediated portfolio. A database-driven electronic portfolio is primarily using the web as a distribution technology. The web becomes a way of having multiple readers look at a series of documents; but, the portfolio is still based primarily on the advances made in the move from the scoring of single essays in a holistic fashion to the evaluation of a print portfolio developed through processes of collection, selection, and reflection. In the case of database-driven electronic portfolios, the process of reflection is still primarily a print-based, textual affair. In the design-driven portfolio, the student reflects on design elements, and the digital elements of the portfolio are not merely an afterthought but are integral to the project's development.

CLOSING: ASSESSING MULTIMODAL MULTILITERACIES

It is not without irony that I note that every time I type "multimodal" and "multiliteracies," MSWord inserts a red squiggly line under my words. I know I could turn off the automatic spelling and grammar check, but to tell you the truth it has become embedded in my writing process. I know the option of right clicking is there, and I know that whenever I mistype, or let's be honest, I misspell a word (e.g., mistype, which I just spelled with two *s*'s for some reason), I right click and keep on typing. Using MSWord has become part of at least one of my composing activities. Sure, I still write with pen and paper, but I've also started talking into a portable tape player. Soon my copy of Dragon NaturallySpeaking 7.0 will arrive, and I will talk into the computer as well as type into it. Each of these tools provides a way for me to compose, and ultimately, mastering these tools give me access to media for sharing my ideas with others.

But composing is no longer only about writing or saying. Chapter 9 of this book could not have been composed without looking at the screen shots of student compositions. The visual elements within the student compositions, as well as my ability to embed them within the word processing document that would become the book you are holding, all influenced my composing process. Writing extended out into visual design. Cognition is not separate from the tools and materials of everyday life, as Jean Lave (1985, 1988; Lave et al., 1982) has shown. The tools for composing, and through electronic portfolios the tools for assessment, are no longer only based on language but on incorporating visual processes. Spatial organization of the screen and the ability to see a relation between textual and visual elements are some of the skills that will develop as students become more proficient with multimodal literacies. The trick will be to design assessment systems that are flexible enough to adapt as these forms of writing emerge. The New London Group, the College Board, ETS, Bertelsmann, and AOL Time Warner suggest that literacy is already changing—the challenge that I take up in this book is thinking through the classroom and assessment practices that will teach student multimodal literacies more effectively.

2

Writing (About) Sounds, Drawing Videos: Multimedia Compositions and Electronic Portfolios

In the summer, a graduate student runs a workshop on technological literacy for lower income, middle school students. The students won't sit still. They bounce around the computer lab. They poke each other. They laugh. They look at Web sites that they are not supposed to; the university's filters catch some of the sites, others slip past.

The graduate student hands out an assignment sheet. "Before the end of the week—that's in four days—you will create a multimedia composition, most likely a website, on a topic you choose. All the specific directions are on the sheet. We will go over them quickly, but you should feel free to ask me about them as you work."

Between running to help one group of students and another, the teacher notices that a group of three boys who have been determined not to participate actually begin to work on a project. They look at music. They look at Web sites about Marilyn Manson; they look at Web sites about Tupac Shakur.

They "steal" pictures from these sites. They open Netscape Composer. They begin to type. They change fonts. Maril*yn* mA*n*son. They change colors. Tupac. They argue. "Man." "Whatever." They include the stolen pictures on their site.

They do not listen to the teacher, much. But they do ask her questions. "Miss. Hey miss." One of them waves his arms frantically, "Miss, how do we add a link to an image?"

She moves around the desk and into their row of computers. "You select the image. And then you click here." She pauses. "You then select the file or URL that you want to link to here."

"Ok."

They add the link. When confused, they ask questions. When the technology stops working, they ask questions.

In 3 hours, this group of three has created a site with 8 html pages, 24 internal links, 10 to MP3s, 7 external links, and 27 image files (both jpeg and gif).

Walking out the door, one asks, "Can we make our own recordings?"

"We could talk about the music, have links to the files and links to our files."

"Yeah, can you get us a mic?"

"I'll see what I can do."

WHAT IS IT ABOUT MUSIC?

The pedagogical sampler, with a computer or without a computer, allows cultural criticism to save isolated moments and then juxtapose them as a final product. The student writer looks at the various distinct moments she has collected and figures out how these moments together produce knowledge. Just as DJs often search for breaks and cuts in the music that reveal patterns, so, too, does the student writer look for a pattern as a way to unite these moments into a new alternative argument and critique. (Rice, 2003, p. 465)

What would an electronic portfolio or composition that relied on Jeff Rice's notion of "a pedagogical sampler" look like? Do they resemble the multimedia, electronic portfolios envisioned by Miles Kimball in *The Web Portfolio Guide: Creating Electronic Portfolios for the Web* (2003)? Kimball sees web portfolios as "much more powerful than paper portfolios" because of "their ability to incorporate multimedia elements—pictures, sound, and even video" (p. 87). In a rhetorical move that recalls Jay David Bolter and Richard Grusin's (1999) critique of new media advocates' desire to claim that their media are immediate—that is, not mediated, not constructed, as old media are—Kimball says that "these elements give you an opportunity to communicate some ideas much *more directly and vibrantly than with text alone*" (p. 87, italics added). Kimball further explains the engagement that electronic portfolios create in a section called "Why Use Audio and Video?" He writes,

Audio and video can make a significant impact on the audience viewing your web portfolio. For audio, rather than merely reading what you have to say, the audience can actually hear you say it. This is particularly useful if a web portfolio includes elements that would benefit from a voice-over explanation. For example, if a web portfolio included a picture or chart that needed commentary, it could include a button users could click to hear the commentary while looking at the graphic. It could even start the voice-over automatically as if the web portfolio were a slide show.

KEEPING IT REAL, RELEVANCE, AND *WHATEVER {IS PLAYED BACK IN JUXTAPOSITION}*

In talking about music—and the technical possibilities for multimedia eportfolios—I would be remiss if I did not ask, "How does the use of popular music in an English classroom relate to the many debates about the 'cultural wars?' about what the curriculum of secondary and post-secondary English classes should be?" The technical ability exists to have students compose multimedia portfolios, but do these portfolios, particularly when they draw on popular music, still "count"? Do they still facilitate the teaching of writing?

In *Teletheory*, Gregory Ulmer (1989) argues that

> the failure of the Humanities disciplines to communicate with the public may be due in part to the fact that what separates specialized humanists from laymen is not only our conceptual apparatus and the discourses of the academy, but the very medium in which we work—the printed word. It is time for the humanities disciplines to establish our cognitive jurisdiction over the communications revolution. (p. vii)

Ulmer goes on to develop "a rationale and guidelines for a specific genre—mystory—designed to do the work of schooling and popularization in a way that takes into account the new discursive and conceptual ecology interrelating orality, literacy, and videocy" (p. vii). The discursive and conceptual ecology of orality, literacy, and videocy that Ulmer predicted in 1989 has emerged; however, its popular forms do not resemble the erudite mystory, "Derrida at the Little Bighorn: A Fragment" with which Ulmer ends *Teletheory* (e.g., pp. 212–243). Rather, multigenre mystories exist on rap/music CDs—the oral/audio songs, the CD jackets with their printed text (lyrics plus), and videos and Web sites. This genre exists and engages with writing instruction when teachers such as Ernest Morrell, Jeffery M. R. Duncan-Andrade (Morrell & Duncan-Andrade, 2002), James Dickson, and Patrick Camagian (Hayasaki, 2003) teach in ways that make music and videos and writing and rap and Shakespeare plays relevant to each other and to the students reading, listening, and watching—and, hopefully, creating their own works in response to these cultural artifacts.

As English teachers in an urban high school in northern California, Morrell and Duncan-Andrade (2002) developed a curriculum that had students analyze and create hip-hop songs/poems "as a post-industrial art form right along side other historical periods and poems so that the students would be able to use a period and genre of poetry they were familiar with as a lens with which to examine the other literary works and also to encourage the students to reevaluate the manner in which they view elements of their popular culture" (p. 90). Although they contextualized hip-hop within a traditional literature curriculum, Morrell and Duncan-Andrade argue that "hip-hop music should stand on its own merit in the academy and be a worthy subject of study in its own right rather than necessarily leading to something more 'acceptable' like a Shakespeare text" (pp. 89–90). Their article suggested the range of ways in which hip-hop can influence the curriculum in a writing course.

Furthering the ideas advanced by Morrell and Duncan-Andrade, Rice's pedagogical sampler urges an incorporation of the composing processes of hip-hop into written compositions—and I am arguing by extension into multimedia composition. While Duncan-Andrade and Morrell believe that hip-hop "should stand on its own merit in the academy," their assignments are carefully located within the traditional curriculum. They must engage students in ways of learning that are recognizable to others more familiar with the traditional literary canon of high school English instruction. Still their assignments ask students to prepare an oral presentation, a 5- to 7-page critical essay, and an anthology of 10 poems. Within the anthology, students could apply composing techniques drawn from hip-hop. The essay could remain uninfluenced by sampling and hip-hop in Duncan-Andrade and Morrell's pedagogies, but teachers following their lead could easily draw on Ulmer's (1989) and Rice's (2003) work and incorporate methods from hip-hop into their composing tasks.

In "Reading, 'riting, and Rap," Erika Hayasaki (2003) notes that teachers across the country have found that having students write about rap music "can be intellectually provocative, shedding light on the grand themes of love, war and oppression." In Madison, Mississippi, James Dickson, a high school English teacher, has students compare Tupac Shakur's poem "In the Depths of Solitude" from *The Rose that Grew from Concrete* with William Blake's "Infant Sorrow." Dickson says that "When students see Tupac . . . writing about the same things that William Blake wrote about, it suddenly makes the poetry of these old, dead white guys much more accessible" (Hayasaki, 2003).

By acting as a bridge between the world outside of school and academics, the use of hip-hop not only makes the words of dead white guys accessible, but also remakes the school environment, the situation within which learning occurs. The language, the words, and the modes of communication that are valued, include, but also expand beyond, the written word. To judge a rap song as a composition, one must understand the situation in which it was created. This act of evaluation includes not only understanding the genre of the song but also the context—the social situation—within which the piece was composed (Johns, 1997; Swales, 1998). This may mean turning to rich interactions between genre or discourse conventions and material conditions. It may also mean turning to the "you just don't get it" response that teenagers so often give their parents when discussing music—or so many things!

"You just don't get it" is often an assertion that speaks about context, that is, your situation is so foreign to mine that you could not *possibly* understand. American teen culture projects parents as foreigners, despite parents having been teenagers themselves. The dedication page of Lester Faigley's (1992) *Fragments of Rationality* spoke wonderfully to this attitude: "Face it, Dad. You're totally out of it. Your last good year was 1976, the year you had me. *Ian Faigley*." "Getting it" is vital in the culture of teenagers. But, before dismissing teenagers in one fell swoop, return to Ulmer (1989); he writes that the "desire to speak, write, and perform in the context of knowledge will be treated now as an explicit feature of academic discourse" (p. 1). I would say that the desire to communicate "in the context of knowledge" is not only a feature of academic discourse, but is also a feature of hip-hop and popular teen music. The performers and the teenagers want to "get it." Once the audience "gets it," they are into "the context of knowledge." In fact, they are part of creating a context of knowledge that values the particular communicative practices championed within a discourse community. Whether that community is a group of physicists studying particle acceleration, a group of high school students listening to hip-hop, or a group of computers and writing researchers talking about iMovie, "to get it" is vital.

But what does "getting it" mean in an academic context—particularly an English or writing classroom that is producing its own genres, neither professional academic discourse nor street lingo? Does getting it mean the ability to produce a five-paragraph essay? At worst, then, "getting it" might mean being taught how to write what Ken Macrorie (1970b, 1975) derided as "Engfish"; at best, "getting it" might mean composing a mystory within the formulation that Ulmer has put forward. The question of what genres are, or should be, taught in high school and first-year college composition courses is contentious, and despite reports such as *The Neglected "R": The Need for a Writing Revolution* (2003), sponsored by the College Board, a vision of writing instruction and assessment that takes into account the revolutionary potential of information technologies has not yet been articulated.

Although the technologies exist to bring music (i.e., audio compositions) into the writing classroom, it is not entirely clear that teachers should. Nor is it entirely clear what types of music or audio compositions should be included. To be honest, the choice among an Ira Glass selection of *This American Life* from Public Radio International, a Rush Limbaugh show, or gangsta rap album seems rather large. If I was to pick one of these shows, play it for a class, analyze it as a composition, and then have students use digital recorders and a sound editor to make their own audio compositions, the choice among Glass, Limbaugh, and a Tupac album would be as great as between reading a work by Matthew Arnold and William S. Burroughs.

Ulmer's (1989) *mystory*, Geoff Sirc's (2002) *composition as happening*, and Rice's (2003) *sampler pedagogy*, what I will call *myhappening sampler* for short, encourage teachers to reach beyond having students write about rap, hip-hop, or whatever music they listen to. These three pedagogies foster a "potential for critical understanding" that "contrasts with the potential for student cynicism (we know how the practice resists dominant thinking, but we still accept the dominant anyway)" (Rice, 2003, p. 469). These pedagogies and the idea of *whatever {is played back in juxtaposition}* suggest the importance of situation in evaluating either a musical composition or a composition about music. How are teachers going to "get" what these pieces are about if they do not understand the situation in which they are composed? What is the value of the 8 html pages, 24 internal links, 10 to MP3s, 7 external links, and 27 image files (both jpeg and gif) created by the middle school students in the summer workshop discussed at the beginning of this chapter? How can they be evaluated beyond a simple catalogue of their existence? What more can be done than a nod toward their mere form? For anything to occur, the teacher must understand the genre in which the students are writing and the social situation(s) within which that genre works.

ACCESSIBILITY, RELEVANCE, AND SITUATION

Because binary opposition is a useful tool for thought as well as a useful tool for writing instruction, let me pit Sirc (2002, 2000, 1998, 1997) against Michelle Malkin (2003) and Allan Bloom (1987). Liberal, perhaps radical, teacher against conservative newspaper columnist and University of Chicago professor. What do they have to say about teaching writing, music, and the relevance of popular music for writing instruction?

In a series of articles ("Never Mind the Tagmemics, Where's the Sex Pistols?," 1997; "Never Mind the Sex Pistols, Where's 2Pac?," 1998; and "Words and Music," 2000), Sirc articulates a "punk" pedagogy that takes the relevance of music to general education students at the University of Minnesota as the starting point of a pedagogy of engagement, a pedagogy of meaning making centered on everyday life. Some of these articles have been collected—the singles made into an album—in Sirc's *English Composition as a Happening* (2002). In the book, Sirc interweaves his discussion and analysis of music and written composition with the composing processes of dadaists such as Duchamp and action painters such as Jackson Pollock and Happenings artists such as Ken Dewey. Sirc sees "the parallels between writing instruction and the visual arts, both seen as composition" as "compelling." The book itself is an "allegory," a look "at the spaces of writing instruction through/as spaces associated directly and tangentially with the Happenings movement (including its pre- and post-history)" (2002, p. 19).

Sirc makes the parallels between avant-garde visual art and technologically mediated compositions clear: "If a Happening or Duchamp's *Large Glass* or a Rauschenberg combine-painting or a Beuy's multiple or a Koos sculpture are typical examples of avant-garde art, we might think of synchronous/asynchronous conversation transcripts, Story-space hypertexts, Web pages, emails, or even informal drafts as species of avant-garde composition" (2002, p. 19). Although Sirc's appeals to high modernism offers a certain intellectual delight, the real guts of his work gets done—and its usefulness happens—when he talks about his classrooms and gangsta rap. Sirc sees "gangsta rap [as] so commonplace as to almost be a readymade, especially given the way so many rap songs are based on sampling of previously-recorded material. . . . Gangsta is consumed by so many of my students; it's a fairly cheap, easily available addiction" (pp. 44–45). As an example of a gangsta rap composition, Sirc takes a "print-out of some stuff, which is no more than a series of hip-hop definitions, that a student of mine found on the net":

Sexual Chocolate = a dark boldheaded nigga with a proper ass car and some tight ass gear
Medusa = a fly bitch who'll make yo dick turn to stone <kistenma>
rims = wheels for yo sweet ass ride
regulate = to creep on some sorry ass fool (see creep. . .) <fhurst>
Here is some stuff from the bay.
money = scrilla, scratch, mail
bad = bootsie, janky
good = saucy <crystalt>
baller = a player wit ends in a benz <Ifunderburg>
ballin = I have game <79D9407A6>
P=Pimpish, the same as tight, slick, dope <Berry>
Bammer = busted and disgusted like half the definitions up on here <mold7316>
(p. 45)

What's happening here? What type of writing is this? Are these compositions or garbage? Or, perhaps, are they a bit of both?

Sirc claims that "all the writers on this list are doing, when they post their definitions, is *inscribing*—cataloguing words, ideas, material that might become useful for the next writer" (p. 46). If the point of the composition is inscription, is the use value for the next writer, then the question about this gangsta-based composition must be: In what ways is this list useful? And, to be useful, does the work need to be accessible?

In some ways, the definitions are useful and accessible to students in a way that high academic texts such as the readings in Donald Bartholomae and Anthony Petrosky's (1987) *Ways of Reading* are not. Yet, they are also inaccessible, *if* the reader does not know the discourse, the lingo. If academics, teachers, and parents[1] cannot "get it," if they cannot bring the correct context to bear on these words—

---

[1]And what if this range of not "getting it" is extended to include some of the students in first-year college composition courses? What about the 35-year-old returning mother of two, the 18-year-old boy who went to yeshiva, and the 22-year-old immigrant from Brazil? And what if this range of not "getting it" is extended to include some of the students in high school English classes? What about the middle-class kids in the suburbs who have decided not to imitate urban youth culture? What about students who are far more comfortable with Christian rock than gangsta music? They won't "get it"

sexual chocolate—then the composition lies there dead, partly dead, forgotten with no future for us. (Faintly, all but forgotten, sampled into the background, again, hear Johnny Rotten of the Sex Pistols screaming "No future! No future for you!") And perhaps this means no future for the student writer trained in this mode of "happening" composition—the "keepin' it real flavor" of teaching English, as conservative newspaper columnist Malkin (2003) derisively calls any teaching that involves rap music.

Rather than following Malkin and dismissing Sirc and others who incorporate rap into their teaching, consider Sirc's earlier work to understand how he arrived at this pedagogy. Sirc argued that composition studies was fascinated with popular music in the late 1960s, but turned away from that energy in the 1970s in favor of the study of academic discourse conventions. Sirc (1997) locates the dismissal of punk music by composition studies with the field's history, and he sees scholars such as Patricia Bizzell (1992) and Bartholomae (1993; Bartholomae & Petrosky, 1986, 1987) as key figures in the field's turn away from students' everyday discourse into academic writing. Sirc believes that "Bizzell spoke for many at the time when she framed our students' problem: they 'are socialized in language usage much more through watching television than through reading and writing academic discourse' " (1997, p. 13).

While Bartholomae is also part of the academic discourse work that turns away from popular, everyday language, Sirc ends "Never Mind the Tagmenics" (1997) by citing Bartholomae's (1993) trouble of letting go of a certain student essay. The student wrote an essay that was clearly a failure. Yet Bartholomae could not get rid of the essay. It stuck with him. It was powerful and moving, but meaningless. It was not hollow—hollowed—academic form, but rather a subtle rejection of form—a punk composition—a loss. But it was one that stuck because it was powerful—as the three-chord progressions of the Ramones are powerful. ("Beat, beat, beat on the brat with a baseball bat." Softly sampled in, from somewhere in the 1970s, a live performance, static covering most of the music; or, perhaps, yet again better a cover of the Ramones by a later band, Seven-minute Hate, "Beat, beat, beat on the. . . ." How do you write or compose when this is the textual landscape that you live in? that is piped into your ears 24/7? But yet, they—we—did and do. . . .)

Here is the failed, "fuck you" (p. 7) essay, as Bartholomae calls it, and some of his comments to readers of the *Journal of Basic Writing* about the piece:

---

either. If the modes of composition that Ulmer, Sirc, and Rice are advocating are going to have any validity, any play, then the criticisms and the critiques from right-wingers, such as Malkin and Bloom, must be considered. If the inclusion of audio elements in multimedia compositions and electronic portfolios is not going to be simply an avant-garde experiment but rather an integral mode of thought and composition for a wide variety of students, then the discussion must move beyond the narrow music genres outlined and ask how the diverse everyday concerns of a wide range of students can be reflected.

The writer's name is Quentin Pierce:

> If existence precedes essence main is responsible for what he is.
> This is what stinger is trying to explain to us that man is a bastard without con-
> science I don't believe in good or evil they or meanless words or phase.
> Survive is the words for today and survive is the essence of man.
> To elaborate on the subject matter. the principle of existentialism is logic, but
> stupid in it self.

Then there is a string of scratched out sentences, and the words "stop" and "lose"
written in caps.

Then there is this:

> Let go back to survive. to survive it is neccessary to kill or be kill, this what exis-
> tentialism is all about.
> Man will not survive, he is a asshole.
> STOP
> The stories in the books or meanless stories and I will not elaborate on them This
> paper is meanless, just like the book, But, I know the paper will not make it.
> STOP.

Then there are crossed out sentences. At the end, in what now begins to look like a
page from *Leaves of Grass* or *Howl*, there is this:

> I don't care.
> I don't care.
> about man and good and evil I don't care about this shit fuck this shit,
> trash and should be put in the trash can with this shit
> Thank you very much
> I lose again. (p. 6)

Bartholomae admits:

> I was not prepared for this paper. In a sense, I did not know how to read it. I could
> only ignore it. I didn't know what to write on it, how to bring it into the class I was
> teaching, although, in a sense, it was the only memorable paper I received from that
> class and I have kept it in my file drawer for 18 years, long after I've thrown away
> all my other papers from graduate school. (p. 6)

Sirc does not quote Bartholomae this extensively, but he does point back to
Bartholomae's "The Tidy House: Basic Writing in the American Curriculum"
(1997) as a way of continuing the debate and questions Bartholomae raises there.
What is the meaning of Sirc's use of Bartholomae and Quentin? What is the
meaning of Quentin's composition? Is it more or less meaningful than the list of
gangsta definitions that Sirc's student ripped from the web? What weight does
Quentin's composition give itself? Sirc sees the piece as being less *Leaves of
Grass* and more Johnny Rotten. If so, what does it teach about music as a subject

to compose about? As a metaphor, an allegory, for composition? As a method of composition?

INCOMPREHENSIBLE TEXTS

As a method of composition, music seems good at producing incomprehensible texts. It seems good at producing failures. Both the gangsta list of definitions and Quentin's punk-based composition do not work in any conventional sense of written, academic compositions. But bear with me. I want to stick with this for a while, and see how the ideas of Rice (2003) and Sirc play out. Part of Sirc's interest in Duchamp opens an answer. "Like many," he writes,

> I'm interested in Duchamp. I'm interested, for example, in failures that really aren't, in works barred from gaining the prize which end up changing the world. Brief, personal jottings that become a litany for posterity; apparently impoverished writing that proves a rich text. I'm interested in Duchamp, then, the way I'm interested in writing, writing done by anyone—whoever, useless, failed, nothing-writing by some nobody that turns out to be really something. (2002, p. 35)

I hear echoes in Sirc's work and Mina Shaughnessy's (1977) careful look at errors—errors that aren't errors, but appear to be when looked at through the logic of standardized English. Errors that operate according to a different, extra-academic grammar. And so I like Sirc, am interested in failed writing, failed compositions. But, unlike Sirc, I am not moved by "litanies for posterity." Instead, I wonder about works that do not "work" in a given context, but might speak powerfully in another. Are these works useful? And if they are not useful at first, how can teachers make these works useful?

It is not simply a question of having the academy make room for—acknowledge—rap, hip-hop, and gangsta as valid discourses for exploring complex ideas. Instead, I want to pose a series of questions about the *accessibility* of various forms of discourse, the *relevance* of these discourses, their forms and media for 21st-century academic, civic, and professional lives, and the *situations* (both academic and non-academic) in which different discourses and modes resonate and are valued. The question of evaluation, of course, lurks in the background of the word *value*, and hence this brings up works on aesthetics and philosophy of value such as Barbara Herrnstein Smith's (1988) *Contingencies of Value* as also informing assessment theory and what Trudy Banta (2002) called the scholarship of assessment. Smith's ideas remind us that evaluation is always already situated, but that situatedness does not equate to an inability to judge and apply criteria. Indeed, contingencies of a value judgment make that judgment possible. Without a situation within which to be made, the very idea of value becomes meaningless. Banta's work places assessment not simply as an activity that allows people to learn about another subject (e.g., the organization, activity, or skill being assessed) but as a field of inquiry itself.

Unlike Sirc, I am not depressed by "collections on what makes writing good in the digital age, taxonomies of email, or standards for evaluating web pages" (p. 24) or by the rise in research on software programs as readers and evaluators of writing. I see these tools—just as I see rap, hip-hop, and gangsta music—as potentially valuable ways of understanding and improving students' compositions and communication skills, when employed in specific contexts. It is necessary to become better at articulating the importance of *situation* to writing assessment and evaluation, or perhaps not simply articulating the importance but rather designing assessment systems where situation is incorporated into the evaluation.

"YO, YO, YO": SITUATIONAL RELEVANCE AND IRREVERENCE

Acknowledging *situation* as part of an evaluation system brings up the accessibility of a composition and its relevance to the composer and the audience. Although the gangsta composition that Sirc's student found on the web and the punk composition that Quentin wrote do not appear particularly accessible or relevant when read from the perspective of an English teacher, they may be more useful when analyzed within the dynamics of their own situations. The list of gangsta terms is highly "accessible" both as a web page and as a form of writing that gives information quickly. Quentin's composition is a relevant answer to Bartholomae's question: "If existence precedes essence, what is man." Quentin's answer is "Survive is the words for today and survive is the essence of man." As Bartholomae notes, "The document [is] also a dramatic and skillful way of saying 'Fuck you—I'm not the loser, you are.' . . . The essay had an idea, 'existentialism is logical but stupid' " (p. 7). Quentin's essay supports this conclusion, although the support is not provided in a traditional academic form but rather through a destruction of that form. (Again, Johnny Rotten, is sampled in to faintly scream in the background: "There's no future for you. We're your future"). A situated assessment of these two pieces could recuperate them, could look at their validity in terms of representing particular concepts that tend to be antithetical to the goals of formal schooling. But, I have to admit that any such move would be greeted with a good deal of disgust by many traditional teachers and readers. And I suspect that even a good number of progressive teachers might wonder, as Seth Kahn-Egan (1998) has in *College Composition and Communication*, about the value of honoring or encouraging forms of discourse that embrace nihilism and a disdain for school.

Because the negative responses to these two compositions is likely to be so strong, I want to think about these negative responses before assessing these two works in terms of their situations. I want to honor these opinions even as I disagree with them; there is a way in which I am trying to read and write as inspired by the practice of dialogue found in hooks–Barlow (1995). Paulo Freire's work stressed the dialogic in teacher–student interactions, but his works also put dialogic principles into practices through his many collaborations with other writers (e.g., Freire & Shor, 1987; Freire & Faundez, 1989). Dialogue is a challenge to learn from others. As Martin Luther King, Jr. (1987) said, "Be transformed by the renewing of your mind." That process of renewal is not accomplished through only reading and encountering the same, but by talking with others conceived of as different from one's own point of view. As author of *The Closing of the American Mind*, Bloom (1987) would clearly disagree with any attempt to read either of the above compositions as college-level work in *any* situation. In addition, Malkin (2003) would hold up to ridicule either of these compositions, and anyone caught championing either writer as literate. Interestingly, both Bloom and Malkin addressed the issue of music in American popular culture and its influence on students.

In his jeremiad about the state of American culture and schooling, Bloom admits that

> Though students do not have books, they most emphatically do have music. . . . Today, a very large proportion of young people between the ages of ten and twenty live for music. It is their passion; nothing else excites them as it does; they cannot take seriously anything alien to music. When they are in school and with their families, they are longing to plug themselves back into their music. Nothing surrounding them—school, family, church—has anything to do with their musical world. (p. 68)

Instead of asking how this musical world and students' great enthusiasm for it could be made relevant to schooling, Bloom believes that "such polluted sources issue in a muddy stream where only monsters can swim" (p. 74). "Nothing noble, sublime, profound, delicate, tasteful or even decent can find a place in such tableaux. There is room only for the intense, changing, crude and immediate, which Tocqueville warned us would be the character of democratic art, combined with a pervasiveness, importance and content beyond Tocqueville's wildest imagination" (p. 74). Here then is the problem: Gangsta compositions that include lines such as "baller = a player wit ends in a benz <Ifunderburg>" and punk compositions that include lines such as "I don't care about this shit fuck this shit, trash and should be put in the trash can with this shit" are part of the intense, passionate, and relevant world of music. They are not only compositions written about themes in music, but they take the musical forms, thumping bass, distortion, and give them written, textual form. But, yet again, it is hard to debate Bloom's claim that these forms of composition are "intense, changing, crude and immediate." They are. And that makes them suspect when they are wrenched out of their situational context—a club, a car, a dorm room—and placed in an academic context.

Rather than dismissing music, teachers such as Morrell, Duncan-Andrade, Dickson, and Camagian have incorporated it in ways that make it "a bridge linking the seemingly vast span between the streets and the world of academics"

(Morrell & Duncan-Andrade, 2002, p. 89). There are also theories of composition and pedagogies developed by Rice, Ulmer, and Sirc that use technology to not only write about hip-hop and punk culture, but also to incorporate the modes of composition associated with what Bloom acknowledged is students' passionate embrace of music culture. In the context of the classroom, these compositions— or at least the two textual examples of these compositions that we have been looking at—feel inadequate when compared with their academic task.

Given this inadequacy, it would be easy to follow Bloom's argument by turning to Malkin's dismissal not only of teachers such as Rice, Ulmer, and Sirc, but also of the more moderate Morrell, Duncan-Andrade, Dickson, and Camagian. Malkin began her Friday, January 17, 2003, column "Hip-Hop Hogwash in the Schools" with a derogatory "Yo, yo, yo." She went on to lament *LA Times* reporter Hayasaki's (2003) "enthusiastic" description of how Camagian, a Los Angeles high school teacher, "got his students talking about the 'lyrics' by the late Shakur." Malkin acknowledged that "teachers are using rap music to 'make classical literature relevant,' " but she believes that this attempt is misguided. These teaching methods replace the major conflicts that Malkin studied when she was in school "(Man vs. Self, Man vs. Nature and Man vs. Society)" with the trivial and insulting conflict of "Man vs. Ho."

Malkin attacks Camagian for the sin of making students' music relevant in the classroom, or vice versa. The word "relevance" winds up in both the opening and closing paragraphs of Malkin's column. In the opening, she quotes Hayasaki "make classical literature relevant" and in the closing paragraph she dismisses urban "relevance" (using scare quotes around the word "relevance") as "the false art of 'feelin it' and 'keepin it real.' "

It is at this point—that rap music is relevant—where Sirc and Malkin would agree. Malkin would like to hollow out the word "relevant" and show how it is a code for replacing education with false arts, Sirc would—and has—written about how and when rap and other forms of popular music should—and do—make their way into his writing pedagogy.

Malkin's attack on Camagian's pedagogy is similar to Lynn Cheney's (1992, 1995) attack in *Telling the Truth* on the Modern Language Association (MLA) and other academic organizations. Malkin and Cheney see the truth, standards, and the great conflicts of the past being neglected in favor of a curriculum that includes the everyday and the mundane. They see racism and sexism and drugs as unworthy of academic investigation. Rather, students should be learning, and writing about, the great truths of the past by using vehicles such as simile—forms of poetry rather than the content. Simply using language, "words & music" as Sirc (2000) put it, to feel it, to keep it real, is a betrayal of the academic enterprise.

How should their critique be answered? Shouldn't music, particularly rap music such as Tupac and punk music such as the Sex Pistols, be irrelevant for writing instruction? Do teachers really want to *value*, or have to evaluate "Sexual Chocolate = a dark boldheaded nigga with a proper ass car and some tight ass gear" and "about man and good and evil I don't care about this"? Wouldn't the great works of literature provide a greater leeway, a greater incentive, actually a better learning experience? As Malkin wrote, shouldn't teachers read—or have their students read—Shakespeare, Melville, and Hawthorne? Shouldn't students "cop[y] famous quotations in [their] marble composition notebooks, memorize[] verses and soliloquies that have stood the test of time, and immerse [themselves] in the creative genius of men and women who lived and loved centuries before [them]"?

It is precisely in Malkin's descriptive language that one begins to sense the fault of her own and Bloom's arguments. "Copying famous quotations in marble composition notebooks" will do nothing to prepare students for the communicative environments they will encounter in the next 10 to 20 years. It will also do nothing to overcome what Bloom identified as students' views that school and ordinary life are "at best" "neutral, but mostly . . . an impediment, drained of vital content, even a thing to be rebelled against" (p. 68). How will "copying famous quotations in marble composition notebooks" convince students to be passionate about their cultural heritage, to be seriously engaged in school-based scientific inquiries, or, even, to be see the relevance of schooling to their daily lives and the ways in which power operates and influences their everyday existence? Students know music. Students know the computer screen. Hiding in a pastoral retreat, a Spenserian eclogue or booklined study as Sven Birkerts (1994) advocated in *The Gutenberg Elegies* will not work for most of the population. If "marble composition notebooks" are the answers provided by schools, the irrelevance of schooling and the unpreparedness of students to encounter the technologically sophisticated world of the 21st century will fast become apparent.

Students know the computer screen is flashing by and it is a space where Tupac and Shakespeare do rub shoulders: Just check the interview with Nas on MTVAsia.com (2002) or the reviews of *Shakespeare in Love* on metacritic.com (1998).[2] Or read Janet Murray's (1997) *Hamlet on the Holodeck*. Web-based literacy is, in fact, not only bringing these folks together, but is also bringing in the music, the sounds of folks like Tupac, and opening up avenues for writing and composition that resemble the works in *Pretext* 3.1 edited by Victor Vitanza or in *Enculturation* 4.2 edited by Byron Hawk. Here writing is out there, the compositions hang in the air, and although one could say that these scholarly journal pieces are avant-garde art—and that would be right—they are also art that is not out of the technological range of many 17-year-olds.

I began this section with the hope of reading Bloom and Malkin in a sympathetic light. I am not sure that I accomplished that goal. But I do see some of their points. Bloom is dead on when he says that the influence of popular music is immense, and he is right when he talks about the principles of these musical and written compositions as "intense, changing, crude and immediate." The forms of

---

[2]http://www.mtvasia.com/news/International/Items/0212/0212012.html
http://www.metacritic.com/video/titles/shakespeare/

and values expressed in Quentin's essay and the list of gangsta terms are "intense, changing, crude and immediate." Honestly I don't know that I like the gangsta list from Sirc's class. I don't get the definitions as "slick" from the word "get-go." I do, however, like Quentin's punk composition as the destruction of the essay question: "If existence proceeds essence, what is man." I wish I had had the guts to write that essay in my undergraduate existenialism class, not because I hated my teacher as Quentin did but because Quentin's essay so forcefully captures existence as I saw it at that stage of my life. Camus and Sartre and Johnny Rotten were right: Existence was everything, and there was no greater point to it all. I did not have the courage, or perhaps not a self-destructive impulse in terms of my presence in the university, to turn in an essay as bleak as Quentin's.

CLOSING: *WHAT EVER IS PLAYED BACK IN JUXTAPOSITION,* CHANGING CONTEXTS, CHANGING MEANING

Even in the differences of my reactions to these two compositions, I begin to see a point about situation and the assessment of student compositions emerging. *whatever is played back in juxtaposition* does provide meaning. This chapter is, or has been, an academic argument that is and is not marked by the classical and print-based rhetorical moves advocated for by Stephen Toulmin (1958, 2003); it has also been a sampling, a happening, a timid mystory. The discussion begins to turn toward the chapter's coda now, the closing, the musical fade. Despite hypertext, everything is listened to and read in a linear version—we live in synchronous spaces and time moves step, by step, by step. And here within the printed text, an academic argument unfolds itself.

I understand Quentin's essay because I "get it." I lived in the second wave of punk. High school and college happened to me during the prerecorded dying notes of The Clash and Sex Pistols and Ramones mingled with The Replacements, The Butthole Surfers, and The Dead Kennedys. Here was an aesthetic of nothingness, of rebellion, of the "intense, changing, crude and immediate" that went along perfectly with my reading of Camus, Sartre, Levinias, Dante, Marx, Garcia Marquez, Anaya, and Brecht. Reading Hal Foster's (1983) *The Anti-Aesthetic* and listening to Jello Biafra of the Dead Kennedys, I composed a view of the world that allows me now to understand—or at least believe that I understand—Quentin's composition.

But unlike Rice and Sirc, I have not listened much to gangsta rap. Public Enemy, Snoop Doggy Dog, and Eminem are simply names, not sounds, not aesthetics that I have a deep knowledge of. I cannot pretend to have the situational knowledge—what E. D. Hirsch (2003) and other reading theorists (Gee, 2001, 2003; Kintsch, 1998; Recht & Leslie, 1988) have called domain knowledge—necessary to evaluate the list of gangsta terms found by Sirc's student. Hirsch's conclusion that "experiments have shown that someone comprehends a text, [when] a background knowledge is typically integrated with the literal word meanings of the text to construct a coherent model of the whole situation implied by the text" (2003, p. 13, 16) resonates with the idea of situation-specific evaluation. Extending Hirsch's conclusions to multimedia texts, teacher/reader/users can only be expected to "get" the value of a Web site about hip-hop if they *already* understand rap music; that is, they would only "get" the work if they already had a good deal of "domain knowledge." Given this lack of situational knowledge, it is no surprise that the list of gangsta definitions does not appear "slick" to me. In Marjorie Goodwin's (1990) terms, I lack the participatory framework to make meaning of this conversation; in Smith's (1988) terms, I like the contingencies necessary to make an informed value judgment about the quality of this composition.

Assessments of the multimedia compositions that I have been hinting at in this chapter—html documents with linked images and sound files composed by high school and college students—do not mesh well with existing theories of meaning and communication. In thinking about multimedia literacies as part of the New London Group, Gunther Kress (2000, 2001, 2003) argued that existing theories of meaning and communication

> are based on language, and so, quite obviously, if language is no longer the only or even the central semiotic mode, then theories of language can at best offer explanations for one part of the communicational landscape only. . . . The multimodal texts/ messages of the era of Multiliteracies need a theory which deals adequately with the processes of integration/composition of the various modes in these texts: both in production/making and in consumption/reading. (2000, p. 153)

To develop a praxis of reading and evaluating multimodal compositions, then, requires a willingness to broaden existing views of how "texts" hold complex meanings. Works that may at first appear only to be "the intense, changing, crude and immediate" may on closer examination appear "noble, sublime, profound, delicate, tasteful or even decent." If the list of definitions from gangsta rap were to appear as separate items associated with different web pages and each of these web pages had an image file and a sound bite associated with it, then the terms might open up differently for me. And, of course, the students who composed the Web site explaining these terms would have used multimedia composing skills. As a teacher in an environment where this list was used as a found item to be sampled—to be broken down and incorporated into another composition—I would be part of the new situation into which the work has emerged, and in fact, I would be part of the situation that asked students to create a new multimedia work based on the text of these definitions. The web pages created as a result would remain definitions, but the addition of other media, and hopefully the addition of the composers' own spins on these terms, would create a new text, a new situation in which a different type of evaluation would be possible.

3

Situation(s): Using Descriptive Evaluation

The following three compositions were all produced in the same class for the same assignment:

- a letter to Olga Vives, vice president for Action at NOW
- a Web site intended to inform the public about SSRIs and addiction
- e-mails to doctors and medical researchers to express concerns about the increasing numbers of prescriptions for antidepressants

Yet, in each case, the format appears radically different, and each incorporates computer-mediated communication in different ways. The Web site explicitly uses technology—and a rhetoric that is web based; the e-mails use technology, but in a way that is clearly a repurposing of print-based rhetoric; and, the letter employs the conventional rhetorical moves associated with that genre. Even the letter, however, was influenced by technology; both the research behind the letter and the student's search for information about her audience, the National Organization of Women, were computer-mediated activities. Given these differences, the ability to include *situation*—what Marjorie Goodwin (1990) called *participatory frameworks*—in the assessment of a composition becomes all the more pressing.

SITUATION AND DISTRIBUTION

Situation is important for assessing the avante garde, myhappening samplers advocated by Gregory Ulmer (1985, 1989), Geoff Sirc (2002), and Jeff Rice (2003), and *situation* is vital as a criteria for assessing the aforementioned student-centered, critical literacy projects. These projects reach beyond traditional class-room boundaries not by turning to rap music, but by asking students to research problems they are concerned with and then creating compositions that will reach whatever audience they have identified as key for the success of their project.

An analogy could be made to a camera—that is, the teacher takes a picture of the work, the student takes a picture of the work, and through these pictures and look-ing at the work itself, the teacher determines a grade. The camera's pictures would be descriptive evaluation—"objective" artifacts—but just as photographs are framed and constructed by their photographer's agenda, so are these descriptions. Adding more photos, providing more perspectives on an object, allows a better pic-ture of it and a better understanding of how it works or why it does not work. This is particularly true if the object in the picture is a communicative action. If the photog-raphers are the ones writing the descriptions, and they are involved in either the in-teractive process of creating the composition or they are situated as the audience for the composition, then their descriptions will add valuable perspectives about the work's creation and reception. Having descriptions from either peers involved with a student's composition or with their own related compositions and having descrip-tive responses from the audience is not always possible, but the evaluation process becomes distributive when these descriptions can be included. The teacher and the student-author are no longer the only two describers, but rather there are multiple angles from which a work is described. Distributing the process of evaluation then can increase a writing assessment's validity. The challenge is figuring out ways of implementing distributive assessment.

If a teacher draws on the ideas of a negotiated curriculum and negotiated as-sessment, then the possibilities for distributive assessment become clearer. Still, as an idea, the process of distributing assessment may be the most difficult to grasp. That is, employing descriptive assessment is much like employing narra-tive assessment, and as David Bleich (1997) points out, narrative assessment is al-ready widely used if not acknowledged:

> The solution to the problem of grading is the relatively common practice of narrative evaluation, a practice that has existed as long as grading has in the form of comment, remark, letter, or conversation of recommendation. In a system of scalar grading, a narrative evaluation usually plays a secondary role, as it does today on the report cards of some primary school systems. As students move further along in school, narrative evaluation plays an increasingly important part. To get into college, rec-ommendations are secondary to standardized test scores and to high school grades averages, but recommendations can determine a student's fate if the other materials don't yield a clear decision. In high school and in college, narrative evaluation usu-ally appears on all essays students write, sometimes to justify a letter grade, some-times alone. (p. 26)

Thinking about the importance of domain knowledge and participation frame-works within verbal interaction for the reading and evaluation of a student-created multimedia composition seems appropriate, because the situations within which compositions are created and read are important factors in their meaning. To jerk a work out of its context, and then to read and evaluate it, seems to ignore some of the basic principles of communication. Of course, high-stakes writing assessments create their own contexts, their own standards, and their own situations in which a composition should be judged. These contexts, however, are not situational. And further, they do not account for the multimodal forms of composition that can emerge when looking beyond paper-based academic modes of argument and toward "the norms and forms of electronic communication." The National Commission on Writing (*Neglected "R"*, 2003) has acknowledged what is apparent to many teachers: "Today's young people, raised at keyboards and eager to exchange messages with their friends, are comfortable with these new technologies and eager to use them" (p. 22). Unfortunately, academic modes of assessment have failed to adapt when they encounter compositions informed by gangsta, punk, or new media principles.

The "genre" of a myhappening sampler and its incorporation of rap aesthetics can help students see learning as relevant to their lives and interests. However, the creation of works that only exist within a culture with which students are comfortable does not make the challenge to encounter the Other, to love in the sense that Martin Luther King Jr. used the term, that is, to allow the world to remake one's mind. Myhappening samplers are more likely to challenge teachers to see student interests and concerns as viable and serious modes of academic inquiry, but they may allow students to continue to exist within their own known cultural milieu, rather than inviting them to encounter a culture that they might not yet know or understand.

Remember that, for middle school and high school students, the world of adults may seem like a foreign culture. Taking advantage of this "cultural divide" and the possibilities for learning that it offers, the Cross-Generational Writing Project at the Goodman Elementary School in Chandler, Arizona, had first graders and senior retirees in Sun Lakes correspond via e-mail; they exchanged stories, tales, and life experiences. The process leads to "a mastery of correct letter form, complete sentences, spelling and punctuation, and creative writing" (Hayes, n.d.). Introducing students to the modes of communication used in adult social spheres is an important process, and having this introduction be a serious mode of inquiry is vital. The outcomes are not written before hand, they emerge as students write to each other. They require genuine interaction across cultures and across geographic distances. Inquiries about cultures across local generational differences may also be beneficial. In chapter 2, I discussed how teachers might work to encounter modes of composing with which students might be more familiar than standard academic discourses. What about having students engage in the creation of compositions that reach the other way, that encounter modes of discourse with which students are not familiar? This, too, is a challenge.

The easy solution is to assume that the discourse with which students are not familiar is "academic discourse." However, those scare quotes around academic discourse are meaningful, because there is no one mode of academic discourse, but rather a series of discourse conventions embedded in the social activities of different fields (Bizzell, 1992; Kent, 1999; Petraglia, 1998; Vassileva, 1998). Writing a chemistry lab report is writing, but the rhetorical conventions used there are distinct from the conventions used in a research paper about *Moby Dick*. If the easy solution of teaching "academic discourse" no longer exists for the writing teacher acting in good faith, then what types of writing assignments can be created? If students are challenged to develop their compositions through a process of inquiry that allows them to identify their audiences and the discourse conventions of those audiences, then the difficult—the impossibility—of the teacher applying one set of predetermined, text-based standards in assessments becomes obvious.

However, this problem only exists if the standards are rooted in an assessment of the finished product. Standards that acknowledge composition as a situated activity will ask a different set of questions, and they will judge proficiency, or lack thereof, based on what happens in a student's work rather than what does not. If these writing assignments produce a wide array of finished products, then it is still possible to assess these works with high degrees of validity and fairness. Drawing on the concept of situation that I developed in the last chapter, but flipping that concept around, and asking if students "get it," the next section explores an evaluation system that uses the technique of *description* to acknowledge how composing is *interactive* and *situated*.

DESCRIPTIVE EVALUATION AND END COMMENTS

For the final product in a critical literacy project, a student writes and distributes surveys about classroom behavior and medication to a group of elementary teachers. In a letter, the student presents the findings to the elementary school principal along with an offer to write an article for the school's monthly news flyer. How is this assignment graded? How is it judged? And, because part of the assignment asked the students to use computer-mediated communication in their projects, how does this project represent the student's knowledge about IT and its uses for communication?

Here is the teacher's final descriptive evaluation:

> A survey of elementary school teachers about the misdiagnoses or overmedication of ADHD; followed up by a letter to the principal of the school sharing the information from the survey and the student's research about ADHD; the student also offered to help write an article for the monthly news flyer that the principal distributes to parents. The responses to the surveys were complete and impressive, and suggest that the student engaged in effective rhetorical activity with the teachers at

the school. Hopefully the engagement with the principal will also produce results. (10/10)

This descriptive evaluation differs from the traditional genre of "end comment" found on many student compositions. First, it begins by simply restating what the finished compositions are: *A survey of elementary school teachers* and *a letter to the principal of the school.* The descriptive evaluation also notes the potential of another text to emerge from the assignment, *an article for the monthly news flyer,* even though this piece of writing is not complete at the time the assignment is graded. As summative comments, these opening three clauses simply state what the student produced.

Traditional end comments often begin with a remark that praises the writer. Erika Lindemann's (1987) sample commentary in *A Rhetoric for Writing Teachers* begins in exactly this fashion. "You have a strong sense of organization for the whole paper" (p. 213), she wrote to her student, David.[1] The traditional genre of end comment discourages either a negative statement (e.g., "this paper is junk") or a simple statement of fact (e.g. "this paper has five paragraphs."). Rather, the formula is more likely to produce praise, followed by critique, and then ending in praise or encouraging words "for the next time."

Lindemann's example follows this rule by transitioning through a description of the student paper in her second sentence and into a critique in her third: "The first and last paragraph express the same general idea, and the three body paragraphs break it into 'aid,' 'education,' and 'entertainment.' I would have liked to know more specifically what you like to do with your free time, how your education has changed your attitudes, and what your outlook on life is" (p. 213). The "I would have liked" phrase is a prelude to an analysis and an evaluation of the paper based on what the student did not do rather than a consideration of what the student did. It is, to be sure, carefully couched within supportive words (i.e., the opening praise and a final clause that says "I'll be glad to help"), but the body of

---

[1]Lindemann's (1987) entire end comment:

You have a strong sense of organization for the whole paper. The first and last paragraph express the same general idea, and the three body paragraphs break it into "aid," "education," and "entertainment." I would have liked to know more specifically what you like to do with your free time, how your education has changed your attitudes, and what your outlook on life is. Before you start drafting your next paper, spend at least thirty minutes probing each of the subtopics, jotting down specific examples or incidents to support the general ideas. Then write a rough draft just to get the ideas down. Finally go back over the draft; ask of each sentence *how? Why? In what way? Such as?* To find even more evidence to support each statement. I'd like you to work on ways to let me "see" specifically what you mean by *things, attitudes, lifestyle, outlooks.* Please log the spelling problems (each check in the margins represents one misspelling in that line of your paper) in your journal and bring it to your conference next week. If you can't account for all the check marks, I'll be glad to help. (pp. 213–214)

Lindemann's comment is a critique and a request for the student to write what I-as-the-teacher-would-have-liked. As summative remarks, even the best process-influenced end comments tend to be "teacher talk" about what a teacher would have liked to see rather than reflections about what is in the paper.

Descriptive evaluation can also be guilty of discussing what is not in a paper: "The responses to the surveys were complete and impressive, and suggest that the student engaged in effective rhetorical activity with the teachers at the school. Hopefully the engagement with the principal will also produce results." These sentences turn away from the actual student compositions and begin to report on the interactions that went into creating this assignment (e.g., the responses to the surveys) and the possible interactions that may occur after the assignment is officially complete (e.g., Hopefully the engagement with the principal will also produce results). Even in describing components of an assignment that are not *present in* the student composition, however, descriptive evaluation sticks to what is—it analyzes and acknowledges the results from the composition and its interactive qualities. Lindemann's end comment is also interactive, but in a way that highlights its school-based form of interaction rather than composing as an activity that involves audiences beyond the teacher; she concludes:

> Before you start drafting your next paper, spend at least thirty minutes probing each of the sub-topics, jotting down specific examples or incidents to support the general ideas. Then write a rough draft just to get the ideas down. Finally go back over the draft; ask of each sentence *how? Why? In what way? Such as?* To find even more evidence to support each statement. I'd like you to work on ways to let me "see" specifically what you mean by *things, attitudes, life-style, outlooks.* Please log the spelling problems (each check in the margins represents one misspelling in that line of your paper) in your journal and bring it to your conference next week. If you can't account for all the check marks, I'll be glad to help. (pp. 213–214)

Lindemann's comment is "interactive" in the sense that she is asking the student to "interact" with her directives as a teacher (e.g., "spend at least thirty minutes probing each of the sub-topics, jotting down specific examples"; "write a rough draft"; "go back over the draft"; "ask of each sentence *how? Why? In what way? Such as?*"). But this is not the risky interactions that I have been championing. These are the safe and tame interactions of the classroom. They are exactly the types of interactions that Ulmer, Sirc, and Rice are trying to destroy. These "interactive" directions drive the essay away from its relevance for the student and make it relevant for the teacher (what-I-would-have-liked). Descriptive evaluation is not about what-I-would-have-liked, but rather about what is. It is a way to begin to acknowledge and consider the interactions involved in creating multimedia compositions that reach beyond the traditional boundaries of the classroom. It is also a way to situate the assessment of a composition within its social context.

DESCRIPTIVE EVALUATION AND GRADES

Obviously, the student's survey and her letter to the principal were graded favorably (10/10). But it is hard to tell why these compositions were graded this favorably based only on the descriptive evaluation. The product of a descriptive evaluation alone does not provide access to the situation within which a composition works. Looking at two other descriptive evaluations might reveal the relations between judgments of a composition's value and the descriptive assessments:

> A letter to the Vice President for Action at NOW. The letter is a bit weak in the beginning; the student says "I *inadvertently* found information that suggested that certain psycho-pharmaceuticals or antidepressants are being marketed specifically to women." The "inadvertently" bothered me as well as the wordiness of the sentence. The move to talk about specifics—Eli Lilly and Carla Spartos's article is where the letter moves, engages, begins. The final paragraph that lists action steps for NOW is also good. The targeting of the letter to Olga Vives at NOW is also good. It seems such a shame that the letter backs into the issue rather than starting strongly by saying, this is a problem for women help us fix it! (9/10)

> Letters sent to National Pharmaceutical Association (NPA) and National Community Pharmacists Association (NCPA). These letters asked the organizations to make their members aware of herb-drug interactions. The opening paragraph seemed wordy (e.g., why say "to briefly express my concern," simply state the concern). The evidence in paragraphs 2 and 3 seemed excellent—concise and attention catching. The letter ends with a thank you for allowing me to express my concern; it does not end with an action plan or even a suggested next step for the NPA and NCPA. (8/10)

Both descriptive comments are more textually detailed than the descriptive comment about the composition that was scored 10/10. Both contain quotations from the students' compositions (e.g., "I *inadvertently* found information that suggested that certain psycho-pharmaceuticals or antidepressants are being marketed specifically to women" and "to briefly express my concern"). They also contain language that is more judgmental than the language in the 10/10 description (e.g., *bothered me* and *the letter moves, engages, begins*; and, e.g., *seemed wordy* and *seemed excellent*). The inclusion of these judgments makes these descriptive evaluations resemble Lindemann's end comment—they are judging and asking, or almost asking, for something that is not there, for what-I-would-have-liked.

However, Lindemann's questions may be gentler to her student. When Lindemann uses words from the student's composition, she asks the student to let her "see" more about his words: "I'd like you to work on ways to let me 'see' specifically what you mean by *things, attitudes, life-style, outlooks.*" Analyzing her own comments, Lindemann writes, "The comments don't label problems; rather they emphasize how and why communications fails" (p. 216). No matter how hidden the agency is in this sentence, notice it is the comments that "label" and "communication" that fails not the writer or the reader, the failure is a problem that the student must fix by allowing the teacher to "see."

In the descriptive evaluations, both problems (*bothered me* and *seemed wordy*) and successes (*the letter moves, engages, begins* and *seemed excellent*) are labeled. Because the communication that is being evaluated is not the student's communication with the teacher, but rather the student's communication with another audience, the summative comments and their judgmental remarks document aspects of that communication rather than justify a grade or a method of rewriting. Descriptive evaluation, then, is different from the traditional process-based end comment because the teacher uses language to document how a composition took part in a situated interaction rather than using the end comment to assess a work and recommend changes.

SITUATED INTERACTIONS

Given that the previous descriptions are parts of a classroom assessment system, where interaction and situation are both acknowledged as important standards by which to judge otherwise disparate student compositions, consider how these descriptions capture interactions. Also consider how these descriptions provide a gateway into an evaluative judgment (i.e., the assigning of a grade) that looks at the situation in which a composition was created. All three of the descriptive evaluations explicitly comment on the compositions' interactive qualities.

The descriptive evaluation of the survey about ADHD and the letter to the principal notes that the survey was "followed up by a letter" and that "the student also offered to help write an article for the monthly news flyer that the principal distributes to parents." In addition, the interactive quality of the surveys as compositions is highlighted by the judgmental comment about the responses to the surveys as "complete and impressive." The conclusion "that the student engaged in effective rhetorical activity with the teachers at the school" and the hope that the "engagement with the principal will also produce results" further locates these compositions within a process of situated interaction. The student is clearly engaging with her audiences in ways that reach beyond the texts. If she had written a survey and sent it into teachers at an elementary school where she had no personal contacts and had not spoken to the teachers and principal before distributing the survey, her results—the number and volume of responses—would not have been as good. Texts, or compositions, are embedded in social networks, and acknowledging this is not a disservice. It is a basic lesson in writing—when you compose, you compose for somebody.

The descriptive evaluation of the NOW letter also comments on the interactive qualities of the composition by praising the "action steps for NOW." In addition, the descriptive evaluation notes that the student created a participatory framework by identifying her audience in concrete terms: "Targeting of the letter to Olga

Vives at NOW is also good." These moves are important for the composition's quality, and the lack of interaction seems to be held against the letters to the National Pharmaceutical Association (NPA) and National Community Pharmacists Association (NCPA). In fact, "the evidence in paragraphs 2 and 3" is acknowledged as "excellent—concise and attention catching," but the letter "does not end with an action plan or even a suggested next step for the NPA and NCPA." The quality of the writing is there, but the interactive components of the composition are missing. This judgment call is difficult, because students are used to being judged on the quality of their work—where quality is defined as what is "in" the work. However, quality in communication involves the reception of a text as well as its production. Making students aware of this quality of communication and holding them accountable for it requires diligence and the creation of new types of assignments and new assessment systems. The reward is that composition can be assessed as communication rather than composition as test taking.

If students are told to imagine that they are writing to a doctor and then their work is read and graded while pretending to read "from a doctor's perspective," then this is only reinforcing the boundaries of the classroom and the idea that student work is merely practice. Standards based around textual features and used to evaluate one-size-fits-all essays continue to assume that student writing is only practice. Practice is important in baseball and in violin, but practice without the promise—or even the possibility—of performance is dull, and students soon realize that it is irrelevant. Imagine being told to take batting practice day in and day out, but never being given the chance to play in a game—even in a scrimmage. The dullness of the activity would soon make you bored, and in turn you would not care about the activity anymore. Unfortunately, this is what happens all too often in writing instruction where students are asked to produce what-the-teacher-wants or what-the-readers-of-the-exam-want. Teachers would be better off if they asked students to produce meaningful compositions and then devised assessment systems that looked at those works as interactive and situated communications.

ASSESSMENT SYSTEMS

The National Commission on Writing's emphasis on "students' inherent interest" speaks to the issue of relevance as a motivational tool to encourage student learning, and the National Commission on Writing's concern about new media "methods of creating and sharing writing" underscores the possibilities of interaction as an important component in 21st-century literacies. However, the SAT 2005 writing assessment system that spurred the creation of the National Commission on Writing itself[2] does not incorporate technology in ways that consider the *situated* qualities of student interest nor the possibilities of using IT to document student

---

[2]"The decision to create the Commission was animated in part by the Board's plans to offer a writing assessment in 2005 as part of the new SAT" (p. 7).

interactions. The College Board's innovative use of technology is limited to the distribution of essays to graders, and to colleges' interested in seeing students' essays. Unfortunately, the SAT designers did not, or could not, envision the development of a writing assessment system that took full advantage of IT as part of the students' composing processes. Instead, they incorporated IT as part of the grading and result distribution process.

Still the National Commission on Writing notes:

> If assessment systems are to help improve writing, several challenges must be overcome. Three are of particular concern to the writing community. The first is that no single piece of writing, even generated under ideal conditions, can serve as an adequate indicator of overall proficiency. The second is that students need enough time to plan, produce, revise and edit a single piece of written work under test conditions. While the amount of time required may vary depending on the assessment itself, without adequate time, students cannot provide an accurate picture of their abilities. The third is a sense of concern about the appropriate uses of different types of assessment. Confusion about policy goals frequently confounds measurement purposes and instruments. It is unlikely that the same assessment instrument can be used for program evaluation, institutional accountability, and enhanced student learning. (pp. 21–22)

The first two points address the validity of writing assessments and their alignment with a high-tech curriculum. When writing is thought of as *situated interaction*, the standards of assessment shift into new categories. No longer can a composition be judged as a measurement of learning or a display of skills to meet preset ideals of proficiency. Rather, a composition needs to be judged for how well it works in a given situation. How well do the writers understand their audience? How well do they understand the participatory framework that they, in part, create? The designers of large-scale assessment systems must take up these challenges if they are to help teachers meet the goals set by the National Commission on Writing.

ELECTRONIC PORTFOLIOS

Nationally, the uses of electronic portfolios both inside and outside of writing programs illustrate aspects of the evaluative techniques I am advocating: distribution, interaction, description, and situation. The need to implement these techniques of evaluation, as Eva Baker (1998) points out, is not simply a liberal or radical reaction to the dehumanizing effects of testing and assessment. The pressures brought to bear by changes in the media used for literacy on existing means of reading, writing, learning, and evaluating are driving this reevaluation of assessment.

A refusal to grapple with these issues will produce numerous failures in terms of assessment systems as well as in terms of students' lives. This reevaluation is not an abstract and self-contained process. It involves all sorts of tendencies and agencies working out of different motivations and positions. The question of how to assess student work as literacy practices and media are changing is not just a question asked by teacher-researchers. It is also a question raised by advocates of raised standards and mandated assessments, business coalitions lobbying for higher standards, and boards of education and trustees. Grounding the development of evaluative methods for computer-mediated writing instruction and electronic portfolio assessment in processes that distribute responsibility among a variety of readers and situate assessment within local, social contexts could eliminate the problems of mass, large-scale assessments and the decontextualized pedagogies they encourage.

The College Board, and ETS for that matter, make their money from the students who take the test paying fees. However, the market for the tests is not the consumer who buys the product. The market is admission offices, college administrators, university assessment and measurement experts, and to a lesser extent college faculty who must believe in the accuracy and usefulness of the test. Although the College Board knows that the best determiner of college success is high school GPA, the logic of college admissions relies on outside exams. Why use another factor to determine admission to college? The assumption is that high school teachers are biased and that an "objective" test is needed to determine students' abilities. If high school GPAs are not accepted as trustworthy predictors or demonstrations of proficiency, then it is clear that external evaluations will persist. Is it possible to design IT systems that truly take the National Commission on Writing's advice to heart and assess writing as communication and learning?

The answer is that it is possible but difficult. It requires imagination and the development of new theories about writing assessment (Huot, 2002, 1996). It also requires that teachers and assessment agencies put into practice the insights gained from 20 years work with portfolios. Models in Kentucky and Oregon offer hope for print-based portfolios, extending the insights gained from these large-scale assessments to electronic media could be productive (Hillocks, 2002, pp. 155–188; Kentucky State, 1996). Programs within higher education have also been developing many, many forms of portfolio assessment (Belanoff & Dickson, 1991; Elbow & Belanoff, 1986; Gruber, 1992; Yancey & Huot, 1997).

One of the key components in portfolio assessment is the use of reflection and meta-commentary. Cover letters have become nearly ubiquitous in portfolio assessment as Liz Hamp-Lyons and William Condon (1999) noted. Given the value of reflection and meta-commentary, I want to explore how the students' meta-commentaries help create the situation within which a piece is judged. How do the student responses inform a teacher's or a grader's understanding of the situation in which a composition was put together? A teacher's descriptive evaluations have shown how they can document (or infer) the interactions that occurred both as a student was composing and as they began sizing up their audiences. But the descriptive evaluations do not fully capture the situation within which the student wrote—they do not capture the classroom aspect of the writing, and they do not consider the students' intentions when composing. The assignment that produced the wide array of compositions mentioned at the beginning of the chapter asked students to turn in a bulleted list along with their critical literacy project. The items in the list were:

- the problem you've found
- the action that you'd like to see taken to move toward a solution to that problem
- the audience you've selected to address (i.e., who the heck has the power to move toward a solution)
- the genre/form of writing that you've selected to work in

Although Edward Tufte (2003) decried the effects of PowerPoint and other slideware programs on education and corporate communication, the form of a bulleted list is becoming a mode of writing and presenting information. Bulleted lists are used in PowerPoint slides. They find their way easily into student compositions produced in Microsoft Word. Arguably, they are influencing the way information is being represented. As horrible as it may sound, the effective bulleted list may be a genre of the future. By giving students the assignment as a bulleted list, and asking them to create a bulleted list as an end product, the format of the quick and abbreviated overview is encouraged. However, students can write both within the expectations of the bulleted list genre and against those expectation. The student who created the Web site intended to inform the public about SSRIs and addiction turned in an extensive bulleted list:

- Selective Serotonin Reuptake Inhibitors, anti-anxiety drugs like Paxil and anti-depression drugs like Prozac, are widely prescribed and taken under the assumption that they are not addictive. The claim that these drugs are not addictive is based on the definition of addiction supplied by the FDA, the pharmaceuticals, and many doctors that a drug is only addictive if taking it creates a "drug-seeking behavior," a craving, and if only increasing dosages can allow the user to achieve the state of euphoria that they crave. The SSRIs do not cause a state of euphoria. Patients are not tempted to take increasing dosages there is no craving; enough Prozac is enough Prozac. Using the FDA definition of "addictive" the claim that SSRIs are not addictive is true, but it is not informative. SSRIs create dependence. The drugs do not cure the disorders that they are prescribed to treat, they simply alleviate the symptoms. Counseling, perhaps psychotherapy, with remedial action must accompany the use of the drugs to cure the mental disorders that indicated their prescription. Primary care physicians are replacing the work of mental health professionals with pills too often prescribed as a panacea for a range of disorders often diagnosed, or misdiagnosed, using over-simplified methods. Besides dependence on drugs without necessary accompanying psychological therapy, there is also the problem of withdrawal. Many patients have powerful withdrawal symptoms, often diagnosed as the reoccurrence of the original disorder, and sometimes much worse than the problems that caused the prescription of the drugs. When prospective users of SSRIs are informed that the drugs are not addictive the generally assume that there are no withdrawal symptoms associated with their use. This is not true.

• I would like to see good honest consumer information written in "plain English" made available. Patients need to be their own informed advocates, or have a friend or family member act as their advocate, not only about prescription drugs but also about other health care issues. Most doctors are willing to be paternalistic in the sense of digesting complex information for their patients and boiling things down to a confident recommendation, a prescription. But most doctors are equally willing to work with an informed patient. Doctors are paternalistic on demand. They are not salesmen trying to sell you a used car that you don't want. Patients, the consumers hold the power.

• That said, it is the patient that I want to reach with clear information about SSRIs. People do question drug use these days. I want to show drug users and prospective users a clear essay that points out the benefits of taking SSRIs as well as reports some of the problems that have been reported. I have come to think that anyone suffering from deep persistent depression or overwhelming anxiety should probably take these drugs if they are prescribed by their doctor. For mild or episodic disorders, the benefits and risks should be more closely examined. Doctors know this stuff already. I will target consumers, so in this case, people who have by one means or another been diagnosed, perhaps self-diagnosed as having a mental disorder, mild or not.

• I will collaborate with my son, Doug to build a web page. Researching these drugs I have many times thought, "I have to tell someone about this. Everyone needs to know this." These drugs are widely prescribed. I know many people, young and old, and among those of us somewhere in between, who have taken or are taking them. I will use the Internet to "broadcast" my three-page paper. We will use meta-tags and blog posts and word of mouth to try to get a hit or two. And as with any first-time endeavor, we will learn as we go.

This text clearly reaches beyond the boundaries of the genre of "bulleted list" and more closely resembles five distinct paragraphs simply formatted as a bulleted list, but the student provides a fuller context within which to situate the reading and grading of his Web site. By answering questions about the content of the composition, the intended action that might result from the composition, the writer's awareness of audience, and issues of genre and form, the students provide an explicit articulation of their vision of the participatory framework within which the composition has taken place. If graders read over this list and their own description of the composition, the decision about how to score the essay is then informed by an awareness of the interactions and situations that provide not only the background within which the Web site was composed but also provide the fabric of (i.e., the meaning-making apparatus, or the participatory framework, for) the composition.

What is the value of this extended bulleted list as a reflection? By having students describe their own work, they are putting reflection into action. They are naming the process and making that process public. But, they are also doing more than that. The very act of naming and describing what one has done creates an opportunity for reflecting on that action and learning about it. Meta-commentary develops higher order thinking skills, and when meta-commentary takes a written format it is captured and documented so that the student and others can view both the process of creation as well as the product that resulted. The composed artifact is situated within an appropriate context.

The descriptive evaluation of this Web site will further help with understanding how the student's own meta-commentary adds a vital element to the situational understanding of the composition:

A website (collaboratively built by the student and his teenage son) on SSRIs and dependence. The student says that the purpose of the website was "to reach [patients] with clear information about SSRIs. People do question drug use these days. I want to show drug users and prospective users a clear essay that points out the benefits of taking SSRIs as well as reports some of the problems that have been reported. I have come to think that anyone suffering from deep persistent depression or overwhelming anxiety should probably take these drugs if they are prescribed by their doctor." The question would be how was traffic directed toward this site? Meta-tags were included: <meta name="keyword" content="selective, serotonin, reuptake, inhibitors, Paxil, Prosac, addiction, dependence"> It might have been better to have Prozac instead of Prosac as a meta-tag. Also, SSRIs should have been a meta-tag. These two changes would have given the site a better chance to get more hits. Posting the site name on blogs (the student's and perhaps his son's might also have helped direct traffic and increase the website prominence on search engines such as google). It is funny how a rhetorical stance becomes so dependent upon technology, and the technology of the meta-tag. Just a note: using the keyword serotonin, the site is not in the top 50 hits on google—not a failure since the keyword is crowded, but it does underscore the difficulty of reaching patients with clear information about SSRIs if you are simply another person. (9/10)

The descriptive evaluation here is distinctive from traditional process-influenced end comments such as Lindemann's. Like the descriptive evaluations of the letter to NOW and the letters to NPA and NCPA, it is more textually detailed than the descriptive comment about the school survey and letter to the principal. However, the textual details above are html-related rather than details from "the composition itself" (e.g., Meta-tags were included: <meta name="keyword" content="selective, serotonin, reuptake, inhibitors, Paxil, Prosac, addiction, dependence">). The scare quotes around "the composition itself" are intended to underline the fact that html-related details are now part of the composition, even if they are not recognized as such.

The descriptive evaluation is much better at capturing *interaction* than it is at representing the *situation* within which the student composed. It notes that the student collaborated with his son, that the student considered his intended audience, and that some of the hoped for interaction was limited by particular meta tag choices. The description misses situational elements that are brought forward by the student's own meta-commentary, such as the major problem that the student has identified and the actions that the student envisions coming out of his writing. In the bulleted point about the hoped for results from the Web site, the student reflects on details about the social situation:

> Patients need to be their own informed advocates, or have a friend or family member act as their advocate, not only about prescription drugs but also about other health care issues. Most doctors are willing to be paternalistic in the sense of digesting complex information for their patients and boiling things down to a confident recommendation, a prescription. But most doctors are equally willing to work with an informed patient. Doctors are paternalistic on demand. They are not salesmen trying to sell you a used car that you don't want. Patients, the consumers hold the power.

These details about doctors and patients are similar to the social and genre knowledge (i.e., the domain knowledge) that would be required for a teacher to understand a gangsta rap composition. Whereas many of the details in the previous passage are "common knowledge," the student's framing of his work in terms of those details keys the reader into the particular participatory framework within which the student sees himself working. The student's reflection provides part of the situation that the reader needs to infer in order to be able to read, interpret, and grade the composition.

CLOSING: SITUATIONS AND PARTICIPATORY FRAMEWORKS

As the discussion has been moving around the descriptive evaluations of critical literacy projects, it has looked at how descriptive evaluations acknowledge interaction. The interactions between students and their audiences have been situated, but there is also a way in which the compositions are situated within the classroom. The works emerged from classroom assignments and were produced for a grade, so they are not removed from schooling but are situated within the discourses of school at the same time that they reach beyond those conventions.

When students are able to choose not only the subject about which they are composing but also the media through which they reach their audiences, the selection of the composition media becomes a significant rhetorical choice. What do you want to do with a composition? How do you most effectively persuade NOW to look into how a pharmaceutical company, such as Eli Lily, is marketing drugs to women? How do you convince teachers as a general group that they need to be aware of, and perhaps critical of, the growing tendency to medicate students for disruptive behavior? Are letters sent through the mail the most effective way to make these groups aware of these issues? Would e-mail be a more effective means? Are there other forums that writers should consider? Public Internet discussion boards? Faculty meetings at local schools? Would a phone call to NOW be as effective as a letter? Would it be more effective? Do the students need to combine media, depending on the civic engagement or advocacy project that they are working on?

The choices that students make here are as important as the choices they make about where to place a period or an html tag. If a student's letter to a congressperson has sentence fragments, then that letter is not likely to be read very seriously. But, if the student cannot find the congressperson's address, then the letter will never reach its audience. Both would constitute failures of communication, because an intended message did not get through. Writing teachers' jobs should include making students aware of the situations within which they compose. This approach does not ignore grammar, does not ignore standards, but it makes grammar and standards have a point, a real-world communication agenda that is meaningful for the student.

Using computer-mediated communication forums to facilitate critical literacy projects does not have to lead toward the avante garde form of a myhappening sampler composition (Ulmer, 1985, 1989; Sirc, 2000, 2002; Rice, 2003). The use of computer-mediated communication forums to facilitate critical literacy projects can lead to the production of multiple forms of traditional texts or speech acts, which are themselves dependent on the composer's goals and audiences. Fundamentally then, teachers still must confront, and ask the developers of large-scale assessment systems to confront, the need to consider situation when evaluating these works. Description and reflection allow for the documentation of the situations within which compositions occur. Associating teacher description and student reflection with a multimedia composition in an electronic portfolio or database helps situate the complex, challenging and always newly emergent forms within the intentions of the writer and the demands of the audience.

4

Negotiating Assessment and Distributive Evaluation

While Marjorie Goodwin's (1990) concept of participatory frameworks leads me to stress the need for a teacher to descriptively evaluate the situation within which a communication act takes place, the idea of a participatory framework also suggests that multiple agents are evaluating a speaker. When a child on the streets of Philadelphia speaks and that speech is inflected for an audience, and opens to invite members of that audience into the debate—to take sides—then, the audience members are always evaluating and creating the meaning of the participatory framework. For the teaching of composition, this multiple interactivity urges moving beyond a student–teacher vision of the composing process and to see the student within a framework of other students, the teacher, and potential audience members outside of school.

Because the processes of composing and communicating are distributive, the process of assessment should also be distributed among multiple agents. However, creating a system of distributive assessment does not necessarily mean having students grade one another. In fact, a far more effective method of distributive evaluation is to employ techniques for collaborative learning. If the concept of collaborative learning in composition studies emerges from anywhere, it is from Kenneth Bruffee's work (1993, 1984, 1973), as well as from the practices employed in some electronic portfolio systems and from the ideas of learning contracts and negotiated curriculum developed in critical pedagogy. The best way to sink into the concept of distribution is to turn to a classroom and see how distributive assessment grows out of a process of negotiating evaluation criteria.

STUDENTS KNOW HOW TO LISTEN

Students know how to listen. They are surrounded by what Don DeLillo (1985) described as the white noise of who we are, where we are, when we are. Now the cul-de-sac of the 20th century opens into the 21st century, and within primary language arts classrooms, secondary English courses, and college writing courses language is used over and over and over again—even by the most caring teachers—in what Hugh Mehan (1979) identified as the IRE formula: Teacher initiates, student responds, teacher evaluates.

In his study of class discussions and teacher preparation, James D. Marshall (1991) identifies two conflicting ideals about interaction with students that many highly successful teachers have. By interviewing secondary school teachers, Marshall finds that "on the one hand, teachers felt discussions were an opportunity for 'interaction, a chance for students' self discovery.' . . . On the other had, though, teachers also felt that discussion should 'go somewhere,' should stay 'on track' and away from 'irrelevancies' " (p. 41). Although the teachers claim that they want to allow the students to control classroom discussion, Marshall's observations of their teaching lead him to conclude that these teachers, all with established reputations for excellence, "dominated most of the large-group discussions" (p. 42). The teachers voiced their concerns and maintained classroom order by controlling the ebb and flow of the discourse and by keeping the students focused on the teacher-selected subject matter. By the time students arrive in college composition classes, they have already been socialized into the modes of school discourse. They know the social behaviors that are appropriate. And they know that when an English teacher asks for discussion, it means controlled discussion. In "Getting Together, Getting Along, Getting to the Business of Teaching and Learning," Margaret Cintorino (1993) recalls her own schooling in the "legacy of student silence." She wrote, "We learned to still our young clamorous voices, to be quiet, and to remain quiet for much of the school day. We inherited, from the beginning of our school years, a legacy of student silence" (p. 23).

SCENE: NEW JERSEY SPRING

How can I pretend to represent the complexities of the compositions of 53 students over the course of a semester? Thick description and ethnography are popular in composition studies these days. Yet, I have so few insights, and you already know the traditional furniture arranged in rows or circles—the comfy instructor's chair that is padded, behind a large desk, and the uncomfortable students' desks, just slightly too small to spread out on and really write. Their hard plastic shells gleaming in the light, there are scribbles—graffiti—on a few desktops.[1] Although

---

[1]For more on institutional furniture see Shor (1980, pp. 56–65).

Stevens is an expensive school and the undergraduates receive laptops during orientation, I have not managed to draw one of the three newly renovated classrooms in the Humanities' Pierce building this semester. The renovated classrooms have network connections for the students' laptops, shared tables where groups of four or five can sit in a semi-circle and work, and a data projector on the ceiling for the instructor's computer. In this classroom that I have, we will use the laptop computers to write and we will connect to the network sockets that are in the walls, when we need to access the network. I will also reserve the old-fashioned computer lab across the hall with its ring of desktop computers and plethora of network hookups whenever possible.

The 53 students in two sections of Humanities 104—a second semester introduction to the humanities and writing course—are an amalgam of ethnicities, but are mostly male. There are only 6 young women among this set of aspiring engineers. Some of the students are upper middle-class, Italian, German, Jewish, Polish Americans who grew up in the suburban sprawl of the BoWash corridor. Some are children of the Indian subcontinent from elite cultural, educational, and economic backgrounds. Some are from Africa—Nigeria and South Africa. Some are immigrants or the children of immigrants from China, Korea, and Indonesia. Some have student visas, and one day hope to return to South America—or not. Some are scholarship boys and girls from Jersey City, Union City, and western Hoboken. These nonelite students "clump" together in groups that are far tighter than any of the other sets of students. There are 4 local students in one section, 5 in the other. They are not deep Siberians, not back-row dwellers, but rather they sit near the front of the class, waiting. All of them—elite and nonelite, men and women—are on a path toward careers in technology—engineers, physicists, and mathematicians. Some are moved by a passion for their subject; some are moved by the promise of wealth. Some are not moved at all, and they do not know why they are here at this small, technical research-oriented institution. But they are here nonetheless, and the promises of computer-mediated communication loom large for them.

None of this reveals anything about these students' abilities as communicators. None of this begins to get under the skin of computer-mediated writing instruction and the evaluation of student compositions. However, it does begin to sketch out the context within which I worked with these students, and within which they tolerated—and perhaps enjoyed and learned from—my questions about writing, computer-mediated communication, and assessment.

Asking the Students a Question: What Is Good Writing?

After telling the students a little about myself and asking them to tell me their names and something memorable about themselves, I begin class by asking them to write down the criteria they consider important for good writing. I do not tell them what type of writing; I do not say academic or fiction; I simply ask them to write for a few minutes from their experience and explain to me what makes a piece of writing good. Paulo Freire and Antonio Faundez (1989) argued for a pedagogy of questions, the initiation of inquiry that begins with open-ended questions based on student experience rather than teacherly expertise. Although student choices of readings and student-centered classroom activities are important for critical-democratic curricula, remember that each of these pedagogical practices can easily be negated or adapted as part of the status quo of traditional schooling. Ira Shor (1996) argues that

> singular practices like seating [in circles instead of rows] must be situated in an overall critical-democratic curriculum oriented toward change. Defining circle seating as empowerment by itself is simply too easy and too "utopian" (in the sense of being uncritically detached from power relations in the system as a whole). It misses the complex strategies and resistances involved in the transformation of students and teachers in the rhetorical setting of a classroom. (p. 65)

By beginning with the content of the course (i.e., writing) and the activity of grading (i.e., assessing the value of writing), I hoped to provide the students with some control over the curriculum and the ways in which their learning was evaluated. By opening up the process of assessment for discussion, I hoped to flip the instruments of the institution back on themselves. While circle seating and process writing pedagogies have been adapted to serve the status quo, I wondered what would happen if we took a pillar of the educational status quo—assessment—and used it for democratic-critical ends.

So, on day one, I began with open-ended questions about value, about evaluation, and about the classroom activity, the learning experience we were supposed to be taking part in this semester. John Seely Brown and Paul Duguid (2002) noted that

> learning is usually treated as a supply-side matter, thought to follow teaching, training, or information delivery. But learning is much more demand driven. People learn in response to need. When people cannot see the need for what's being taught, they ignore it, reject it, or fail to assimilate it in any meaningful way. Conversely, when they have a need, then, if the resources for learning are available, people learn effectively and quickly. (p. 136)

What was valuable about writing, about communication, to these technical students? All too often I have experienced student rejection—especially among technical students—of the basic premise, the basic value of writing instruction.

All too often the writing instruction in American colleges continues to pursue subjects of inquiry and methods of evaluation that students of technology see as irrelevant to their academic lives or their professional careers.[2] In these courses, I was determined to ask students about what they wanted to write about and how we should evaluate that writing. I needed to know how they saw writing and communicating in terms of their own needs. So I asked, and they wrote and then they read out loud:

> A good piece of writing is concise. It is clear. It uses correct grammar.

> Writing is good when it gets the imagination going, when it makes you think.

> Good writing has a thesis statement. It supports this thesis with examples. In order for a person to consider whether a piece of writing is good or bad, it must be correct.

> Poetry is good writing when you can't understand it (quickly). Newspapers are good writing when you can understand them (quickly).

> Good writing uses correct English. A good essay has a thesis statement and there is structure to it. It meets the needs of the audience.

I let the definitions wash over the class. I let them hear each other's words, and I kept my mouth shut until after the fifth definition. Some of the students had begun to lose focus—their attention was drifting to the windows, the hallway, away from the reader's words.

I said, "So we've got different definitions of good writing. Let's see if we can write some of these down and come to some sort of agreement. I heard 'concise.' " I wrote "concise" on the board. I was trying to back load my comments here; I wanted student discourse, the students' own words to serve as the basis for our evaluative criteria. Later in the semester, I often moved away from the front of the room during these types of activities, handing the chalk to students so that they can write on the board. By displacing my White, male teacher's body, by moving the talking head from the front of the room, I forged a different dynamic among students and instructor.

However, teaching at a technical institute where most courses are either lectures or labs creates expectations for students. And although I do envision my classroom as more like a lab than a lecture hall, I do not want to create a permissive environment. Science labs have TAs who monitor students according to pro-

---

[2] A quick survey of college textbooks for composition courses reveals readers that focus on multiculturalism, readers that focus on cultural studies approaches, readers that draw on popular magazines. All of these books reflect general humanistic inquiry as the vehicle for teaching writing. Students of technology correctly recognize these books as well as rhetorics that prompt general writing skills as irrelevant to their interests. Using a generative themes approach with technology students does not mean there is no room for critical thinking, rather it means the critical thinking gets directed at subjects relevant to them—and toward areas they may have influence in during their careers—rather than toward domains that they will never work with once they leave the writing classroom.

cedures designed by faculty members; writing courses have instructors who are supposed to monitor students according to the traditional, unspoken procedures that instructors and students have learned through years and years of schooling. Inviting students to create a focused, democratic-critical learning environment can be mistaken for an anything-goes pedagogy, if one is not careful. The students' previous experiences of schooling and their current arrangement of science courses at Stevens coupled with my age—I was born around the time that 10 out of the 11 full-time faculty members in the Humanities department earned their PhDs—makes my implementation of student-centered learning challenging. I want to share control of the course with the students, but I also need to demonstrate the seriousness and validity of discussing writing and my expertise to facilitate these discussions. As a result at the beginning of the semester, I remain at the blackboard, a funnel, a secretary scribbling down the students' words. Working as a "scribe" instead of a speaker, I lower my profile and allow student discourse to fill the room. Later, I will curtail my presence even further and try to pass more control over to the students, but at that moment I tried to move the discussion forward by asking, "What other things did you hear?"

Community of Practice

I was hoping that they would tell me what they heard rather than my filtering the experience and selecting the valuable criteria for deciding whether or not a piece of writing is good. Whereas Marilyn Cooper and Cynthia Selfe (1990), Gail Hawisher and Charles Moran (1993), and Michael Spooner and Kathleen Yancey (1996) all pointed toward the potential of using asynchronous forums to make discussions less teacher-centered, I opted here for standard, face-to-face discussion because I wanted the students to feel themselves becoming part of what Jean Lave (1985, 1988; Lave et al., 1982) called a "community of practice." Lave's work on situated and distributed cognition argues that thought is not made up inside an individual's mind, but is rather constructed through interactions with material environments and other human agents. In her study of mathematical cognition and the everyday activity of grocery shopping, Lave has shown how humans adapt their stated goals and tasks based on local material conditions. In the case of the writing classroom, students should feel a connection not only with each other's ideas about writing, but with the person speaking. They can develop into a community of practice that bridges across media rather than working only in computer-mediated forums.

We were grounding our discussion of evaluation criteria within the local situation, as it seemed counterintuitive to exclude the rich set of contextual clues created in face-to-face interaction. We would draw on the benefits of computer-mediated asynchronous discussions after this face-to-face session. By creating an e-mail list, I would extend the conversation into the space between classes; however, I was determined not to use this asynchronous discussion forum as "a constantly accessible record" of the students' work for "monitor[ing] their out-of-class activities" (Thompson, 1990, p. 52). Rather, I wanted the face-to-face conversation to create the momentum that would spill over into the e-mail list and would allow me to remain silent—or nearly silent—online. As a result, I had decided to use an e-mail list forum instead of the asynchronous discussion board provided with the WebCT platform Stevens Tech supported. I had spoken with students from previous classes and they associated the discussion boards with observed and required assignments from other humanities courses that used WebCT. They told me there was a general feeling among students at Stevens that discussion boards were ways for teachers to "check that you had done the reading" instead of places where "real ideas got discussed." Because the asynchronous discussion boards had a reputation among students as tools for monitoring their work, I decided to use an e-mail listserv instead. For our purposes, e-mail discussion would allow for conversation outside of class, and I hoped it would seem different enough from the discussion boards to allow the students to feel that they were working on "real ideas" rather than going through dictated motions.

Before the students could create an active discussion list, I had to convince them that their words were more than the completion of a formal task. I had to demonstrate that learning to write—or that their comments, their dialogue about learning how to write—would have significance for them in terms of their material and institutional worlds. To ask students about what they value in writing without making their answers significant and influential in terms of the class—and in terms of grades for the class—merely shifts the mode of information delivery from teacher–student to student–student. This sort of student-centered curriculum is a sham; it is a continuation of the current hierarchies of power and modes of teaching under a rubric of interaction and dialogue. When asking students about the criteria they value in writing, teachers must be willing to show them—to take the risk of showing them—that their comments matter not only in the world of ideals but in the material world of institutionalized education. Still, this process is not instantly achievable.

Just as Shor (1996) notes the impossibility of walking into a classroom and declaring that the class will be democratic, I could not walk into the classroom and declare that students were going to determine the standards for grading. This process had to be open, dialogic, and negotiated. Students would have ideas about the qualities of good writing. Some would come from previous English teachers. Some of these ideas would come from the students' pleasure readings. Their ideas would conflict as well as compliment one another. I would agree with some of what they said and disagree with some of what they said. We would work on it. The students and I would discuss intensely the ideas of criteria, value, and evaluation over the course of 2 weeks, and then continue to circle back to the issue of assessment throughout the semester. By distributing discussions across media (e.g., face-to-face discussions and online forums) and situating them within powerful and meaningful discourses for students (i.e., assessments and grades), the class could experience assessment as a messy and complex activity that serves as a way of communicating.

Good Writing

But first we had to wrestle with the criteria, the ground rules, and the basis on which we were going to judge effective communication. Hands went up. Someone said, "correct." I wrote "Correct" on the board.

"Thesis." I wrote "thesis" on the board.

"Gets the reader's imagination going." I wrote "gets imagination going" on the board.

"Examples." I wrote "Examples" on the board.

"What about poetry and newspapers?" I asked.

"Poetry is just your opinion." Adam said. "Newspapers tell you the facts."

"So you judge poetry according to your opinion," I said, "and newspapers according to whether they present the facts or not."

"Yeah."

"But how do you know that the facts are the facts? How do you as a reader judge if something is true?"

Silence. I stumped them; I stumped myself. I tried again. "Maybe that's the wrong question," I said. "How do you decide whether to read a newspaper article or not?"

These stumbles are part of a discussion; a neatly planned lecture moves differently. I sort of know where I want these discussions to go, but I'm also trying to let the students talk through what they already know about communication. To lecture about genre and context as the be-all and end-all of writing evaluation would make the criteria predetermined rather than negotiated. By having this discussion, students gain a sense of the struggles we were going to have with writing criteria rather than assume that everyone else knew what THE good criteria were. Of course, the criteria we generated are in some sense always already predetermined. The students' views of good writing, especially in a school context, have already been taught. Most students know some version of the five-paragraph essay like a bad dream, and a good number can recite the steps of the writing process (brainstorm, draft, revise, final version) like a haunting mantra. The action of articulating what we value in writing, and what we want to value in this particular writing setting, helps pull out the stops—the illusions that this teacher, or any teacher, really knows what good writing is. In "Collaborative Learning and the 'Conversation of Mankind,' " Bruffee (1984) demonstrates that knowledge of academic discourse conventions can be created through structured collaborative tasks. This opening discussion was to provide a basis for the online collaborative work the students were going to take part in before the next face-to-face class meeting. I hoped to establish a sense of inquiry with these students, a sense of really questioning with them rather than talking at them. They know about communication and how language works. The trick is getting them to speak and us to listen.

"It depends on what you're interested in," someone says. We flounder around for a while. Eventually, I ask, "What's the difference between the sports page and the business section? Are their styles different?"

"No, they're both journalism."

"Ok," I say. "So what are the qualities of good journalism? How do those qualities differ from the qualities of good poetry?"

"See a newspaper lets you read it quickly. You read it at breakfast. It's got to be concise." He pauses to look at the board. "It's got to be concise, and correct, and it'll have examples. Imagination doesn't matter in the newspaper."

I smile. Ahh the blackboard, security safety, the words I wrote down. They'll help ground us. I turn to the word "thesis."

"And?" I ask as I point at "thesis." "Does a newspaper article have a thesis?"

"No."

"No. That's only in school," Shaun says, "you write a thesis because you're making an argument, a newspaper story isn't arguing it's just telling the facts. Like we said before."

"Ok, ok." I hold my hands up. "I want to ask you about a thesis as a quality in good writing. Do we cross it off the board, if it only works in academic writing?"

"No. You need it in academic writing. But you don't need it in a story about sports. It depends," Shaun says.

"The criteria vary," Joe adds.

Again, we're moving here. I nudge the conversation forward, "Like they do between poetry and a newspaper?"

"Yeah. A poem is one thing. You judge it depending on whether you like it or not. A newspaper article you judge on whether it gives you the facts in concise way."

"And how do I judge your essays?"

"One of our essays you judge according to how well it supports its thesis, its structure, its use of examples, you know."

"You're saying the qualities of a good piece of writing depend on the context?" I ask.

"Yeah, it depends," he says.

I write "CONTEXT" on the board.

"All these other things are important," I say. "But you're right, they vary from context to context, from writing situation to writing situation. If you're writing a newspaper article you write one way. If you're writing a history essay, you write another. If you're writing a lab report, you write another way. These are all issues of context, issues of genre, issues of audience."

I ask what sort of audience will they be writing for this semester. And the reply is you, the teacher. I ask them how they can anticipate what I'll want from their texts, and they looked bemused. They know, and I know, what I should want—good writing in the form of grammatically correct, organized, and well-argued essays. I also wanted these future engineers to see what Brown and Duguid (2002) have called the social fabric around information and information technologies. Brown and Duguid argue that designers often exclude, or do not consider, the social conditions within which an information technology will be used. That is, computer scientists, electrical engineers, and programmers often work in terms of technical needs, or industrial agendas, not in terms of social use. In this argument, Brown and Duguid ran parallel with recent work in composition studies that emphasizes the social context around composing.

"But, what," and I risk looking silly here, "does good writing mean?" I ask. "We've just pointed out that good writing depends on context. That good poetry is different than good journalism, and that both of those things—well at least the poetry—depend on the reader as much as the writer. So I guess what I'm asking here is what do you think the criteria for judging your writing this semester should be?"

This question is an important move because it attempts to situate the assessment and the criteria for evaluating the students' work in terms of the local conditions. Of course, students' responses and their ideas about how writing is assessed will come from their previous encounters with school and with writing classes. They will not produce means of evaluating writing that only reflect literacy practices from outside of school; on the contrary, they are more likely to reflect the values and means of assessment associated with school-based literacy. Still, we are not creating a means of assessment that evaluates nonacademic writing. Rather, we are developing evaluative methods that will be employed to judge their schoolwork. These criteria are situated and negotiated. However, all the criteria offered previously would seem to suit almost any writing class anywhere, secondary or postsecondary. Have the students been parroting rather than developing criteria? Does saying that we have "created" these criteria obscure how prefabricated they are? These are tough questions. Of course, the students are parroting what they have heard before. The game of telling teachers what they want to hear is old hat for them; in moments of despair, I can almost hear them thinking, "Lets just tick off the magic words and he'll let us out of here early." Still, by spreading this process out across a few weeks, by asking students to talk about issues of the qualities of good writing in a variety of media and by considering how we will apply these criteria in our local situation, the generic qualities of good writing will take on narrower and more contextualized nuances. Asking students to generate the criteria for assessment and talking about the importance of context for determining the effectiveness of a piece of writing, we come not only to see that effective communication depends on context but also to take part in a process that embodies this idea.

Final Words

I say, "You've all been in English classes before. You've all had at least a semester of humanities here at Stevens. What do you think the criteria should be? Don't answer now. I'm going to ask you to make up a list of five criteria for judging good writing in Humanities 104 and post it to our email discussion list. I'll email you-all a post that says criteria, and I'll let you talk. I really want you to think about the criteria you expect me to look for and the criteria you'd like me to use. Think about how you could argue for the criteria that you mention, ok? And bring a list of five criteria that you personally value to class next time."

"Can they be the same ones we use online?" Kim asks.

"Yes," I say, "Sure, they should be drawn from the email discussion. Think of the criteria—yours or someone else's—that you like best. And bring that to class."

My voice has shifted; I've already done something to indicate that I'm in the teacher's final word mode, because they are putting away their books, zipping up backpacks. It is amazing, how well they can read teachers. Our actions, our inflections, are transparent. Even the students who hate the classroom are experts at reading teachers. They've been so ingrained in the culture of school, they know the nuances, the twists and turns of classroom at the first signal of the final word, they pack.

As they prepare to depart, I say, "That's it for now."

NEGOTIATING ASSESSMENT CRITERIA

By asking themselves and their students questions about the criteria for assessing writing, teachers can provide a means of situating assessment not only in local classroom practice but also in an authentic communicative environment. "Authentic" communication, as Mikhail Bakhtin (1981) noted, is always affected by imbalances in power relations: It is never dialogic in a utopian, fully two-sided sense. The achieved utopia of negotiated assessment will always be compromised; it will always involve power relationships between the grader and the graded. Yet, asking students questions about how teachers evaluate writing also uncovers some of the dynamics around how and why they value writing. What do the students value in writing, about writing? What do they value about communicating with each other? What do they value about communicating with others outside of the classroom? And how will I, in this case, evaluate their actions, their words? Where do we begin a conversation about communication and writing in a course where computer-mediated communication will play a major role in the students' composing processes and in the processes of providing feedback and in the assessment of the students' work?

The Online Discussion

After setting up an e-mail listserv, I sent out an invitation to all the students. After the formalities of welcoming them to the list, it read, "so we're still thinking about criteria for judging writing. . . . Can you carry on the conversation we were having in class? Use this list as a way of testing out ideas before the next class. Cheers, Carl."

Within 3 hours, five students had responded:

"Hi Prof. Whithaus, I think good writing has a fire to it. It tells a story. Well, at least that's what my high school English teacher said. But that really does seem like the way to think about writing."

"Professor, I didn't really get what we were doing in class? And I'm not sure how to come up with criteria? Are these suppose to be for our writing or for the stuff we like to read?"

"As you said in class it depends on what context something is in. If we're talking papers for this class, then good writing has a thesis, a structure, uses evidence, has correct grammar, and stays on topic."

"Yeah, I think he wants us to write about class. The things you list make sense to me. I'm not sure how fire or telling a story fits?"

"Our papers should be readable, use effective vocabulary, have a thesis, have an effect on the reader, and support the thesis through structure."

Seventeen more students (out of 53) posted before the following class meeting, but these initial responses show a marked shift in the direction and tone of the discussion.[3] Each of the previous responses is worth thinking about in terms of the rhetorical position the writer takes and in terms of the criteria they list. The first two responses, although they are directed to the list, address me directly ("Hi Prof. Whithaus" and "Professor"). The third response also speaks to me as the teacher, but without the formal salutation (e.g., "as you said in class"). The fourth and fifth responses change the discussion from direct address to me to a dialogue among the students. By writing "Yeah, I think he wants us to write about class," the fourth writer begins to move the discussion toward what Cooper and Selfe (1990) have described as "powerful, non-traditional learning forums" where students can "resist, dissent, and explore the role that controversy and intellectual divergence play in learning and thinking" (p. 849). This change is marked both by a change of tone "Yeah" and by a positioning of the teacher in the third person "he wants us to." He also makes the discussion into an exchange among students by responding to both the second and third writers. When he writes that "the things

---

[3] I did not want the students to feel compelled to post, so I did not make it a requirement. I did want them to post in order to carry our discussions forward, however. The response rate (27/53) of this group is fairly standard from my experiences with a short, purposeful assignments that are not required. There are many, many variables that could go into this response rate—I'm not so interested in the response rate as in the class's ability as a group to carry on a conversation about evaluation criteria that is meaningful and not compulsory.

you list make sense to me," he is addressing the student who posted before him, and whose e-mail is included at the end of his response.

But this writer does more than that, he reaches back to the first post and questions this student's use of "fire" and "telling a story" as criteria. There is also an interesting note of grammar and "voice" inflection here. Although "I'm not sure how fire or telling a story fits" is a statement, the writer ends with a question mark. Why? To indicate a desire to continue the conversation? To indicate that he is not certain about his criticism? To show that the statement is a question? Although I did not ask the student why he used this punctuation mark at the end of this sentence, it is indicative of the new genres created by asynchronous discussion forums that Yancey and Spooner (1996) theorize as occurring between writing and speaking. If teachers build communicative activities around these computer-mediated environments that draw on "casual" modes of communication to address substantial issues, they may move toward a form of discourse where students can gain control of academic writing rather than allowing academic writing to gain control of them. Of course, students have long talked about academic writing in "casual" modes of discourse. Hallway conversations and discussions that spring up as students leave a classroom are full of casual modes of discourse. Some writing teachers reprimanded students for the use of colloquial language in formal academic writing. Aren't these moments evidence that serious, substantial issues can and do get discussed in informal language? Yes, but these moments are not validated by the participation—the observation of an instructor. In fact, when instructors observe "colloquial" language in printed essays, there is a tendency to mark it as incorrect, that is, as below the register of appropriate college-level written discourse. Yancey and Spooner's article suggested that this correction of informal discourse in writing does not make the jump into e-mail. Online discourse allows, and validates, academic communication in registers previously considered unsophisticated.

Although some of computer-mediated asynchronous communication spaces may have already established norms (e.g., the association at Stevens Tech of the WebCT discussion boards with teachers monitoring students), it is possible to work around these conventions by creating social spaces in face-to-face discussions that invite students to communicate their views. This strategy creates a dramatic shift in the age-old debate between educational technologists such as Ellis Page (1968) and Hunter Berland (1996), who argue for the use of the computer as a tool to evaluate student writing, and computers-and-writing specialists such as Patrick Finn (1977) and Liz Hamp-Lyons (2000), who argue for modes of writing assessment that are centered on teachers' knowledge of local conditions. By inviting students into the process of creating evaluation criteria, the low-stakes, interactive, student-centered discussions advocated for by Cooper and Selfe (1990) become staging grounds for discussions and writing activities about the institutional power structures—assessments—that influence students' everyday lives.

Day 2: Evaluation Criteria

The students return with their printed or handwritten lists of criteria. The classroom is warm; the heat is on high today, and someone has already tilted a window open. These windows do not slide up and down, but rather swing on a hinge placed in the middle so that the entire frame—both panes of glass as well as enclosed venetian blinds—moves at once when opened. I shuffle through papers. The day is already disorganized.

"Divide into small groups," I say. "Four or five to a group."

Six different groups form. Mostly groups of four. One group has six members, but I figure I'll let them work where they are comfortable for now. "As a small group, read your criteria out loud. Look over each other's criteria and decide on five that you want to put on the board."

"Remember whatever criteria we end up with today will be the criteria I use to evaluate your essays. We're going to go through this whole process today of moving from your individual criteria to group criteria to criteria for the entire class. So speak up. Remember you can argue for your criteria. Use this as a chance to call my attention to some aspect of writing that you think is important, that you want feedback on, ok?"

The groups work for about 15 minutes, and then I have one member from each group go to the board and write down the criteria the group has come up with. I ask them to explain the criteria when they are writing them down. Sometimes the group member writing the criteria explains them, sometimes another group member does. The important thing here is that the students are articulating what they see as valuable in a piece of academic writing.

After 25 minutes, the following list wraps around two walls of the room:

Important Content

Supporting Examples

Relevant Research

Transition (putting together the work)

Readability—smooth transition between ideas

Vocabulary—spelling errors and minor grammar errors that do not detract from the paper should be ignored

Structure—does the author utilize structure in a way to strengthen the thesis of the paper (e.g., Hayakawa's use of others' opinions)

Effect—is the paper unique

Structure

Focus

Content

Grammar

Quality of Information Presented
Reach on Overall Objective
Strong Intro. And Conclusion
All topics should be discussed

Organization
Subject Matter
Strong Intro. And conclusion
Quality not quantity

Content
Effectiveness
Creativity
Enjoyability

"Ok, what we want to look for now is commonalties," I say. "That is, ways of reducing this list down to four or five things.[4] If something appears in more than one list it is probably important, but if something appears only once that doesn't mean we're going to discard it."

"I really like the idea of 'enjoyability' as a quality. I like the idea of having a bit of fun when I read these. But that's not the only thing to consider." These criteria are collectively negotiated, but they will be applied individually. That is, for all the collaborative work that occurs in the class when I read or when the students read, we read and evaluate the paper or the screen that is in front of us. Our readings—our interpretations and applications of our negotiated criteria—will be filtered through our subjectivities. The reading experience—as many fiction writers have claimed, Jorge Borges, Italio Calvino, Paul Auster, and John Updike—is individual, and yet our readings and our evaluations are informed by complicated layers of conditioned responses. As a criteria, "enjoyability" will always be subjective, but a group naming and agreeing on a subjective criteria creates a shared experience, a shared acknowledgment that reading and evaluation are simultaneously radically subjective (e.g., Stanley Fish, 1980) and socially constructed

---

[4]I limited the number of criteria to four or five items because each term is pregnant with discussion possibilities. Having students select the most valuable criteria produces a discussion of those criteria and the selection process used for establishing them. Beyond that, it also shows the network of lines and ideas that intersect when one begins to talk about evaluating writing. It highlights the idea that a reader's subjectivity is informed by a series of, often competing, values and methods of reading. A list of four or five terms produces a neat and manageable list that can be written around and over, and the process of limiting criteria in itself is valuable because it forces choices AND forces individuals to articulate why they are advocating for those choices.

(e.g., David Bleich, 1988). Exposing the lines along which consensus and conflict about the value of a piece of writing is achieved can be as important of an act as evaluating the writing itself. In a pedagogy of questions, the process of raising questions creates the opportunities for learning along with the activity of answering the questions does.

"Ok I'm going to take the chalk and you tell me what to cross off the list and what is really important. I'll put a star next to the items we consider definite keepers."

This method of creating evaluation criteria does not ignore what Berland (1996) argued for as the "certain amount of standardization, particularly in writing mechanics," that "is an essential part of writing and writing assessment" (p. 256). It includes the students, which make up the community within which the communication is actually taking place, in the articulation of what standards will apply. Given the rapidly changing modes of communication noted by scholars of hypertext and computer-mediated communication such as Jay David Bolter and Richard Grusin (1999) and Steven Holtzman (1997), as well as Brandt's (1995) claims about residual literacy strategies and styles, composition teachers (especially those working in computer-mediated environments) must admit to the ever-increasing difficulty of defining effective style and standard usage. Not only has English studies seen the rise of web style guides (e.g., Nick Carbone and Eric Crump's *Writing Online*, 1998; Janice R. Walker and Todd W. Taylor's *The Columbia Guide to Online Style*, 1998), but discussions of the varieties of appropriate online language have made their way into the ever-present composition handbooks. For instance, in the second edition of Andrea Lunsford's (2002) *The Everyday Writer*, there is a section with the chapter on composing called "A Matter of Style: Considering Tone Online." Here the student writer is advised:

> Remember that closeness to online readers doesn't happen automatically. Your tone in online exchanges, then, should be based on how well you really know your audience as well as on what is most appropriate in the context of a specific piece of online writing. The company president may also be your very good friend, but when you write to her about company business, you should adopt an appropriately businesslike tone. (p. 30)

This advice to student writers is embedded within a larger section called "Consider Specific Online Issues." The passage from Lunsford and Horowitz's handbook demonstrates how audience awareness ("how well you really know your audience") and context ("what is most appropriate in the context of a specific piece of online writing") are the key factors in determining tone and style. How should one write online? Well, it depends on the context and the audience. Should one use emoticons? Well, it depends on the context and the audience. What about the mechanics that Berland mentions? Does it matter whether you write "to" your friend? "two" your friend? "too" your friend? Or "2" your friend? Well, it depends on the context and the audience. Even handbooks, long harbingers of the enforcement of standard English acknowledge that online discourse varies according to audience and context. Despite what some may fear, the students in Humanities 104 did not discard mechanics and grammar. They insisted that language obeys certain rules. But, by asking what these rules are and by reading and evaluating each others work, we created a set of standards based on situated communicative actions rather than on distilled, prescriptive grammars. We arrived at the advice given in Lunsford's handbook on our own: Audience and context help determine what types of language are considered correct and effective.

"Put a star next to enjoyability," Jason says.

"Thanks," I say and I put a star next to it.

In the end, however, they will argue me away from enjoyability as a criteria. "It just isn't as important as some of the others," Priya will argue. Our final list looks like this:

Important content

Supporting examples

Relevant research

Readability—smooth transitions between ideas

Structure—structure must support thesis

(Quality not quantity)

CLOSING: SITUATED AND NEGOTIATED CRITERIA

What do these criteria reveal about what these students consider important in academic discourse? These criteria are situated and negotiated. They show an awareness of form and content and the relation between the two. This exercise in student-created evaluation criteria helps to contextualize assessment. The meaning of "context" here offers a way of extending Brian Huot's (1996) use of the term for institution- and community-specific evaluations to assessments based on criteria created and discussed by the writers and audience members for the piece. While portfolio assessment, particularly the dialogic methods discussed by Hamp-Lyons and Condon (1999), allow for the creation of evaluation criteria by communities of teachers rather than by outside testing experts, the aforementioned activity suggests that students can also be invited into discussions about assessment criteria. The students will bring preconceived notions about what English teachers value in writing and what should be marked as good, correct, and effective, but an open discussion airs out these assumptions and helps students and teachers begin to consider what they value in writing, and more narrowly— and perhaps more effectively—articulate what they will value in each other's writing over the course of the next 16 weeks. To invite students into a dialogue about writing assessment that reaches beyond preconceived ideas about writing evaluation is difficult. Usually students will return to notions of evaluation based on the value of form that they have learned as part of General Writing Skills Instruction. This move cannot be accomplished in a single class meeting, perhaps not in a single semester. But the invitation to talk about how to read and evaluate the works that are produced in a particular writing lab begins the process of creating localized standards. To allow space for students to challenge their inherited notions of what good writing is, a teacher must stretch the discussion over a number of class meetings, must allow for individual reflection through short writing activities between class meetings, and must be prepared to take the small advances, the small changes to students' conceptions of good writing.

Distributing the process of evaluating writing begins with this move to include students in the creation of localized assessment criteria. The possibilities of distributive evaluation for statewide or universitywide assessment systems are difficult to envision, but their possible use on the classroom level is clear. By involving students in the creation of assessment criteria, the process becomes open and students understand how a work is being evaluated.

5

Interaction

Assessing a student composition as the product of an extended series of interactions opens up questions about how these interactions, and the evaluations of these interactions, are being changed as IT is integrated with print-based writing processes. Situating, describing, and negotiating criteria prepare teachers and test developers for considering how student interactions during the process of composing can be incorporated into pedagogical and evaluative techniques. Advances in IT have changed both how students compose and the products that they produce. Looking at an html composition, evaluating that work from the perspective of a print document and as a Web site contrasts some of the basic differences in rhetorical structures used for the page and the screen. However, simply considering the medium as the context within which a work exists excludes social variables. Ignoring the social situation within which a composition works curtails the validity of a writing assessment.

CITIES AND URBAN LANDSCAPES: READING AND RESPONDING TO A STUDENT HYPERTEXT ESSAY

By acknowledging that a composition is situated within a medium and within a social context, the discussion may turn to questions of assessing not only how the finished product works in its particular medium and context, but also to how interactions that occurred as the student composed the work influenced the final form of that work. The social and technical components of a participatory frame change as students compose, looking at these changes—acknowledging that a student made a change in a document because a teacher, peer, or outside reader requested it—is an important part of evaluating a student's ability as an effective communicator. If students are able to adapt their work based on interactions with their audience, then these students are more skillful composers than those who do not incorporate audience feedback. Traditional testing has not been concerned about measuring interactions as components in judging a student's writing proficiencies. But, in the multimodal and multimedia compositions students are creating today, interactions and the ability to adjust based on those interactions is a vital writing skill.

Take the html essay in Fig. 5.1 as an example. The essay draft, as shown in Fig. 5.2, could easily have been turned in and evaluated as a print document. The student would then rewrite the opening of the essay so that it looked like this:

> In today's society, more and more cities are beginning to develop. But are these cities good for the world, its environment and the people that live in it? The world is a constantly changing place, and even humans are being altered. No longer are we being manipulated by others, however. The cities we live in and the technologies we utilize everyday now dictate our lives and our ways of living. Urban cities and landscapes have begun to alter the way people live. Humans are no longer capable of living on their own, rather they need the city as much as it needs them to survive. People now rely on the city to be there and provide everything an individual may need, from the grocery stores lining the blocks, to the public transport that gets people from place to place. Humans have become a dependent species, dependent on the tools that we have created to make our lives easier.
>
> Cities today are no longer designed based on efficiencies, rather now they are designed to manipulate the behavior of the individuals living inside the city limits. For example, Cityscape Institute is an organization that designs alterations to present cities to improve the overall behavior of the individuals living within the city.
>
>> Today, there is increasing awareness that the physical character and management of public places influences human behavior and that attractive, well-managed places promote greater community self-esteem, increase social order, and, in short, produce a civil city (Cityscape Institute).
>
> This example clearly indicates that there are those that will try to manipulate the masses through the designs of the landscapes of the cities. No longer is it up to the individual to determine his own behavioral habits, rather it is up to the few to decide for the many to alter their behavior through urban landscape design. No longer are cities beautiful, rather they have strategically placed parks and trees to make it seem beautiful, to make people feel comfortable.
>
> Not only is it the case that the city landscape itself provides for influence over the masses that reside there, rather it also relies on the technologies that people utilize in their daily lives that have an impact on their emotions. Mass transportation is a great example of a technology that people rely on. Without it many people would not be able to get to work. It is just something they depend on to be there. Even in homes there exist large numbers of new electronics that change and influence human behavior.

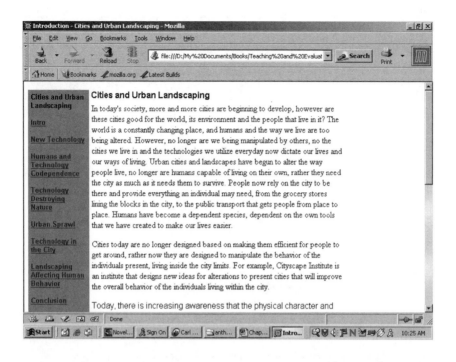

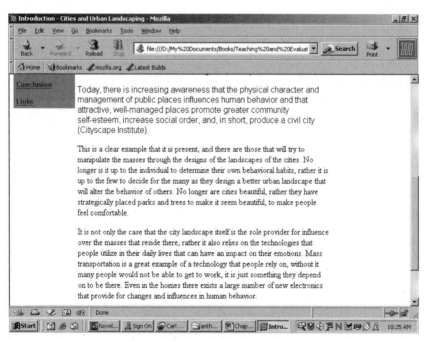

FIG. 5.1. *(Continued)*

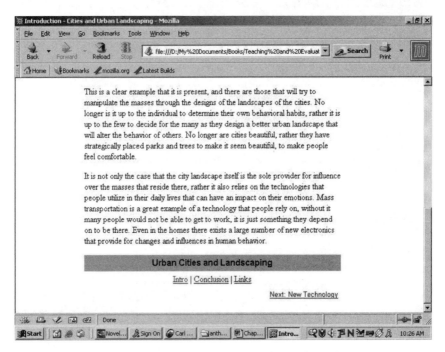

FIG. 5.1.   Urban cities and landscaping: HTML version.

The student has "effectively" interacted with the teacher by literally incorporating her comments into a revision. The paragraph is more effective, both as a decontextualized sample and as a work situated within a classroom and within the wants of a particular teacher. However, the corrections are what I would call "copy-editing plus." They focus on style, mechanics, and clarity. They do not challenge the student's ideas or ask for higher order revisions. Part of a writing teacher's job is to address these "copy-editing plus" issues. The messiness of language requires it. Teachers must respond to and push students to present their ideas in clear and accessible formats. However, the development of students' abilities as communicators demands more than clarity. Student writers need to respond to conceptual challenges. They need to hear how readers respond to the content of their work. They need to hear how readers respond beyond demands for clarity and correct surface features.

How would these interactions be different if the teacher was responding to the representation of the file on the screen rather than to a printed version of the html page? How are the teacher's responses further changed if the modes of delivering this feedback change from writing comments in the margin of the student essay to interacting with the student via an IM conference?

First, the basic unit or node of the text shifts. Whereas in print, the student's writing is "chucked" into paragraphs, on the screen the teacher takes in the lefthand navigation bar, the opening three paragraphs, and the visual design elements of the work. When the teacher begins to discuss the work with the student using IM, they talk about the html pages as the basic unit of the text. They use screens and file names as the way to make references to different sections of the text. The student and teacher are interacting in such a way that it makes it clear that they are thinking about the work as divided by files instead of divided by paragraphs.

In addition to the change in the basic chunks of the text, the teacher and student are also now concerned about the look and feel of the work, about its design fea-

Cities and Urban Landscaping

In today's society, more and more cities are beginning to develop, however are these cities good for the world, its environment and the people that live in it? The world is a constantly changing place, and humans and the way we live are too being altered. However, no longer are we being manipulated by others, no the cities we live in and the technologies we utilize everyday now dictate our lives and our ways of living. Urban cities and landscapes have begun to alter the way people live, no longer are humans capable of living on their own, rather they need the city as much as it needs them to survive. People now rely on the city to be there and provide everything an individual may need, from the grocery stores lining the blocks in the city, to the public transport that gets people from place to place. Humans have become a dependent species, dependent on the own tools that we have created to make our lives easier.

Cities today are no longer designed based on making them efficient for people to get around, rather now they are designed to manipulate the behavior of the individuals present, living inside the city limits. For example, Cityscape Institute is an institute that designs new ideas for alterations to present cities that will improve the overall behavior of the individuals living within the city.

Today, there is increasing awareness that the physical character and management of public places influences human behavior and that attractive, well-managed places promote greater community self-esteem, increase social order, and, in short, produce a civil city (Cityscape Institute).

FIG. 5.2. *(Continued)*

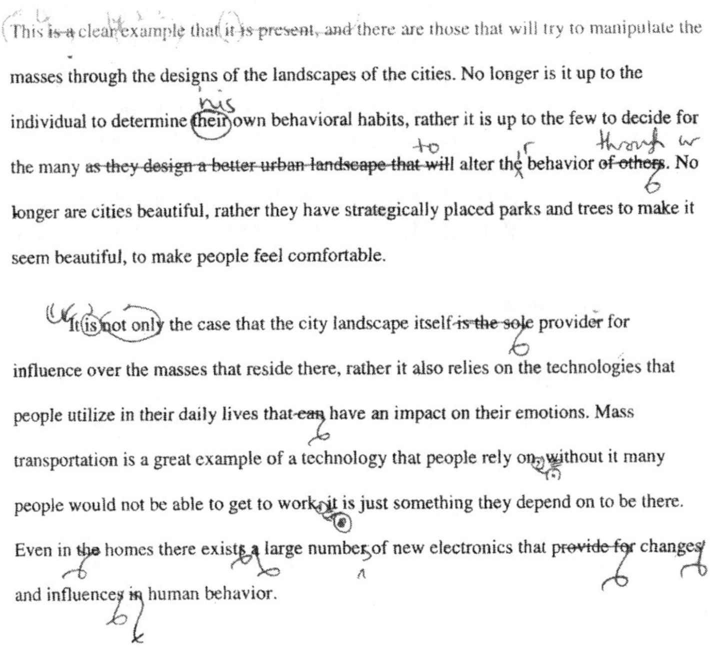

(This is a clear example that it is present, and there are those that will try to manipulate the

masses through the designs of the landscapes of the cities. No longer is it up to the

individual to determine their own behavioral habits, rather it is up to the few to decide for

the many as they design a better urban landscape that will alter the behavior of others. No

longer are cities beautiful, rather they have strategically placed parks and trees to make it

seem beautiful, to make people feel comfortable.

It is not only the case that the city landscape itself is the sole provider for

influence over the masses that reside there, rather it also relies on the technologies that

people utilize in their daily lives that can have an impact on their emotions. Mass

transportation is a great example of a technology that people rely on without it many

people would not be able to get to work it is just something they depend on to be there.

Even in the homes there exists a large number of new electronics that provide for changes

and influences in human behavior.

FIG. 5.2.   Urban cities and landscaping: Print version.

tures and layout in a way that was not discussed when the work was printed. The instructor asks the student if he could add images to the site. The student responds, "Why do I need them? I am not really doing much worth illustrating . . ." (see Fig. 5.3). The implication is that this humanities essay is *not* a technical document, and does not need visual elements to convey its message. In fact, there is still a tendency to see visuals as belittling within academic humanities writing. However, within computer-mediated communication, visuals become key rhetorical elements. If students are to become effective communicators for a variety of audiences that can read in multiple environments, then students need to learn how and when to add visual components. In this case, the instructor responds, "yeah but the site seems to sort of limp along without visuals" (see Fig. 5.4). Viewing the essay as an html file, the look and feel of the composition is now a rhetorical statement and is related to effective communication in a way that was not this understood this explicitly in the 1980s (pre-1993, pre-WWW). The student and instructor move from the instructor's suggestion that a visual be added to a more detailed analysis of where and what types of graphics should be used. When the instructor exclaims, "Sure. A park would work on the Landscaping Affecting Human Behavior page!" the visual element that will be added in the next version of the html essay has been arrived at through interaction. Not only is the discussion of visual elements markedly different from the red pen comments in the printed

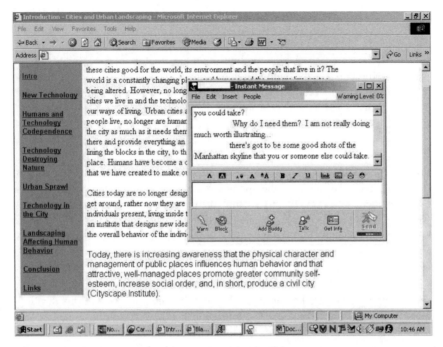

FIG. 5.3.   IM dialogue: Adding images.

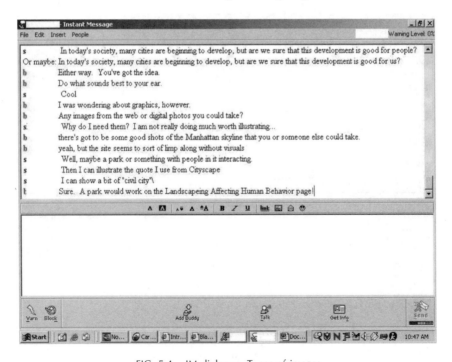

FIG. 5.4.   IM dialogue: Types of images.

essay, but the means of commenting, the depth of the interactions, and the student's active role within the interactions are intensified in the IMs. In the IM, the teacher comments on the navigation bar and the lack of graphics. Later, the teacher comments favorably on the change in the font when the student is quoting. The visual display of the text is brought to the foreground, whereas the textual and linguistic elements occupy a later place in the teacher–student interactions.

The teacher also addresses some of the same issues about the opening that were addressed in the commentary on the print version; however, in the IM dialogue these comments have a very different and more open-ended feel to them (Fig. 5.5). Instead of dividing the opening sentence into two sentences and changing the student's "however" into a "But," the instructor says, "so I was wondering what you meant in the opening sentence when you said 'more and more cities are beginning to develop.' " With the typical stutter-step dialogue of IM, the student responds, "I was trying to say that we are creating more cities and I am trying to explore the consequences of this creation" (Fig. 5.6).

After a couple of more exchanges, the student suggests a revision: "In today's society, many cities are beginning to develop, but are we sure that this development is good for the world . . . ?" The teacher then goes on to praise the last sentence in the student's opening paragraph. This praise leads the student to decide on a further refinement of the *opening* sentences (Fig. 5.7). The opening sentence

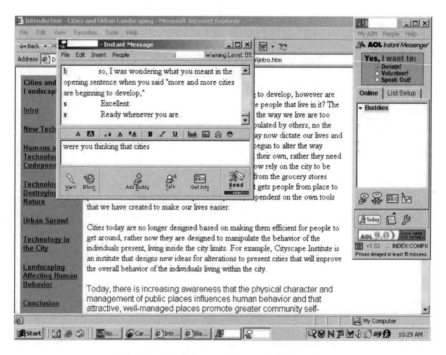

FIG. 5.5. IM dialogue: Open-ended discussion.

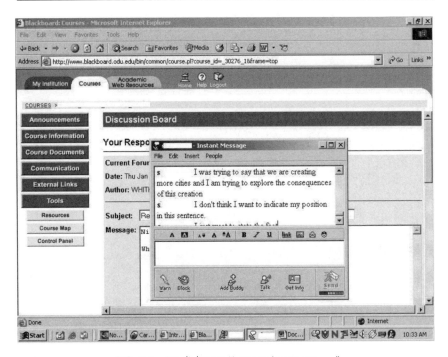

FIG. 5.6.   IM dialogue: "I was trying to say . . ."

now reads: "In today's society, many cities are beginning to develop, but are we sure that this development is good for the world?" Contrast this with the revised opening sentences from the print-based exchange: "In today's society, more and more cities are beginning to develop. But are these cities good for the world, its environment and the people that live in it?" There is not a major difference in the final product, but the social interaction that drove the changes was remarkable. The student arrived at the changes through a process of negotiation. In the print exchange, the teacher's red pen enforced the teacher's will on the student's work. Learning about writing was a form of responding to a command rather than an act of dialogue.

Still the time-intensive nature of the IM exchange, especially when working with surface features and stylistic comments, will drain teachers and students quickly. Employing an Automatic Essay Scoring (AES) system as a feedback agent in the process of revision could allow students and teachers time to work on the dialogic components of learning about writing. If the textual elements of this html essay passed through e-rater or IEA, then the student would get the equivalent of the "copy-editing-plus" comments that the teacher gave on the printed essay. Given the needs and situation of a particular writing course, a teacher could make a decision about when to most effectively turn to e-rater or IEA in the process of composing an html essay. For instance, a teacher could have an IM or face-to-face dialogue with

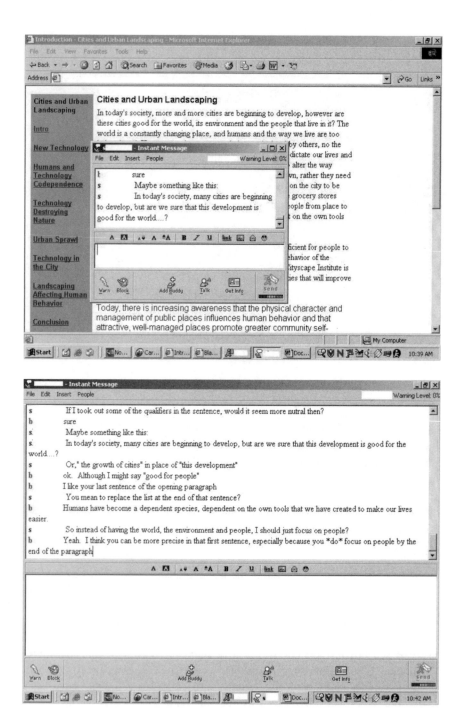

FIG. 5.7.   IM dialogue: Refining the opening sentences.

students and then have them use a software agent as a final editing tool. In a different course, where mechanics and style presented greater difficulties, this editing could be done earlier in the students' writing processes, followed by a student–teacher or student–student dialogue and then a final e-rater or IEA response could be coupled with the teacher's final evaluative reading.

Although the student and teacher interacted in the print-based example, their interactions occurred within a traditional discourse of schooling. The student's revisions reflect a direct implementation of the teacher's will. In the interactions about the html essay something different is happening, the dialogue breaks away from the easily known and becomes a process of discovery—a dialogue that involves risk. This interactive dialogue makes student learning reach beyond the already known and become a process of creating knowledge for both teacher and student.

hooks–BARLOW: THE RISKS OF DIALOGUE AND LEARNING

Teacher-researchers working in critical pedagogy have teased out the implications of dialogic learning. Turning to their works provides a frame for understanding learning as dialogue. The works of Paulo Freire (1970; Freire & Shor, 1987; Freire & Faundez, 1998), Ira Shor (1987, 1992, 1996), and bell hooks (1994) emphasize learning as dialogue. Freire (1970) observed that his work, *Pedagogy of the Oppressed*, asked the reader to be open and to engage in a dialogue: "The reader who dogmatically assumes close, 'irrational' positions will reject the dialogue I hope this book will open" (p. 19). The dialogue that Freire (1970) began in *Pedagogy of the Oppressed* took the form of many co-authored works. Rereading the list of Freire's works, I am reminded of hooks and John Perry Barlow's discussion in *Shambhalasun* (1995). The piece began with descriptions of hooks and Barlow:

> On paper, you are my polar opposite [bell hooks: iconoclastic feminist, leading African-American intellectual, progressive Buddhist, self-proclaimed homebody], yet I feel none of that in your presence.
>
> I've never met anyone from Wyoming before [John Perry Barlow: cyber philosopher, retired cattle rancher, world traveler, Grateful Dead lyricist, self-proclaimed Republican]. I sought you out. I wanted to hear your story. (¶ 1–2)

Within their discussion, hooks says,

> In this past year when I went around to so many colleges and universities, I found people deeply and profoundly cynical about love. I spent this week re-reading Martin Luther King's sermon "Strength to Love," and I was somewhat saddened by the idea that what we remember about him revolves so much around fantasy and dream-

ing and hope for the future, when there was this real concrete message, particularly during the later period of his life, which was all about love and the rigor of love. Not easy love but that love which really requires of us the willingness to be dissenting voices, the willingness to stand alone, the willingness to be transformed. He's constantly stating, "Be not conformed to this world but be transformed by the renewing of your mind." (Categories ¶ 1)

Barlow responds, "It seems to me that what we're here to do is to learn about love in the presence of fear." For both hooks and Barlow, discussion and learning involves encountering others with radically different ideas and still acknowledging their humanness.[1] hooks reflects,

And what I see in a lot of young folks is this desire to be only with people like themselves and only to have any trust in reaching out to people like themselves. I think, what kind of magic are they going to miss in life? What kind of renewals of their beings will they never have, if they think you can have some computer printout that says this person has the same gender as you, the same race as you, the same class, and therefore they're safe? I feel that intuition is so crucial to getting beyond race and class and gender, so that we can allow ourselves to feel for and with another person. (¶ 9)

Barlow responds,

I think that among the great errors of the political correctness movement is that it reduces things to their externalities and avoids the essence. I think that there is something about that whole academic, literary, critical culture that spawned a point of view that is anti-intimate. (¶ 10)

hooks and Barlow encourage thinking about literacy work as communication. And they do not just mean communication as telling a person who is similar to you what they already know. No, this communication is interaction; it is risk taking; it is writing to learn, but writing to learn with others rather than about yourself. The idea of feeling for and with another person is vital for critical pedagogy. Intimacy, or a willingness to think of students as humans rather than as papers to be graded, can become a central aspect of teaching writing. This sense of intimacy with others, with people of different backgrounds and beliefs, is not only a practice that should occur when the teacher reads student writing but should also occur among students.

---

[1] Emmanuel Levinas (1969) wrote extensively about this encounter with the other, with the face of the Other: "even when I shall have linked the Other to myself with the conjunction 'and' the Other continues to face me, to reveal himself in his face. . . . These relations which I claim form the fabric of being itself, first come together in my discourse presently addressed to my interlocutors: inevitably across my idea of the Infinite the other faces me—hostile, friend, my master, my student" (pp. 80–81).

One way teachers can facilitate student interactions with others from radically different backgrounds and with radically different beliefs is through the Internet with e-mail and synchronous chat. If scholars champion writing-to-learn, what better way to learn than to actually interact and communicate, to write back and forth between different cities in the United States, perhaps even different countries, different continents. An 11th grader in Ohio reads *The Speaking Tree* (Lannoy, 1971), a book about Indian culture, and corresponds with a 17-year-old student in Bombay. The student in Bombay reads *Wish You Well* (Baldacci, 2001), a novel set in American Appalachia. Both the books and the e-mail correspondence shape a rich, layered understanding of everyday life in the subcontinent and in the United States. Claims made by a scholar and novelist are challenged, qualified, or annulled by the sharp wits of students, their dismissal of the pompous, the wordy, and the merely academic. Yet, at the same time, the e-mail voices do not alone represent the totality of the students' experiences of other cultures. The writing in the books seeps into their ideas, thus changing and altering their views.

INTIMACY AND DIALOGUE

A powerful, and deeply troubling, example of open dialogue can be found on Ted Nellen's Web site (2001). As a teacher in New York City, Nellen lives in lower Manhattan. Following September 11, he engaged in exchanges with Rehmat Ebrahim, a teacher in Karachi, Pakistan, and posted the work of her students online. Their work is anti-American and anti-Semitic, and yet it is the writing of children trying to respond to the events and the images they are seeing in the Pakistani media. Nellen does not champion their views nor does he support an anti-interventionist position about the war in Afghanistan. But he allows the writing of students in Karachi to accompany his own, and his son's, terrifying accounts of September 11.[2]

Given the value, and challenge, of intimacy and dialogue in critical pedagogy, I'm coming to believe that as a teaching technique within computer-mediated communication it is neither left- nor rightwing. Rather, critical pedagogy is about

---

[2]About 70 of the 660 students were left around 10 a.m., when the school was ordered to evacuate. Teachers grabbed kids by the hand and rushed to the street—and found it clogged with acrid smoke, fleeing pedestrians and the sounds of screaming sirens. Second-grade teacher Mary Jacob, 26, got out with a 7-year-old boy Tom Nellen just as the second tower collapsed. She didn't think she could outrun the thick cloud of blackness roiling toward them; when her legs gave out, she let go of his little hand and told him to run. "God forbid something was to happen, I didn't want it to happen to him" she recalls. "So I was like, 'Go, you'll be OK.' " Then Jacob realized the black smoke had stopped its inexorable rush forward—and it was her turn to be saved. The little boy came back for her and said, "C'mon. Let's go." (*Newsweek* Commemorative Issue, September 2001).

a radical willingness to listen to the experiences of others. As hooks pointed out, people learn by talking with those who are not the same as they are. Learning about writing may involve the opening up of a dialogue that contains the potential to transform students' ideas and actions as well as their written sentence structure.

The value placed on *dialogue* in works of critical pedagogy is precisely what makes it valuable as a teaching praxis for computer-mediated writing. Proponents (Bromley & Apple, 1998; Cummins & Sayers, 1995; Egnatoff, 1992; Selfe, 1999) of computer-mediated instruction see it as *potentially* democratic, as empowering, and as primarily about communication. If writing, at some fundamental level, is about communication—about passing along ideas, feelings, and emotions and in the process having your own ideas, feelings, and emotions changed—then critical pedagogy provides a body of teaching methods and activities that help open ways for thinking about teaching and learning in computer-mediated environments. These ways of thinking and acting acknowledge that the still unstable forms of communicating online are socially situated activities. They don't always translate into conventional forms of writing assessment. What happens in computer-mediated environments is that students learn how to think rather than regurgitate memorized information.

In the online journal *Kairos*, Lori Mayo (2001) describes a series of critical writing activities that she used at Jamaica High School in Queens, New York, as part of a "Using the Internet to Teach for Social Justice" project. These activities grew out of Mayo's sense that her students were "complacent." Yet, Mayo's initial attempts to focus her curriculum on social issues lead to some frustration because "the work that [her] students were doing wasn't reaching anybody outside [the] classroom door." At first, for Mayo, critical pedagogy led toward the questioning of social norms, but only within discussions in the classroom. The sense of connection, of engagement, and of dialogue to the world was missing—that is, having students talk to others who were different, who might not see the injustices they saw as injustices. That vital sense of dialogue with the other that hooks points toward was not present in the classroom, despite Mayo's best efforts.

Mayo saw the Internet as a way to put into practice Randy Bomer's (1999) advice that critical pedagogy should "call for public attention to problems and possibilities" (p. 2). However, Mayo and the students quickly moved beyond the issue of gaining public attention and began to focus on forming "alliances with groups that are trying to do the same good work." Students not only read and wrote about social problems, but also implemented local responses to the social problems they were investigating. For instance, Golam Karim researched the 1971 Bangladesh Liberation War and created a web page that honored those who had given up their lives fighting for social justice during the war. Karim's work did not stop with the making public of past violence against individuals who worked for social justice. He also helped form a Bangladeshi student club at Jamaica High School. Although the formation of a student club may seem like an inconsequential action when compared to the violence of a war, Karim helped shape the club's goal so that "the objective of the Bengali Club [was] not only to diffuse the culture, but to stand up against discrimination and racism against our race and society." In a small way, Mayo's exploration of social injustices and her encouragement to students opened possibilities for them not only to learn about writing, but to move from writing about society to taking an active part in shaping their own local society and its goals.

Mayo also had students take part in an e-mail exchange with Galen Leon's students in rural Idaho. Leon's students were reading Jonathan Kozol's (1996) *Amazing Grace*, an account of the impacts of social inequities on students in New York City. Mayo and Leon had their students write back and forth to one another about Kozol's book. Karim and Jessica Nelson, a student in Idaho, discussed the trouble of students in a poor urban school district. Interestingly, Karim insisted that the students in Kozol's book should really be responsible for their own behavior, and Nelson, who had begun reading *Amazing Grace* with the same attitude, changed her mind. The e-mail dialogue then is not the cause for the change in Nelson's opinion in any direct fashion (i.e., Karim says, "life is hard here," and Nelson says, "oh, ok now I pity you and see Kozol's point"). Rather, the two talk around the issues raised in the book; they agree, and they disagree. But they talk, and, through that interaction, both Karim's and Nelson's writing and views develop.

Computer-mediated communication provides a contact, a connection, between students from radically different educational backgrounds, but Nelson's final journal points toward a reiteration of the conclusions reached in her assigned book and not toward an opening up of questions and dialogue with Karim. While Mayo believes that "the educational experience was so enriched by this collaboration, that Jessica and many of my students learned far more from this project than Galen or I could have hoped," some of the situated complexities of the exchange (e.g., Karim's vision of himself and the girl in *Amazing Grace* who died of an overdose as active agents not victims of a social system) vanish in favor of a overarching narrative of transformation. The New York City–Idaho interactions are powerful and sensitive, yet the closing note of the exchange is a turn to the book's—in this case *Amazing Grace*'s—authority. Kozol's discourse produces the critical agency, the imperative toward social justice in Nelson's writing. The subtleties that are reminiscent of the hooks–Barlow dialogue that Nelson achieves through interactions with Karim vanish when Nelson encounters the ideological power of Kozol's progressive voice. Teaching for social justice seems to be happening, but I also see a loss in Nelson's writing. She trusts the book's representation of reality rather than the intimate denials of poverty insisted on by Karim. Still, interactions have occurred. Mayo and Leon have stepped back, facilitated a dialogue, and allowed students to interact across great cultural and spatial distances. Online student discourse has not replaced the power of the printed word—school learning, books, Kozol's ideas—but rather authentic student discourse has had a chance.

RISK AND EXPECTING TOO MUCH

Can engaged writing teachers consider student writing, student learning, and the knowledge produced by students as on par with the knowledge produced by intellectuals? This move would be difficult to make for teachers trained in traditional English departments and in the reading of literary works. They expect student writing to be less than published work. They often think of students as engaged in a process of learning how to write rather than actually producing knowledge. The old adage that "you must learn the rules before you can break them" comes to mind here. Writing teachers cannot think of student writers writing the way that Salman Rushdie or Gabriel Garcia-Marquez write—with their long complex, entwined sentences—because students are, well, students. They are only learning. They are not yet at the level of a hooks or Barlow, Rushdie or Garcia-Marquez. But this idea is precisely one that they might want to disabuse themselves of. If they seek to engage students in intellectual and social actions, then shouldn't they read students' work with the aliveness, with the mind-set that they bring to reading literary and philosophical works? Can teachers think of student writing as producing knowledge—insights—for both the students and for them?

How do teachers read that way? How do they function as readers as well as graders? The issue becomes especially pressing when the student writing is littered with surface errors the way that Karim's pieces are. Shouldn't teachers correct the student writing first before having students go public, that is, before they "call for public attention to problems and possibilities," shouldn't teachers insist that their writing at least be grammatically correct?

These questions are significant. They focus on issues of student needs. Do students really need to know the rules before they can break them? Do students need to be able to diagram a sentence before they can write one? Do students need to be able to talk about the parts of speech in order to improve their writing skills? These questions can be answered, at least in part, by returning to a history of computers and writing instruction in American education. Because technology embodies ideology, the development of tools for computer-mediated writing instruction has reflected changing visions of how best to teach writing. Unsurprisingly, issues of grammar and usage as well as communication have often been considered by researchers working in educational technology and writing instruction.

GRAMMAR

Like a good many English teachers who have been intrigued by the computer movement, I have been disappointed by the content and quality of many language arts computer programs on the market. Whether one looks at elaborate packages put out by the major publishers and computer manufacturers or at the "basement programs" produced by computer hobbyists, language programs seem inordinately concerned with drill, especially in spelling and grammar. Now a computer can do that sort of drill very effectively, more effectively than an English teacher, but such programs seem to me pedagogically obsolete, putting the proverbial "old wine in new bottles." The new bottle of the computer will have to offer more creative kinds of language programs if it is to be more than an educational fad for English teachers. (Stephen Tchudi, 1983, p. 10)

The idea that going over grammar rules and then having quizzes on those rules will help students become better writers was a generalized method of teaching writing that was adapted in early Computer-Assisted Instruction (CAI). What happened in terms of writing instruction is that a particular idea (grammar drills lead to better writing) became inscribed in both writing technologies and teaching methods. This inscription of grammar drills in teaching machines perverted a decent, age-old idea that knowledge of grammar helps one understand how language works. Today, it is not unusual to encounter someone—a parent, a school board member, even a fellow teacher—who believes that students will become better writers if they would just learn their grammar lessons. A teacher committed to the process movement would insist that these people were simply wrong—a writer needs to write, not do grammar drills. This teacher could easily turn to Braddock et al.'s (1963) research summary that claims: "In view of the widespread agreement of research studies based upon many types of students and teachers, the conclusion can be stated in strong and unqualified terms that the teaching of formal grammar has a negligible or, because it usually displaces some instruction and practice in actual composition, even a harmful effect on the improvement of writing" (pp. 37–38). Braddock et al.'s claim has only gained strength with additional studies (e.g., White, 1964; Gale, 1967; and Bateman & Zidonis, 1966). As paradoxical as it might seem, I would argue that the grammar-promoting school board member and the teacher who believes that writing is a process are both right.

A knowledge of descriptive grammar does help one understand how language works, but drills on the rules of grammar do not translate into students becoming "better, more effective" writers in any valid, measurable way. The problem arises when the methods of learning grammar move away from context-based lessons about communicating to decontextualized, universalized "skills." This shift from thinking about grammar as a way of talking about language to grammar as a drill-based skill occurred in the 1960s, just as researchers were trying to develop teaching machines, programmed instruction, and early CAI.

Teachers hear advocates of skills-based grammar instruction and proponents of the process approach to writing instruction endorse different things. By understanding how grammar became separate from writing in computer-enhanced writing instruction, teachers may be able to realize a way to bring these two competing camps back together. That is, their students will be required to display proficiency on standardized grammar exams, but they will also be required to write effectively in a variety of situations. If teachers see these as opposite goals—the way they have been portrayed by advocates of skills-based standards exams and by proponents of process approaches to teaching writing—then they will have to become schizophrenic to teach in the public schools. But, if the division is viewed as a product of the adaptation of writing instruction to behavioral science, programmed learning, and CAI, then teachers may be able to chart a course that proves this division is artificial. The separation of writing and grammar is a legacy from the limited technologies of the 1960s and 1970s, and the ways in which test makers, instructional designers, and computational linguists have tried to adapt these technologies to writing instruction.

Quickly looking at Virginia's Standards of Learning (SOLs) for secondary writing instruction, however, can produce the feeling that progress and sequence are rather jumbled (see Table 5.1). Ninth graders are expected to "develop narrative, literary, expository, and technical writings to inform, explain, analyze, or entertain," whereas 10th graders must "develop a variety of writings with an emphasis on exposition." At first glance, it appears that 9th graders are expected to have a greater range of competencies than 10th graders. That is, 9th graders must present "narrative, literary, expository, and technical writings," and 10th graders must focus on "exposition." However, taken within the overall context of the SOLs, a careful progress is being developed. Ninth graders are introduced to a wide variety of writing styles (narrative, literary, expository, and technical) and purposes (to inform, explain, analyze, or entertain). Tenth graders still employ a variety of styles, but the focus is on "exposition." Eleventh graders turn to "persuasion." Twelfth graders return to exposition and technical writing in a sort of overview of the students' secondary writing experiences. Narrative and literary writing skills are embedded within exposition and technical writing exercises. In addition, students have learned how to read and critique pieces of writing from professionals and peers in the 10th grade, and these skills are drawn on in both 11th- and 12th-grade writing assignments.

CLOSING: INTERACTION AS RETURN TO DIALOGUE

The arc of a sequence for a student's development as a writer does not at first blush appear to offer much room for the messy and complicated notions of intimacy, dialogue, and interaction. How would the hooks–Barlow and Karim–Nelson dialogues from earlier in this chapter be charted in terms of student progress? Where are these open-ended face-to-face and e-mail conversations placed in the sequence of a student's development? In the sequence of a composition's development?

The most common answer would be to suggest that they are prewriting or brainstorming activities. The Daedalus Integrated Writing Environment (DIWE) developed in the late 1980s and early 1990s used synchronous discussion in this way. However, that move denies the validity and the power of these works as they currently stand. Reading hooks–Barlow and Karim–Nelson, I found myself as moved as I have found myself when reading a more finished, more formal student

TABLE 5.1
Writing Standards for Virginia Secondary Students

9 The student will develop narrative, literary, expository, and technical writings to inform, explain, analyze, or entertain.
  • Plan and organize writing.
  • Communicate clearly the purpose of the writing.
  • Write clear, varied sentences.
  • Use specific vocabulary and information.
  • Arrange paragraphs into a logical progression.
  • Revise writing for clarity.
  • Edit final copies for correct use of language, spelling, punctuation, and capitalization.

10 The student will develop a variety of writings with an emphasis on exposition.
  • Plan and organize ideas for writing.
  • Elaborate ideas clearly through word choice and vivid description.
  • Write clear, varied sentences.
  • Organize ideas into a logical sequence.
  • Revise writing for clarity and content of presentation.
  • Edit final copies for correct use of language, spelling, punctuation, and capitalization.
  • Use available technology.

The student will critique professional and peer writing.
  • Analyze the writing of others.
  • Describe how writing accomplishes its intended purpose.
  • Suggest how writing might be improved.
  • Apply knowledge of critical analysis to writing.

The student will use writing to interpret, analyze, and evaluate ideas.
  • Explain concepts contained in literature and other disciplines.
  • Translate concepts into simpler or more easily understood terms.

11 The student will write in a variety of forms with an emphasis on persuasion.
  • Develop a focus for writing.
  • Evaluate and cite applicable information.
  • Organize ideas in a logical manner.
  • Elaborate ideas clearly and accurately.
  • Adapt content, vocabulary, voice, and tone to audience, purpose, and situation.
  • Revise writing for accuracy and depth of information.
  • Edit final copies for correct use of language, spelling, punctuation, and capitalization.

The student will write, revise, and edit personal and business correspondence to a standard acceptable in the work place and higher education.
  • Apply a variety of planning strategies to generate and organize ideas.
  • Organize information to support the purpose of the writing.
  • Present information in a logical manner.
  • Revise writing for clarity.
  • Edit final copies for correct use of language, spelling, punctuation, and capitalization.
  • Use available technology.

12 The student will develop expository and technical writings.
  • Consider audience and purpose when planning for writing.
  • Present ideas in a logical sequence.
  • Elaborate ideas clearly and accurately.
  • Revise writing for depth of information and technique of presentation.
  • Edit final copies for correct use of language, spelling, punctuation, and capitalization.

essay. As compositions, these works are engaging. They take risks. They appeal to the type of learning and assessment that Bob Broad (2003), in *What We Really Value: Beyond Rubrics in Teaching and Assessing Writing*, and Brian Huot (2002), in *(Re)Articulating Writing Assessment*, discussed. They are the types of engaged works that teachers as different as David Bartholomae (1993) and Geoff Sirc (1993, 1995, 1997) look for. These dialogues work.

Standardized testing and curricula encourage thinking of students' writing development over time as a general progression and their work on a particular assignment as developing writing abilities in a clear and understandable sequence. However, both the concepts of sequenced writing assignments and progressive development of writing skills are immensely messy when put into practice, and this is especially so when dealing with dialogic forms such as hooks–Barlow and Karim–Nelson. Think about this issue in terms of mathematics education: In math, high school students are often seen progressing along a clearly defined path from Algebra to Geometry to Algebra II to Pre-Calculus and then Calculus. In English education, secondary students within a school district may have a strict progression in terms of literature, moving from, say, the easy Shakespeare play, *Romeo and Juliet*, in 9th grade to the more difficult Shakespeare play, *MacBeth*, in 11th or 12th grade; however, these students are not always exposed to as structured and as specific a sequence in writing instruction.

Statewide standardized testing is one attempt to address the sense that many parents and students have that the teaching of writing is a subjective call that does not correspond to any grade-specific standards. Statewide standards present the image of learning writing as a clearly sequenced acquisition of specific knowable and namable skills. Research (Flower & Hayes, 1977, 1980; Flower et al., 1979) into the teaching of writing suggests that measurable cognitive development does occur in understandable sequences. Research (Lave, 1985; Lave et al., 1982; Gee, 1988, 2001) also suggests that cognitive development of mathematic and literacy skills varies widely from individual to individual and depends on situational factors ranging from cultural to economic to accidents of an individual student's biography. Standardized testing pushes one way; academic researchers push another. So writing teachers must decide what they will do every day in the classroom.

Put simply, teachers hope that students develop their writing skills in ways that will be reflected on standardized exams. But they know that writing is also a highly contextualized activity and that mastery over narrative writing in the 9th grade may be lost when narrative examples are required to be used as supporting evidence within a persuasive essay in the 10th grade. Still, in systems that value accountability, both state departments of education and individual writing teachers must point to the acquisition of specific writing skills at specific grade levels to prove that they are accomplishing their tasks.

Where in the sequence of a student's development as a composer do teachers allow them to interact? Where in the development of an essay do they say *ah-ha* that dialogue is not brainstorming, it is not prewriting, it is actually part of the meat of what the student has to say. The Karim–Nelson exchange is the end in and of itself; the journal entry created by Nelson is an afterthought! The fulfilling of an assignment, the nod to the authority of Kozol and a progressive vision of education. But the work, the writing, the interaction—dare we say the learning—that occurred in Mayo's and Leon's classes happened in those e-mails. The students in Bombay and Cleveland did not give their work to their teachers first. They e-mailed one another. They exchanged ideas.

"Dialogue." "Intimacy." "Risk." The first word is often invoked in writing about education. The second two are not, except as negatives—"A Nation at Risk." Perhaps the insight that interaction through the Internet leads people to is an old insight. Plato or Socrates (1956) could easily have said it, "Then as far as thirst, could it be a desire in the soul for something more than what we mean here—drink? I mean is thirst a thirst for hot drink or cold, for much or little, or in a word for drink of any special kind?"

"Yes to that," [Adeimantos] said. "Every desire in itself is only for that one thing which each naturally wants." (p. 237)

The form of this discourse is a dialogue. The concept of thirst (What type of thirst? What type of desire?) is an intimate subject. It is an inquiry about the everyday. How do you live? How do you thirst? But unlike the exchanges between Cleveland and Bombay, between New York and Idaho, Socrates' dialogues as reported by Plato are without risk. Their outcomes are known. Done. Past. Already said and written. The risk taken on the Internet is more akin to Martin Luther King Jr.'s call: "Be transformed by the renewing of your mind."

Writing, like thirst, is a desire. The object of desire in writing, however, is not consumption, but response, dialogue, interaction. And this is not dialogue with the same, with those people know, but those they do not know. Given the world and its history, what a challenge to think of learning about writing and composing as processes of interacting—dialogue, intimacy, and risk.

It is easy to invoke these ideas when discussing pedagogy and teaching methods, but a technique for writing assessment that acknowledges interaction and dialogue has not yet been formulated. Scholars of critical pedagogy talk about transforming teaching and breaking down assessment regimes; assessment experts try to measure discrete writing skills. In the middle, the concept of judging students' composing skills by the way they interact with each other slips past. If teachers continue to miss interaction, their assessments of students' abilities as composers working with new media technologies will continue to be anemic. And still, the question remains, how can these out of the ordinary student "compositions" be assessed so they—and teachers—are seen as achieving all their objectives?

6

Distributive Evaluation

As a technique, distributive evaluation involves seeking multiple perspectives and responses to student compositions. For instance, works in students' electronic portfolios at Alverno College can be read by multiple audiences—various course instructors, advisors, and other administrators (*Diagnostic Digital Portfolio*, 2000; "Finding Proof," 1997; Iannozzi, 1997; Hutchings, 1996). Each of these audiences brings its own expertise and perspective to readings. If individuals are encouraged to record their responses, and these responses are then associated with the compositions in a database that is available to the instructor and other evaluators, it is possible to build a situated evaluation of a student's composition. This evaluation acknowledges that writing, composing, and communicating are localized social activities by incorporating disparate responses from teachers, student-authors, peers, and outside audiences. Unlike the commonly used 1- to 6-point holistic reading or the more detailed rubric-based multitrait scoring systems, a distributive assessment system does not insist that all readers read alike. Research (Elbow, 1997; Hirsch, 2003) has shown that different readers read differently in nonconstrained settings. The objective of a writing assessment system that values validity—that values an accurate evaluation of how well a student writes—should be to include multiple, and potentially different, responses to a composition.

Chapter 3 looked at how a classroom context can be created for inviting students into the process of reading and describing each other's work. By discussing, and inviting students to help create, the criteria used to evaluate papers, a teacher can situate evaluation criteria within the dynamics and goals of a particular course. This course itself may be located within larger constraints, such as state-mandated standards, in which case these should be acknowledged and incorporated into discussions about what should be valued in particular pieces of student writing. The rubber really meets the road for distributive evaluation, however, when students are asked to formally describe others' works. With the students at Stevens Institute of Technology, I used the following assignment to put both descriptive and distributive assessment into action:

Evaluative Essay 2 (due 5/3)
C. Whithaus
Humanities 104 C&D

The purpose of this essay is to make you engage in a close reading and analysis of a collaborative, hypertext essay written by other students. I will provide you each with the URL of an essay from the other class.

I'm going to ask you to follow a series of steps to complete this assignment. The material generated from these steps will be included in the final essay.

All of the following must be emailed to me (cwhithau@stevens-tech.edu). Send this material in the body of the email message; do NOT send these pieces as attachments. The final evaluative essays will be shared with the group members who wrote the essays; your names will not be attached to the comments.

Steps for Evaluative Essay

1. Your first step is to create a rhetorical analysis of the website. Comment on three aspects of the website: (a) its overall organization, including navigation; (b) its rhetorical effectiveness in terms of a paragraph/paragraph analysis. In this section, you should consider thematic and rhetorical connections among different paragraphs as well as actual links; and, (c) at least, three examples of sentence-level rhetoric. In particular, address the issues of syntax and semantics on the sentence-level. (due 4/28)

2. Next I'd like you to develop an analysis of the essay's content. (a) Provide a one sentence per page summary of the entire web site. (b) Provide a paragraph in which you summarize the entire essay. Try to summarize here (i.e., use Hayakawa's report style of language). Do not try to argue with or respond to the authors' claims, yet. (due 5/1)

3. After you have completed those preliminary steps, I'd like you to write an evaluative essay in which you respond to and evaluate the essay. You should be able to reorganize and include much of the material from steps 1 and 2 during this stage. (due 5/3)

Format for Evaluative Essay

I. **abstract** (a summary of around 200 words about YOUR evaluative essay. You should write the abstract AFTER you have finished the evaluative essay.)

II. **rhetorical analysis**
    a. overall organization
    b. rhetorical connections among paragraphs/pages

    c. sentence-level rhetoric

III. content

    a. page/page summary of the website

    b. paragraph summarizing the entire website

IV. response (This section should include your feelings about the hypertext essay in terms of both form and content. This section is really the moment where you look back on the rhetorical analysis and content and reflect upon the value of the essay. Did you learn anything? Was the essay informative? engaging? boring? Why? What did you like? What did you dislike about the piece? This section is for you to develop your subjective response to the essay).

THE EVALUATIVE ESSAYS:
THE PREVIOUS USES OF HYPERTEXT

To look at the practice of distributive peer assessment, I begin with students' evaluative essays. In their evaluative essays, students developed sophisticated responses that attempted to show both their knowledge of rhetorical structures and their responses as readers or "users" of the hypertext projects. This practice differed from the knowledge produced in previous studies of student hypertexts such as Michael Joyce's "Siren Shapes" (1988), George Landow's (1992, 1994, 1997) *Hypertext, Hypertext in Hypertext*, and *Hypertext 2.0*, and Stuart Moulthrop and Nancy Kaplan's (1994) "They Became What They Beheld," because the evaluative readings and descriptions of hypertext projects here are written by students rather than by teacher-researchers—the process of research as well as assessment was distributed.

Although the hypertext projects themselves were fascinating, I am less concerned with hypertext as a revolutionary writing technology and more concerned with the social process of including students in the assessment of each other's work. The students' responses ranged from praise to criticism depending on the hypertext being read. And, although the tone and the details used in the evaluations varied depending on who was doing the reading, what struck me as intriguing was the agreement, what assessment experts call the interrater reliability, among the student readers about the quality of the hypertexts they were evaluating. This chapter looks at Moulthrop and Kaplan's (1994) analysis of a work by one of Kaplan's students (Karl Crary), and then examines the evaluation of a highly successful hypertext (Women in Asian Societies) and a less successful hypertext (Sex and Sexuality) from my courses at Stevens Tech (Fig. 6.1).

Thinking about how the students describe works by other students highlights the complexities of composing html documents and demonstrates the value of including student descriptions in an assessment process. Their evaluations solidified around their descriptions of each other's works; their acts of observing pieces of writing, of viewing hypertexts and describing their reading experiences, moved me as a teacher and evaluator away from speculative discussions about students'

FIG. 6.1. Student Web sites: "Women in Asia" and "Sex and Sexuality."

composing processes and forced me to ground my comments on students' descriptions of the effects that texts have on them.

A CLASSICAL STUDY OF STUDENT HYPERTEXT: KARL CRARY'S "GARDEN OF FORKING PATHS"

In their discussions about student work and hypertext, Joyce (1988), Landow (1992, 1994, 1997), and Moulthrop and Kaplan (1994) focus on the students' writing processes. When they discuss reading hypertext, as Landow does when he talks about the Dickinson Web, the focus is on hypertext's implications for reading literature. Moulthrop and Kaplan (1994) blur the lines between reading literature and student writing (pp. 223–228); however, by using Borges' "Garden of Forking Paths" and Moulthrop's hypertext rendition of this story called "Forking Paths" as the basis of the student work, they continue the practice of student writing as responsive commentary about master works of literature. Their study of the hypertext created by Kaplan's student, Karl Crary, is a descriptive evaluation of a student hypertext, but it is a reading of a student work, a student reading, created in response to Borges' literary piece. Ultimately, Moulthrop and Kaplan conclude that Crary's reading of Moulthrop's hypertext version of Borges' story fails in its attempt to create "an anatomy of [this] pastiche, an attempt to classify all its parts according to a comprehensive taxonomy" (p. 233). Kaplan and Moulthrop argue that the medium of hypertext subsumes the student writer into the (hyper)text story:

> In this case, the reader might reasonably consider "Karl Crary" (quite contrary) not an external commentator but just another self-conscious *lector in fibula* (see Eco *Open Work*). As Crary notes, "Forking Paths" already includes several such characters. Crary's fourth category makes as much sense of his own antithetical structure as it does of these previous discursive oddities. Contrary indeed to his textual resistance, Crary's commentary helps the Garden grow. (p. 234)

They suggest that "Crary's failure stems from the very strength of his attempt" (p. 234). By writing in hypertext instead of print, Moulthrop and Kaplan claim that Crary challenged "the medium on its own terms" (p. 234). His strong reading "never stood a chance," because "in this medium, there is no way to resist multiplicity by imposing a univocal and definitive discourse. Hypertext frustrates this resistance because, paradoxically, it *offers* no resistance to intrusion" (p. 235).

I would argue, however, that Crary's "failure" is less the result of hypertext as a medium and more the result of the power Moulthrop and Kaplan give to Borges' literary text and their own (hypertext and teacherly) readings/versions of that work. One simply needs to look at a corporate Web site today to see that it is possible to present "a univocal and definitive discourse" using hypertext. By using hypertext within a literary course, Kaplan's section of the Reading Texts course at Carnegie Mellon University, Moulthrop and Kaplan invariably, and unintentionally, make certain that Crary's hypertext will be subordinated to the literary work. The social structure and the educational process of teaching reading subordinate and contain the textual technology used for reading and writing.

To move toward a course that explores the relation between reading and writing, especially within students' everyday lives, the technologies of textual representation and reproduction enabled by computer-mediated communication must be combined with a question that David Bartholomae (1996) has raised. In "What Is Composition," Bartholomae asked himself and composition teachers: "What does it mean to accept student writing as a starting point, as the primary text for a course of instruction, and to work with it carefully, aware of its and the course's role in a larger cultural project?" (p. 24). This question has immense relevance for the projects about student writing and literary works outlined by Joyce, Landow, and Moulthrop and Kaplan. Joyce, Landow, and Moulthrop and Kaplan envision transformations brought about in English studies by hypertext as a medium. The most student-centered of all these projects, Moulthrop and Kaplan's, aims at transforming students' relation to literary texts through cut-and-paste methods and hypertext commentary on the literary work. Whereas these works describe student hypertext essays and sketch out the implications of these essays for writing pedagogy and literary study, they preserve the role of teacher-researcher as observer and evaluator. The implications of their work combined with Bartholomae's question, however, lead directly to my project. If teachers accept not only student writing but student reading of that writing (really student-to-student communication) as the starting point for a course of instruction, then how do they develop methods of assessment (the end points of a course of instruction) that reflect the complexities, the engagement, and the risks students take as writers and readers? How can learning be measured? How can communication be measured?

The answer is apparently simple (e.g., "Ask the students. Include the students in the process of reading and evaluating each other's work."), but the implementation of this answer in institutionalized higher education is not. An entire complex, a knowledge ecology, drives the process of teaching. Chapter 3 sketched the elaborate setup needed to reach the point where students can read each other's works and evaluate them. Whereas questions about the interactions among reading, writing, and evaluation emerged for me in part through reading Joyce, Landow, Moulthrop and Kaplan, and Bartholomae, they became embodied through the students' hypertext compositions. By ceding some of my control over how the student hypertext works were evaluated, a different classroom dynamic emerged and a new pattern of research became clear. The students would describe each other's work. They would observe and comment and evaluate. And I would listen. I would read. Their comments about each other's writing, as well as their writing and hypertext designs, would gain new weight. They would not become what they beheld and have me comment on their brilliant failures, but rather they would describe what they were learning and what they were seeing, and, I thought, might catch a glimpse of what is to come.

WOMEN IN ASIAN SOCIETIES: STUDENT
DESCRIPTIONS AND DISTRIBUTIVE EVALUATION

The first hypertext project was a group research project on women in Asian societies. This group used chapters 2 and 3 from John Berger's (1985) *Ways of Seeing*, which we were reading in the class, as a framework for discussing the roles of women in Asian society. The group consisted of a student from China, a student from Korea, and two students from New Jersey (one whose parents had emigrated from Pakistan). As a group, then, I could understand why they felt drawn to writing about Asia and Asian culture. The one female student in the group was from China. I was happy that the group was tackling the issue of gender, but I wondered how they would work through what seemed to me an issue fraught with difficulties, especially because Stevens itself has an extremely high male to female ratio, which is reflected in the engineering field more generally.

Readings on gender and feminism that I had introduced to courses at Stevens over the years had almost always turned into criticism of "nonsensical, rabid feminist dogma," as one of my students recently labeled Judy Wacjman's (2000) "Feminists Perspectives on Technology." I have never, at Stevens, been able to have a discussion about feminism and gender that did not turn into an argument between me and a few, very vocal male—and sometimes female—students. Occasionally, after these discussions, a student (more often women, but sometimes a man) would write an essay that showed stirrings of an awareness of gender inequities in engineering. I was worried about how this group would handle the issue. And, if they handled it from a perspective that I could agree with, I wondered how the students evaluating the hypertext would respond.

In responding to this essay, the three student reviewers praised the project's content. Kathy wrote, "overall I thought that the pages were very informative though. They gave an abundance of information. If the reader takes the time to read all of the pages, they will learn a great deal about women's lives in Asia." Mark commented on the differences between his views of women as an American and the views of women described in the essay:

> There are certain thoughts that run through your mind when you view this web site. After living in this part of the world, and in this country especially, one gets a certain feeling towards women. Then after visiting the web site, it proves how different the lifestyles are in a different part of the world. This web site is a basic overview of the particular region, and how the women in this area have evolved, and the life of them.

The final student reviewer, James, pointed out the similarities between this project and a traditional, academic research essay. He wrote, "the website is much like a traditional academic essay, with excellent developed content and a well-organized order of writing. Rhetorical forms in this essay are effective due to the successful of integration in both quotations and statistic data."

I was also impressed with the hypertext's content, and in responding to the group, I wrote,

> overall, I was impressed with the development of the theme about women throughout the website. While the context of Asia helped give the paper focus, I was left wondering about the differences between Berger's EUROPEAN view of women and the different views of Asia your group explored.
>
> I don't think there is a simple binary between Europe and Asia, as one of the readers notes there are many different Asian cultures discussed here. But I do think your

group could have explored the differences between the view Berger attributes to European societies and the views of Muslim and non-Muslim countries you discuss.

While I intended to praise the students for their project and for their handling of the issue of representing women in a careful, culturally sensitive, and yet critical way, my comments may not have come across as praise. In typical teacherly fashion, I opened with a positive comment ("I was impressed"), but then moved forward to raise questions ("I was left wondering"). The student evaluations followed a different format, and as such were able to present their praise in a much more unqualified manner. The comments that the peer-evaluators made about the essay's quality (e.g., "excellent developed content and a well-organized order of writing," "it proves how different the lifestyles are in a different part of the world," and "they gave an abundance of information") might be as effective in terms of feedback to the writers as my praise, followed by critique. There was clearly a different rhetorical structure and flow to the student commentaries and to my comments, and the difference may have been enough to jar the students into seeing the readings of the hypertext as both multiple and as accurate. They may have come to see different responses to the same composition as valid responses, because the readers were different. The value of a text, of a communicative action, is determined by its reception as well as by the structures embedded within it.

Instead of pushing on the differences between Asian and European representations of women as I had done, the student readers criticized some of the design features of the Web site. Mark wrote,

> overall this web page is laid out very neat and organized fashion. You have the ability to link to any part of the page from any area of the page. It has a lot of graphics that make it very nice to look at, but can slow down the time to view the page. I like the idea of a map being the link to all of the sites, and the flags on the side. The use of graphics is good, but the backgrounds take to long to load. This makes the reader have to wait, and they can possible lose interest in the site.

> The way that some of the pages were laid out is very boring. The fact that some pages are just essays posted on the web do not make them appealing to read. When a person is surfing the web for information, it should be easy to find and short, not long and complicated.

The criticism of the site's backgrounds as too complicated, and as a result too slow to load, showed an interesting awareness of the reader as user, and as the end-user occupying different sites of access. There was also a powerful sense of connection between the design feature and its effect on the reader: "This makes the reader have to wait, and they can possible lose interest in the site." The student evaluator was aware of the reader as an agent—a user—engaged with the text and with the text as an embodied feature of a particular technology.

James wrote,

The overall rating of this site is subject to many factors. The overall writing content was rather well. Although the web page is not as great as a commercial site. This is most likely due to the fact that it is for a writing class, and not a web designing class. Also, because there is a lack of knowledge on how to make these sites, as well as the lack of resources and web space, since it is all on free web space. That is the basic overall aspect of the web site in question.

Although this paragraph is not brilliant, it did praise the essay's writing as "well" done. But, it also critiqued the page design as not living up to the standards of "a commercial site." I also read some discontent with this student's response to the hypertext essay assignment itself. When he wrote that there is "a lack of knowledge on how to make these sites, as well as the lack of resources and web space," I suspect that he was feeling somewhat at odds with the overall project. In terms of the evaluative essay, these comments softened his criticism of the design and provided an explanation for the weakness he was pointing out. In this way, his evaluation also took into account the social and academic situation in which the Web site was composed. Thus, this comment placed the evaluation of the student hypertext within the context of this course—something that many professional assessment tools have not yet figured out how to do. Still, his awareness of context was essentially an admission that a criticism he made, besides not being very clear, was basically irrelevant given the context. And his frustration may have been at least as much with his apparent difficulties in articulating criticisms, while still trying to seem knowledgeable and objective, as it was with how he felt "at odds with" the project.

Kathy concurred with her peers on the essay's strength as a piece of writing but weakness in terms of design. However, she presented this combination of strength and weakness not as a product situated within the confines of a writing course, but rather as a product of changing media. She wrote, "However, the con with this website is the same as its pro, it's too much like a traditional essay instead of a world wide web. If the authors can get rid of the minor problems within the website and be more creative to the use of images, sounds, web layouts, and all other multimedia forms, the website would be perfectly developed." Jay David Bolter and Richard Grusin (1999) have noted similar features in their analyses of professional software development and new media forms of communication (pp. 64–87). Kathy engaged with the content of the site and believed that this content had been presented effectively if the criteria of academic writing were applied to the Web site; however, she—like Bolter and Grusin—longed to see the content developed "perfectly" for this new media.

Although the students' judgments about this site expressed a general agreement on the site's strengths and weaknesses, their descriptive summaries and rhetorical analyses showed even greater coherence. I would like to argue that this coherence was based on the fact that the students were observing what was in each other's writing, or what was on each other's Web sites, rather than imagining what the other students were not achieving. Following M. A. Syverson (1999, pp.

192–194), I want to argue that one of the reasons that readers of standardized essays may disagree and have to be renormed is that they are looking at how students' writing does not do certain things. It is hard to come to agreement on what is in a text; it is harder still to come to agreement on what is not in a text.

However, although these three students came to a general consensus that the writing on the Web site was effective but the design was lacking, the explanations they presented about the site's design flaws revolved around what the Web site did NOT do. The students were filtering the site through a rubric of descriptive evaluation but they, like readers of standardized writing tests, evaluated according to absences as much as observation. Each student commented on what was not in the Web site:

- "The use of graphics is good, but the backgrounds take to long to load. This makes the reader have to wait, and they can possible lose interest in the site";
- "Although the web page is not as great as a commercial site";
- "it's too much like a traditional essay instead of a world wide web."

When a composition does not meet readerly expectations, the elements that are not in the text become part of a reader's experience of the work, and they are reflected in the descriptions of the composition.

Another noteworthy aspect of the student commentaries was their adherence to critiquing formal aspects of the writing and design. They did not engage on a substantial level with the site's discussion of women in Asia as a subject for critique, commentary, or agreement. In fact, their comments about the content of the hypertext essay remained summaries. Two students briefly described the contents of the essay, by writing: "If the reader takes the time to read all of the pages, they will learn a great deal about women's lives in Asia" and "This web site is a basic overview of the particular region, and how the women in this area have evolved and the life of them." The third student's summary of content did not even mention "Asia" or "women," but rather mentioned only the essay's "excellent developed content" and "quotations and statistic data." On one level, I could critique these student comments as mere summaries instead of analyses or extensions of the essay's topic.

The questions I would like to ask involve a triangulation among the agreement that all evaluators expressed about the quality of the Web site's writing, the student evaluators' agreement on the Web site having design flaws, and the contrast between a teacherly questioning of the essay's content and the students' terse summaries of that content. The students and I agreed that the writing on the Web site was for the most part effective; and, one could claim that within this very limited sample then, there is something that resembles the more formal assessment criterion of interrater reliability. However, our consensus on the work's quality as a piece of writing is undercut by the different articulations of the work's design flaws. One student evaluator wanted the work to be simpler (e.g., "the backgrounds take to long to load"); another student wanted the site to be more like "a commercial website," but reserved his critique for the course and not the student authors (e.g., "this is most likely due to the fact that it is for a writing class, and not a web designing class"); and the final student argued that the writers did not make their composition enough like "a world wide web." All of these critical comments about the work's design presented different reasons for their critiques and hence shattered the interrater reliability: They agreed that there were flaws in the design, but what those flaws were varied widely. And to make matters more complicated, the flaws were explained in relation to a readerly expectation, not to a feature that was already in the essay but to a component that had NOT been included. Observation and description were not only about what was out in the world, what the students saw in other students' essays; they were also about the expectations that student evaluators brought with them.

Finally, this process of evaluation breaks down along a teacher–student divide. As the teacher, I felt compelled to comment on the work's theme; and as a teacher concerned with critical pedagogy, I felt compelled to comment in a way that I hoped would provoke more questions for the student authors. The students, in contrast, focused on the work's form in terms of both the writing and the hypertext design. Their comments stressed the staying power of the formal modes of assessment associated with what David Russell (1991), Joseph Petraglia (1998), and Charles Bazerman and David Russell (2003) have analyzed, and critiqued, as General Writing Skills Instruction (GWSI). When I invited students to take part in a process of negotiating evaluation criteria and then employing those criteria to make assessment a communicative process, I unwittingly ran the risk of having the negotiated criteria applied in ways that revalidated comments about form. As evaluators, students applied not only what they had learned in my course, but also what they had been taught about commenting on essays in primary and secondary school language arts and English classes.

Trying not only to negotiate the criteria for assessment but also to make the process of evaluation into a series of communications among students and teachers provides few neat answers. Teachers and students move toward interrater reliability, and then we see that consensus break down when criticisms of the work are developed. Teachers and students move toward evaluations based on observations of what is present in student works rather than absent from those works, and then we see that readers are already bringing to bear expectations about what is not in the work. We move toward a process of negotiating evaluation, of centering the process of assessment within the context of student-generated criteria, and then we observe that the application of those criteria reinstates the status quo of commentary on form rather than content. Yet, it is in these movements toward an amorphous, new type of "reliability," toward "descriptive" evaluations, and toward the application of situated and negotiated evaluation criteria that I sense a foundation for accurate, valid, and useful methods of writing assessment in computer-mediated composition courses.

SEX AND SEXUALITY: THE STUDENTS' ASSESSMENTS
AND THEIR BASIS IN DESCRIPTIVE EVALUATION

Looking at the work of two students, who reviewed a hypertext essay on "Sex and Sexuality," contributes to a better understanding of how a new, less quantifiable interrater reliability might be achieved through descriptive evaluations. These two students presented detailed descriptive summaries of the group's homepage. The first student wrote,

> Overall the website is well organized. The introduction, on the first page, explains that the website will be about Sex and Sexuality and that it will be split up into different topics: Sex and Sexuality in the Media, Sex as a Metaphor, Sex and the Roman Catholic Church, Sex as a Basic Biological Look, and Sex, Nudity and Art. These topics each have a page dedicated to them, which allows for navigating through the site smoothly, as well as links on each page that give additional information. These topics were chosen because of the everyday relevance they have in our lives. This keeps the reader interested while informing them of the writers' views on this subject. Throughout these pages, sexuality is discussed first and then sex is mediated. This gives the web page consistency and orderliness. Although each page does not refer to any ideas from another page and no obvious connections are made between the pages, the different topics all address the influence of sexuality and sex in our lives on a daily basis. The words sexuality and sex show the interrelationship between each of these topics, and are redefined in each of the different contexts.

The other student, working entirely on his own, described the homepage as follows:

> The web site that will be evaluated is entitled "Sex and Sexuality". To start off the title is catchy and in today's society most men and women will click on such a link to see what the website is all about. The page loads rather quickly, which is always a plus, as most people will give a web site three seconds to load before closing the page. The homepage is very well set up, with links and an overall summary of the website. There are five links on the upper left side of the page that link to the other five pages that contain the five sub topics. The first page contains the title of the website on the top of the page. At first glance the rest of the page appears to be a standard essay set up which is correct and it works very well for this type of web page. The first paragraph is an introduction for the entire page. Each following paragraph contains a summary of each individual person's page with a link to that page incorporated somewhere in the paragraph. This is a very clever touch, because as the reader looks over the topics he can easily click on one while still interested in the topic at hand. The only problem is there is no closing paragraph; still with this type of a setup there is not always a need for a closing paragraph.

These two descriptive evaluations of the site's homepage noted the way the page's text and organizational links present "Sex and Sexuality" to the reader. They both noted the site's division into five subtopics, and the opening page's descriptive introduction to the topic. These descriptions lead both readers to evaluate the site, at least the opening page, favorably. The first reviewer commented that the page was "well organized," that he was able to "navigat[e] through the site smoothly," that the "topics were chosen because of the everyday relevance they have in our lives," and that the web page had "consistency and orderliness." The second reviewer noted that "the title is catchy," "the page loads rather quickly," and "the homepage is very well set up, with links and an overall summary of the website." Whereas these two responses did not duplicate each other, they stressed similar features in their description of the page and then incorporated praise for the site around these descriptions.

As the students moved through the hypertext, they continued to describe what was actually present in the text. They did not judge the text here, but this did serve as a basis for their critique. While viewing the page on "Sex as a Metaphor," one of the reviewers noted:

> Sex as a Metaphor gives the different sports metaphors used for sex. The writer starts with the most famous baseball metaphor, comparing the crossing the bases to how far one has gotten. Other sports metaphors dealing with hockey and basketball are explained. Furthermore, the writer gives metaphors that are not related to sports, and discusses the stereotype of crude construction workers.

The student did not critique the page at this point, but merely noted what he had observed. The other student evaluator commented on the page in a bit more detail, but was also not particularly negative. He wrote,

> The second topic is "Metaphors", which gives many examples of how people speak about sex without actually using the word itself. This page however starts out with examples about the topic in the first line. It goes on this way throughout the page. A new topic, which are all sports related and how key phrases in sports actually stand for a sexual act. This is affective and works yet the thing missing is links. This page contains no links to related pages that would support the claims. A way past this is using pictures to provide a support for the topic being discussed, however no pictures are used either. At the end of the page however, there is the author's name, which is a link that opens up a window to send mail to the author regarding the essay. This link to send mail to the author occurs in each person's individual page.

The extra details in this description did provide a bit more of a judgmental flavor to the description. By commenting on the absence of links and the presence of a mailto link, this reviewer established the technical qualities of the page and did note that the page was "affective."

While the students worked on description in the rhetorical analysis sections of their evaluative essay and did not include many evaluative comments on the "Sex as Metaphor" page here, they both returned to the "Sex as Metaphor" page in their responses. The first student criticized the page for "grammatically and spelling errors that sometimes leaves the reader confused." He also noted that "the title, Baseball and Sex, is misleading because not only is the baseball metaphor used but sex is also compared to other sports, hockey and basketball, and other metaphors that are not related to sports." The other student concurred on the weaknesses of this page. While criticizing the overall hypertext for "miscommunication" among pages and overall brevity, he wrote, "a good example is the metaphor page" because it "speaks about how sports are related to sex and how athletes or just anyone uses a key phrase from a sport to represent something concerning sex." He singled out this page because it was effective in terms of catching his interest, but it did not relate to the other pages very well. In addition, it was short and skimmed over the topic.

In the end, both students moved away from their praise of the site's homepage by the time they got to their closing responses and evaluations. While describing the site on a page-by-page basis in terms of its content and its form, they discovered substantial flaws. When they began their responses, they returned to, and in some cases expanded on, their summaries and rhetorical analyses of individual pages. Their evaluations of the site did not rely on a letter grade but they did describe the site in terms that relate to what they saw on the site and included notes of dissatisfaction with the overall product. The first student noted that "while the essay was informative and very well organized, some grammatical and spelling errors made the information being presented hard to follow at times." The second student decided that the essay "could have been better." Although these evaluations did not have the traditional interrater reliability dictated by numbered systems of assessment, they clearly corresponded in their sense that the hypertext essay did not live up to its potential. Their dissatisfaction as readers was clear, was based on their descriptions of the Web site, and was situated within the context of a first-year writing course at a technical, research university.

CLOSING: STUDENTS AS READERS
AND ASSESSMENT AS INTERACTIVE,
DESCRIPTIVE, SITUATED, AND DISTRIBUTED

For the Humanities 104 classes at Stevens Tech, our descriptive evaluations took the form of rhetorical analyses and content summaries. By working with these students and watching how they decided on evaluation criteria, adapting those criteria for hypertext compositions, and then using a method of describing each other's work as a means of making judgments about the effectiveness of the work, I learned that teaching writing involves more than the passing on of information about language. Teaching writing in a society where academic, workplace, and interpersonal communications are becoming increasingly computer-mediated affairs requires the creation of environments where students have opportunities to learn. This process of learning should not be confused with a simple articulation of already-learned criteria and then an application of those rules to new writing tasks. Rather an invitation for students to learn—to think critically and creatively—about what is valued in computer-mediated communication is also an invitation to teachers to think, and re-think, their methods and criteria for valuing writing.

These invitations are not benign but are difficult challenges, seams along which teacher-researchers risk their theories and ideals within the testing ground of classroom experience. Attempting to have students read and describe only what was in other students' works and not speculate on what was absent from them soon reminded me of the varying subjectivities and expectations people bring with them to the reading process. Attempting to establish a system of interrater re-liability based on students' descriptive evaluations splintered as soon as things moved toward criticisms of what the hypertext essays could have done better. And having students act as generators of evaluation criteria and readers who ap-plied those criteria soon revealed the staying power of their previous educational experiences. The students at Stevens Tech know how to play the game of school very well. My attempt to say let's discard the game, or at least one of the basic rules of the game (i.e., the teacher as grader), meet not so much with resistance as with tolerance. But it was within this very tolerance, within the students' willing-ness to negotiate evaluation criteria and write evaluative essays that applied those criteria, that I discovered students' persistence in commenting on the form of a piece of writing. The students "know," and I "know," that critiques and commen-tary in a writing course should be about "writing," not about inequities in the way men and women are treated.

As a technique to build a situated evaluation of student work, distribution em-phasizes multiple readers describing their experiences with a student composi-tion—for example, the students within the Humanities courses discussed in this chapter. These various audiences create a distributive process of composing. They make the student aware that they are writing for particular individuals and for multiple individuals at the same time. By having the teacher read the descriptive comments from multiple readers, distribution helps transform composing from an activity about pleasing the teacher (i.e., "Just tell me what you want me to say") to an activity that situates composing within the interactions of a writer and her audi-ence. For the development of pedagogy and learning, distribution makes sense. It makes the learning of higher order thinking skills more likely. If, however, evalu-ators cannot figure out ways of designing large-scale assessment systems that also incorporate and honor distribution, that acknowledge different readers read differ-ently, then teaching and learning will be curtailed when teachers and students go into "test prep mode." Creating databases that associate the descriptive responses of multiple readers with students' multimedia compositions provides a technical solution for implementing distributive evaluation techniques for large-scale as-sessment programs. Developing these systems is a far more worthy and useful en-deavor than the current push by the College Board to enhance writing instruction through implementing a multiple-choice exam and a single 25-minute essay.

7

High-Stakes Testing
and 21st-Century Literacies

8 a.m. September. A group of 18- and 19-year olds look at me through bleary subway, bus, or Long Island Expressway eyes. Having taught in Brooklyn before
coming to Queens College and having worked as an editor on English as a Second
Language (ESL) textbooks, I know and do not know these students: Most are
products of New York City public high schools; many are immigrants from eastern Europe, southeast Asia, and the Caribbean; a few are native New Yorkers
from a grab bag of ethnicities. They are remarkably young for a basic writing
course at CUNY. Most basic writing classes here include a large number of non-
traditional students. In fact, so many students are nontraditional that friends of
mine who teach at other CUNY campuses say that traditional students are a slim,
sometimes nonexistent, minority in their basic writing courses.

I know and do not know these students already as I know and do not know the
anxiety that creeps into my stomach on the first day of classes. The elevator doors
open and I see the narrow fifth floor hallway. Seventeen students wait—well at
least the roster tells me there will be 17 students waiting—and, indeed as the dull
silver doors slid apart and I blink into the claustrophobic hallway, I see quite a
collection of students.

Some are standing. Some, slopped against the wall, sit on the carpet. They are
waiting to be allowed into the room. Around 17, I guess. There will be stragglers.
But not too many. They have not yet figured out the differences between high
school and college. Try teaching an upper-division English class at 8 a.m. and the
late comers will be legion, but for now—they are on time. It is the first day of college for many of them and they want to make a good impression. Actually, there
may well be more trying to enroll in English 95. If the section met later in the day,
then there would be more. But at 8 in the morning. It's not too likely. They are

here not because students naturally bang down the doors to get into a writing course, but because students are supposed to take English 95 before they retake CUNY's infamous Writing Assessment Test (WAT).

HIGH-STAKES TESTS

Although the WAT has its own unique history, which I will talk about a little bit later, the use of high-stakes tests has been on the rise nationally as part of the standards movement within education. One could almost see the passage of the No Child Left Behind Act, signed into law January 8, 2002, by George W. Bush as the culmination of the decades-long standards movement. The rhetoric of programs such as No Child Left Behind is inclusive, even the program name has been lifted from the progressive Children's Defense Fund. The Department of Education Web site declares:

> [The No Child Left Behind Act of 2001] redefines the federal role in K–12 education and will help close the achievement gap between disadvantaged and minority students and their peers. It is based on four basic principles: stronger accountability for results, increased flexibility and local control, expanded options for parents, and an emphasis on teaching methods that have been proven to work. (*No Child Left Behind*, 2001)

However, the lynchpin in this act is the first of the four points, stronger accountability. Holding administrators and teachers responsible for student performance requires a system of determining effective performances—in short, it requires testing. The other three points—"increased flexibility and local control, expanded options for parents, and an emphasis on teaching methods that have been proven to work"—all emerge only through the filter of standardized accountability in the No Child Left Behind Act of 2001. Thus, commendable goals (e.g., local control of schools, parental involvement, and teaching methods that work) may be lost under a scrim of standardized forms of accountability.

Although the College Board intends to promote writing instruction by including writing as a major area on the SAT, the W-component of the new exam could actually reduce the amount of time that high school students spend on complex research-based writing. It could also reduce the number of opportunities students have for working on multimedia compositions such as those discussed in chapter 9. Because the W-component of the SAT values the quick organization of evidence possible within a 25-minute window, correct surface features, and sentence structure, these areas will be focal points for secondary writing instruction. The multiliteracies documented by the New London Group, the Educational Testing Service, and even the College Board itself will be taught less often because one of the most important exams a high school student will take does not value these sorts of compositions.

Coupled with the rise in standardized testing at the state level and No Child Left Behind, the shift in the SAT could actually signal a decline in students' higher order composing skills. Eva Baker (1998) has shown that many of the tests commonly used in school tend to focus on easily measured basic skills and facts. Audrey L. Amrein and David C. Berliner (2002) of Arizona State University argue that by assessing basic skills "we may fail to measure important and complex areas of student knowledge, skills, and strategies" (p. 1). "Even more importantly," they noted, "what is tested becomes the de facto standard for what students are expected to know. Tests of low-level skills and facts not only reflect but also reinforce low expectations for student achievement. Students, parents, and teachers come to believe that if something is not tested, it is probably not very important to learn" (p. 1). As Amrein and Berliner make clear, standards-based testing may have negative as well as positive impacts on schooling and students' learning. If the challenge of a writing curriculum, particularly in the age of the Internet, is to have students learning to communicate effectively in a variety of rhetorical situations, then tests of low-level skills are probably not the most effective way to achieve that end.

Teachers have to deal with the current policies instituted by state governments. Yet they are obligated—ethically obligated in a Levianisn sense (Levinas, 1969), I would argue—to prepare students to meet the academic and real-world communication situations they are going to encounter, as well as to prepare them for whatever standards-based test is in place at the moment. Providing students the scaffolding to investigate problems on their own, to turn their writing activities into social initiatives as well as academic exercises, is indeed a challenge. This is a challenge that has only been made greater for writing teachers by many of the state-sponsored exams that students will encounter.

To make matters even more complicated, computer-mediated communication (CMC) technologies emerge faster than traditional assessment tools can be created to evaluate those skills. In these discussions, what surprises me over and over again, is the resilience of teachers and their sense that given time they will both come to understand what, if anything, a test can add to their curriculum and what parts of their teaching are too valuable to give up to test prep time. It is never an easy balancing act, and perhaps the best way I can talk about grappling with a high-stakes test and computer-mediated communication is to return to that stifling classroom on the fifth floor of Klapper Hall, early on a September morning.

CONTEXT

The WAT was the hotly contested and now thankfully retired entrance requirement for CUNY—an institution once centered around City College, "the poor man's Harvard." By 1997, CUNY had become an extensive urban institution with 21 campuses beset by political critics. Writing in *The City Journal*, Heather Mac-

Donald claimed the "once . . . loose aggregate of elite colleges for the ambitious poor [had become] a bloated bureaucracy that jettisoned academic standards in the face of a flood of ill-prepared students" (1998, p. 65). The WAT and its sisters, the RAT (Reading Assessment Test) and MAT (Math Assessment Test), were installed as entrance requirements along with the first tuition bills in 1976. During CUNY's 129-year prior history, tuition had never been charged—City College "was a highly competitive, tuition-free institution that catered to gifted but poor immigrant students" (*Profile*, 2000, ¶ 2). This progressive ideal had been expanded in 1969 to include open admissions, in other words, any New York State high school graduate could attend CUNY. But the fiscal crisis of the late 1970s brought Mayor Abraham Beame and NYC to a screeching halt; tuition was instated, along with these entrance exams, to control skyrocketing costs through limiting enrollment.

Ironically, the entrance exams were designed as rising-junior exams. They were supposed to be a way of testing competence after 60 credit hours had been completed, not as a tool for assessing *readiness* for college-level written work (CUNY Assessment Review Report, 1996).[1] But the teachers who designed the test did not control its implementation, and 21 years later, 17 students and I were left to grapple with the legacy of an assessment tool designed for the educational and economic crises of another era. The misuse of assessment tools is an all too common story in education. For instance, in the late 1990s, some colleges were still using verbal SAT scores for placement in college writing courses, despite the Educational Testing Service's insistence that this multiple-choice based aptitude test is *not* an indicator of writing ability (Fairtest, 2003).

Politicians and boards of education cling to the idea that cookie-cutter assessment tools, whether or not used appropriately, reflect students' knowledge and skills. Over and over, there has been a willingness to believe that rising test scores equals rising ability levels equals rising standards. But this equation is a charade, an elaborate disguise. When Virginia public schools' Standards of Learning (SOL) writing scores went from a pass rate of 70.66% in 1998 to 85.04% in 2000 (English Standards of Learning, 2000) does this mean that one set of students—

---

[1]Current universitywide assessment has its roots in the 1976 board policy for certification; for students wishing to progress beyond the 60th credit, that policy mandated "evidence, in accordance with a standard to be determined by the Chancellor, that they have attained a level of proficiency in basic learning skills necessary to cope successfully with advanced work in the academic disciplines." Determination of the nature of such assessment was delegated by the chancellor to the vice chancellor for academic affairs, and a universitywide testing program was instituted in 1978. Developed to certify achievement of the board-mandated level of proficiency by the 60th credit, the tests of this program also determined remedial or freshman-level placement. In fact, these tests—the Mathematics Assessment Test (MAT), the Reading Assessment Test (RAT or DTLS, for Descriptive Test of Language Skills, developed by the Educational Testing Service), and the Writing Assessment Test (WAT)—were and are known collectively as the Freshman Skills Assessment Program (FSAP). From the outset to the present, they were used for initial placement, exit from remediation, *and* 60th-credit certification.

simply 2 years younger—is that much smarter than the previous set? When local newspapers trumpet "Seniors clearing SOL hurdle: Roughly 9 out of 10 pass tests now required for graduate" (Bowers, 2003, p. A18) in 2003, should it be assumed that real gains, measurable by outside assessment tools, have resulted? Or have teachers improved in their teaching methods so dramatically in 2 years that students are really learning that much more? Isn't it more likely that teachers have learned how to teach to these tests, and that administrators have worked hard to make sure that teachers can adapt their curriculum to meet these tests? The tests are not measurements of students' knowledge, but measurements of their test-taking abilities and measurements of teachers' adaptability to different examination criteria. In discussing the SOLs and their impact on Norfolk schools, Matthew Bowers writes a telling paragraph: "This year, however, the [elementary] division . . . will adminster[] SOL-like tests every quarter in third through eighth grades. A new computer system will get the results back quickly . . . so teachers can use them to shape lessons and review sessions." (Bowers, 2003, p. A18)

In addition, outside consultants such as Douglas Reeves of the Center for Performance Assessment are brought in to help poorly performing schools. He helps schools "create unique strategies based on their data. Julie A. Keesling, chief information officer for Norfolk schools, acknowledges Reeves provides "tailored attention." What does this tailored attention mean? It means that the exams are driving the curriculum, that teachers and administrators are working hard to adjust and to succeed within the new rules for "educational success." For the writing portions of these exams, then, it is clear that teachers are preparing students to meet (i.e., to write within the particular confines) the particular goals of a particular test.

Now it could be argued that if the tests are designed correctly, then when teachers teach toward them they are teaching better, more meaningful, material than the curricula they taught previously. To a degree that argument makes sense because a statewide testing regime does enforce a standard curriculum and *if* that curriculum develops students' skills more effectively than the one a certain teacher had in place, then students would learn more and will have developed more meaningful skills. Invariably, some teachers will have their curricula improved by outside mandates, and invariably some will have their curricula dumbed down because of outside mandates. However wide and deep the changes are to teachers' language arts and English curricula across a state, the success of these changes in terms of students' writing cannot be calibrated by the exams themselves. Because teachers have taught toward these tests after they were implemented, the tests scores will go up. A real comparison of students' knowledge and writing abilities before and after the implementation of a state-mandated test would require readings of student writing samples not related to the test from *before* the test began to shape the curriculum and *after* the test had been in use for at least 4 years. Until such readings are done, claims that standards are rising because test scores are rising are only so much political hot air. Meanwhile, writing teachers are losing control of the curriculum. They are becoming disenchanted with teaching. They are deprofessionalized by testing experts, the way doctors are deprofessionalized when administrators at HMOs make systemwide treatment decisions rather than relying on the expertise of local practitioners.

Systemwide assessments appear in simple numerical terms to lead to improved writing instruction and improved writing skills. They provide sound bites for politicians: 70% pass in 1998; 85% passed in 2000; therefore, I—Mr. Politician, Mr. Mayor, Mr. Governor—have improved education. But the deeper and harder questions of increasing knowledge, increasing the challenges of curricula, and increasing composing abilities to prepare students for 21st-century communication environments remain unaddressed and unresolved by government-mandated testing agencies.

21ST-CENTURY LITERACIES:
WHAT THE EXPERTS THINK/PREDICT

Further, technology standards and computer-mediated communication (CMC) suggest that the skills needed to survive in the 21st-century academy and workplace are not the same as the skills developed for print-based literacies. The research of Carol L. Winkelman (1995), Michael Joyce (1988, 1995), Stuart Moulthrop and Nancy Kaplan (1994) on hypertext and literacy and the work of Charles R. Cooper and Lee Odell (1977), Myra Barrs (1990), and M. A. Syverson (1999) on descriptive assessment suggest that the evaluation of student compositions in electronic writing environments requires teachers, as the Bertelsmann and AOL Time Warner report (21st century, 2002) also suggests, "to revisit many of our assumptions and beliefs" about measuring student achievement. Reflecting on, and rejoicing in, the difficulties of evaluating electronic texts, Winkelman argued that "the criteria for text and text production must constantly and contextually change. The criteria must capture the radical intertextuality, the seeming anarchy, of postmodern literacy" (p. 435). This awareness of evaluation criteria as shifting categories underscores the ways in which computer-mediated writing theory and pedagogy fostered a view of writing as a course about communication rather than about the production of academic discourse in a formally defined, standardized English. Communication, or the exchange of information and the creation of knowledge, has become a pressing issue in discussions of how the evaluation of student work in computer-mediated composition courses should progress into the 21st century.

Joyce's (1988) classic study of early hypertext and writing pedagogy, "Siren Shapes," not only made the distinction between constructive and exploratory hypertext, but also described the writing process of a developmental writing student using the hypertext composing program Storyspace. Constructive hypertexts for Joyce are open structures, spaces, and compositions that are complex and ongoing. They allow readers to build their knowledge, their responses, their continuations of a narrative into that text. Exploratory hypertexts allow a greater flexibility for readers in accessing information, but they do not allow readers to substantially change the text. In today's terms, an exploratory hypertext would be the help menu in a word-processing program or an encyclopedia on CD-ROM; a constructive hypertext would be a collaborative composition by a group of students or one of the many open-story sites, such as the X-Files site where readers create alternative episodes to Chris Carter's famous TV series, now on the web. Perhaps the greatest constructive hypertext in practice today are wikis such as *wikipedia* (2003; Fig. 7.1), a free, "open-source," collaborative encyclopedia that rivals, if not surpasses, *Britannica*.

However, Joyce's "Siren Shapes" did not limit itself to a tautological definition of two different types of hypertext. Rather, "Siren Shapes" described the composing process of Les, a student in Joyce's developmental English class, when Les worked in Storyspace. By examining Les' process of "journaling" in Storyspace and then turning those journals into a linked hypertext essay, Joyce turned to an evaluative method that is descriptive of the student's writing process, the organizational links the student saw within his own writing, and the final written product—the Storyspace file. As a teacher-reader of Les' hypertext essay, Joyce occupied a new and different space from the teacher-reader of a printed student essay. Joyce's choices made a difference in how he saw the text. And his responses to Les' work, and the works of all the developmental writing students working in Storyspace, brought into question not only the relation of students as writers to the texts they were composing but also the relation of teachers as readers of students' constructive hypertexts.

In "They Became What They Beheld," Moulthrop and Kaplan (1994) argued that these new computer-mediated reading systems physically embody the reader-response theories of Wolfgang Iser (1989) and Stanley Fish (1980) by blurring "distinctions between reception and production" (p. 221). One of the key questions Moulthrop and Kaplan asked was, "What value do these changes [in writing technologies] have for students and teachers of texts" (p. 221)? To explore pedagogies that accommodate changes in students' interaction with and production of texts, Moulthrop and Kaplan turned to Gregory Ulmer's (1985) "textshop" approach to teaching surrealism. They noted that "Ulmer treats students' production of texts not as a vice to be regretted (or corrected) but as a source of essential dynamism in the pedagogic process" (p. 225). Digital media embody student writing as dynamic text, as writing physically in dialogue with and against literary text, and as composition electronically written around and over the words of the old master texts. As cut ups and ready-made novels, electronic student writing becomes "a form of literature (or 'paraliterature' or 'paracriticism') open not only to interpretation but also to expansion and revision" (p. 227). By describing and evaluating student hypertext created in response to Moulthrop's hypertext pastiche of Borges' "The Garden of Forking Paths," Moulthrop and Kaplan worked toward a method of descriptive evaluation.

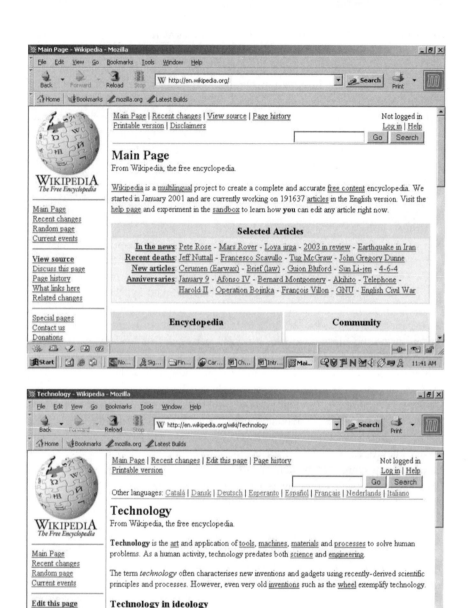

FIG. 7.1. Wikipedia.

IMPACT OF INFORMATION TECHNOLOGY
ON ASSESSMENT SYSTEMS

"Shakespeare shakes, I heard . . ." Walking across the Queens College campus after teaching, I heard this exchange between two students slopping out of Klapper
Hall. The Manhattan skyline was visible on a clear, cold Fall day. I was heading
toward the bus stop where I would catch the bus heading toward the Forest Hills
subway stop. What was it about the Shakespeare course that had moved these two
students, I wondered. I knew two of the Shakespeare instructors: One was a re-
nowned scholar and researcher of kingship and politics in early modern England,
the other was a graduate student who was writing his dissertation on early modern
England. I wondered which one had taught the "shaking Shakespeare" course,
and what that meant. Was it a good class? A bad class? I couldn't quite tell from
the comment. Something about the double "sh"s had caught my ear, but then the
rest of the conversation had fell away from me.

Catching part of a conversation but not having the context, the situation within
which to evaluate the phrase "Shakespeare shakes," I held the words in my head
and later wrote them down. Really, they are meaningless without a context. They
were meaningful to me, because I could recall when I heard them and then describe that situation. But, even with my description, they are useless as evaluations of the Shakespeare class because I do not know if they are positive or negative assessments. In addition, I do not know whose class or what aspect of the
class they apply to.

They are nearly as meaningless as an A or a B or a C or an F placed on a student's transcript for her achievements, or failures, in a writing course. However, a
grade on a transcript does have more meaning than just a letter, because a grade
for one course is read in the context of the grades for all the other courses a student
took. It has a particular significance within the context of the transcript (and there
is some systemic use to this letter), but as a full descriptor of what a student has
done in a writing course, a single letter, even marked with a plus or a minus is a
paltry, and ultimately decontextualized, marked evaluation. What does saying
"Shakespeare shakes. . . ." or writing "B" mean? They do not mean anything
without the situation, without the context. They do not mean anything without the
interaction that leads to their meaning, that lends them meaning.

The idea that new information technologies (IT) can improve the testing and
observation of students' work has not only occurred within computers-and-
writing studies but has also occupied the minds of assessment experts. Assessment and measurement experts are turning to information technologies to help
provide richer contexts within which to evaluate student learning. In her 1997 presentation at ETS, Eva Baker (1998) focused on how information technologies can
be used to improve the quality of what is tested, the efficiency of the test, and the
means of communicating test results to the community (pp. 5–17). Baker ac-

knowledges that "large-scale testing has depended in great measure on the refinement of machine-scorable approaches to the processing of student papers" (p. 7). Here Baker calls attention to the ways in which technology is always already a part of writing assessment—without technological advances in card-punch computing, without advances in scantron sheets, the dominance of indirect, multiple-choice writing assessment methods in the 1950s and 1960s may not have occurred.

As a result, the arguments of process movement adherents and holistic-scoring proponents such as Edward M. White (1985, 1992, 1994) and Karen Greenberg (1988, 1992, 1993) for the testing of writing skills by actually looking *at* samples of student writing rather than at tests of knowledge *about* writing would not have been needed. But history cannot be rewritten, and one cannot speculate for too long on what could have been "if only. . . ." Rather, there is a need to engage with the contemporary structures for assessing writing as they are. There is a need to examine how teacher-researchers and assessment experts have moved forward in the last 17 years to develop tools for writing assessment that measure what Baker (1998) calls "domains of performance in areas heretofore inaccessible on a broad scale" (p. 7). Developments in information technology, in fact, suggest that the nature of argument and the value of communication skills will shift as computer-mediated communication increases.

TECHNOLOGY

On that morning in September at Queens College, I felt a keen tension. The institutional realities were that an outdated writing assessment system mandated by a bureaucracy and supported by politicians had created a roadblock for my students. I knew that the most effective way to get the largest number of students to pass the exam was a semester of cramming five-paragraph themes and sentence-level grammar work down their throats. I knew how to coat these materials in engaging activities, feel-good process movement adventures with some personal writing thrown in as a treat. But still, the most direct route to a 100% pass rate was through a formalized test prep course. "Do this to pass the exam," I could have told them. And then I would have added, "but come back and see me next semester in Composition 1 and I'll show you how to really write."

However, another set of institutional realities, and my own inclinations, were also at work. I had been hired to help with establishing a "cyber" presence in the composition program. Surely that involved teaching some of my classes in a computer lab. I felt this imperative even if we had to move from the conference room on the fifth floor of Klapper to another building in the middle of a class meeting, because the computer labs did not open until 9 a.m. As an institution, CUNY supported the use of technology for teaching purposes. In fact, on March 14, 1997, CUNY Chancellor Ann Reynolds called attention to the University's plans to improve access to the Internet in her Testimony before the City Council Committees on Education and Finance.[2] She said,

> Nationally, we are witnessing the trend toward the acquisition of educational materials from the Internet and World Wide Web. The emerging importance of Internet access for communications and research and the workplace demands for computer-literate individuals produce an immediate need for the University to ensure that its students are skilled in these areas. The appropriation of $3.4 million in last year's capital budget for the Educational Technology Initiative is a step towards fulfilling these needs and I thank you for your support of this initiative. To further our efforts in this area, the University has proposed a program to promote student ownership of computers. Called the Computer Ownership Matching Program (COMP), it is a three-way partnership combining the resources of the City, private industry and the students themselves to make computer ownership feasible for the Fall 1997 incoming class. (1997)

In addition, at Queens College, there were internal faculty development grants available for work with computer-mediated teaching.

On the flip side of the coin, the writing teachers and director of composition valued WAT pass rates for English 95 students. Queens College had small basic writing classes (17 students, compared to 35 at some community colleges) and a higher than average pass rate. The tension between assessment-based writing instruction and the development of computer-mediated writing skills is not an external play between forces of light and darkness, but this tension is encapsulated (i.e., internalized in a certain model of psychology) within different agents at work in any given educational system.

I would teach basic composition in a computer lab, but I would also make sure my students practiced for the WAT. In retrospect, I may have spent as much as one third of the class time on explicitly test preparation activities (Whithaus, 1998). This compromise occurred even though I believed that the students would have learned more in terms of academic and workplace writing skills if more time had been spent on computer-related activities.

CLOSING: BACK TO THE FUTURE
(QUILL AND THE EARLY 1980S)

This chapter has been about the tensions a teacher encounters when using computers in an educational system that values standards based on high-stakes testing, so I want to end by returning to an example from the early 1980s. High-stakes testing does not play into this example, but computer technology does. In a sixth-grade

---

[2]Reynolds resigned the following Spring amid debate about the WAT and graduation requirements for students at Hostos Community College.

classroom in Hartford, Connecticut, Jim Aldridge had one stand-alone computer in the early 1980s (Bruce, Michaels, & Watson-Gegeo, 1984). He used the QUILL system, which included a retrieval system (Library), a proto-e-mail/message system (Mailbag), an organizer (Planner), and a text editor (Writer's Assistant). Aldridge allowed students to type up papers on the computer and read each others' work there. When Bertram Bruce, Sarah Michaels, and Karen Watson-Gegeo observed Aldridge's students' writing processes, they noted "that changes in the pattern of social interactions in the classroom as a result of the computer may be even more significant than any simple technological effect" (p. 4). Finally, the researchers commented on the act of printing student essays as a form of publication: "Writing comes off the printer typed and formatted, like published print (newspapers, magazine ads). It can then be seen on the wall (where its neatly typed format makes it easier to read and hence more accessible to classmates and outside visitors)" (p. 15). This is simple by today's standards. However, Aldridge's class was working with a new medium—a new machine—and yet he also carried forward simple and effective pedagogical practices like posting essays on the walls as a way of sharing and making public and valuing student work.

A computer entered the classroom, but the teacher and the researchers watching him kept their heads. They did not rely solely on the technology. Rather, they carried forward the pedagogical practices that had worked before, studied how the students worked, and continued to adapt and improve their methods of teaching. For me, this example has relevance not only for our treatment of technology but also for teachers' responses to high-stakes testing. Pedagogical responses to both technology and testing need to retain teaching techniques that work. If teachers throw out their intuitive sense of what lesson plans work and only teach according to rubrics for writing proficiency or technology standards, then something valuable is lost.

8

Tools (AES) and Media (Blogs)

How do writing teachers and administrators integrate new and emerging forms of literacy with existing testing regimes? How do they prepare high school students for success in college and the workplace? How do they prepare undergraduate college students for success at work and in graduate studies? And, how do they, at the same time, boost their test scores on the new W-component of the SAT and on standardized, statewide, high school exit exams?

One solution is suggested in the Bertelsmann AOL Time Warner 21st-Century Literacy Summit: "build on reading and writing—and then expand media literacy" (2002, p. 6). However, this solution is shortsighted and doomed to failure because the multimodal literacy skills fostered through information and communication technologies are becoming increasingly intertwined with basic reading and writing skills. Children in middle-class families are playing on PBS's www. pbskids.org and Hasbro's mylittlepony.com, as well as reading Dr. Seuss' *Green Eggs and Ham*. In fact, many of these children are reading and playing with *Green Eggs and Ham* in CD form as well as reading the book. Interacting with multimedia texts from early childhood means that when these students reach high school and college, literacy will mean *both* the screen and the printed page. Hybrid literacies, multimodal forms of reading and writing, will come into the academy embedded in the bodies and minds of students. Testing will change, and teaching will change. But how?

"PILING UP" LITERACIES

The past is not a perfect predictor of the future, but the "piling up" of literacy practices that Deborah Brandt (1995) notes suggest the outlines of how multimedia literacies will enter the academy. There will be strange and complicated nego-

tiations among emerging, multimodal literacy practices, the existing status quo of
student academic writing (i.e., the Toumlin inspired five-paragraph essay based
on thesis and support and conclusion). At moments students will appear wedded
to the status quo, and teachers and institutions will push the incorporation of
Blackboard discussion boards and blogs in educational settings. At other moments, students will want to compose digital videos and teachers will insist that
composition means writing, and the clean, clear, scientific organization of ideas.
"Learning to compose an effective, well-written, tightly-organized five-paragraph
essay is vital for entering the academic discourse community," the argument will
go. It will continue with sentences such as: "This skill shapes how students think,
without it their minds are mushy. They cannot put anything together. Proof goes
out the window."

Brandt calls this back and forth the dull processes of literacy practices, the accumulation and residual methods of reading and writing. For Brandt, residual literacy practices are the skills and strategies acquired by one generation and passed
on to the next, despite changes in public discourse conventions and technology.
These practices do not necessarily become outmoded but reshape themselves according to the form demanded by a particular audience (pp. 650–655). For instance, one of the subjects interviewed by Brandt was Charles Randolph, the son
of a Methodist minister. Randolph had acquired a great deal of his stylistic devices from his father and from sermons. While working in an affirmative action
office in a metropolitan school district and writing his doctorate in school administration, it became clear the that "flowery English major with Ciceronian writing
style" was applying this form of church-influenced writing to bureaucratic memoranda and a manual on affirmative action that he was writing. As Randolph told
Brandt: "My memoranda were very long and pretty or piercing or whatever, but
they were not typical" (p. 663). Randolph explained:

> I never wanted to write anything that was so dull and deadly that you couldn't flour-
> ish every now and then but the manual was tough for me. . . . The interplay between
> what I wanted to write and the way I wanted to write it and what they wanted me to
> write was pretty hard. I remember a couple of times having the writing reviewed and
> having been told they didn't particularly like it—which also frustrated me because I
> didn't particularly like the way they wrote. (p. 663)

Brandt goes on to note that

> Charles Randolph encountered similar tensions with his dissertation committee of
> four white male professors "I was tending to have all these Ciceronian flourishes
> and lots of words and lots of analogies and lots of imagery and the professors kept
> saying, 'You're bleeding on the paper. Stop bleeding on the paper. This is a scien-
> tific piece of work.' " Charles Randolph learned how to compromise, earning his
> doctrorate and serving for several more years as an educational administrator. (p.
> 663)

Literacy practices and writing styles emerge over time and are often applied across genres and media (e.g., the Ciceronian, Methodist sermon style of a southern preacher bleeds into the memos of a school administrator). Although tensions may—and, as in the case of Charles Randolph do—occur, the practice of literacy and the criteria for good and effective writing can adapt to these changing influences. Randolph no doubt compromised his style at certain points, and it is clear that the memoranda genre he had to write in and his audience's expectations also adapted to Randolph's long, pretty, or piercing style. While Randolph provides one narrow example of how genres vary over time and across media, Brandt works his narrative into a braided narrative about literacy practices in the United States over the course of the 20th century.

Brandt's key point about literacy practices in the 20th century is also a key point about literacy practices in the 21st century—genres vary over time and draw on multiple influences. Media and setting do not determine all the features of a particular writer's writing in a genre, but media and setting do have an impact. The ways of writing and knowing the world are not only bound up in formal and technological innovations for reading and writing, but are embodied in an individual's knowledge of the relations among past and present literacy activities. This "piling up" of verbal and textual rhetorical practices is emphasized in asynchronous discussion forums such as discussion lists and blogs. To assume that any form of writing, including academic writing, will always obey the same criteria is to assume that genres are fixed. High-stakes testing tends to promote the idea that writing and ways of knowing are fixed, because effective texts represent effective cognition on the part of students, so Brandt's concept of literacy practices as a "piling up" suggests that textual structures change over time.

New and emerging information and communication technologies speed up the process of accumulation but do not speed up the process of removing residual literacy practices. That is, the thesis–support–conclusion driven five-paragraph essay as a paradigm of effective writing and clean, well-supported argument or issue presentation does not vanish as asynchronous discussion forums (e.g., bulletin boards and blogs) enter academic discourse. Rather, forms of information technology will develop to encapsulate the thesis–support–conclusion driven five-paragraph essay. When thinking of writing assessment as a technology, as Brian Huot does (2002 pp. 137–164), the encapsulation and sustainability of the five-paragraph essay form is not only embodied in the forms of textual organization built into automatic essay scoring (AES) software but its continuity is also assured by the social system of high-stakes testing. The formal conceptual as well as practical technological advances of high-stakes testing and AES systems create a default value for Toumlin's thesis-support driven essay. At the same time, high-stakes tests encourage the development of technological literacy skills. As students accumulate these new literacy skills associated with discussion boards, e-mails, blogs, and web-page design, their ideas about, and their practices of, effective writing change. Associations become more important than hierarchical support structures. Visual elements are not support for textual claims but serve as invention tools and metaphors that change the textual organization and even the textual content. Residual and accumulative literacy practices both gather speed and become incorporated in digital forms of communicating.

First mastering reading and writing, and then building multimedia composing skills preserves an idea of mastery in order to progress. All is beautifully sequenced. But Brandt's research and the penetration of multimedia works into early childhood show how doomed—how wrong—an educational system built around first learning reading and writing and then learning multimedia compositions is. Figuring out how to integrate the residual forms of print-based writing and the rapidly accumulating new forms of multimedia composing in high school and college composition courses is vital for both teachers and test designers.

INTEGRATION

How do teachers, administrators, and test developers adjust during this transition, this period of piling up literacy practices? How do they, as the College Board's *The Neglected "R"* (2003) and ETS's *Digital Transformation* (2002) reports suggest, "integrate" the literacy skills required for success in print-based reading and writing with the multimodal skills required for success with screen-based compositions?

A solution exists in thinking about two very different information and communication technologies: AES and blogs. AES software provides scores and sometimes feedback on student textual compositions through using natural language processing techniques to model human readers' responses to mechanics, rhetorical structures, and effectiveness, and, in the case of e-rater and IEA/LSA, representations of content knowledge. They have been designed mostly for testing environments, although now their applications for classroom settings are being considered (Burstein, 2003; Shermis & Burstein, 2003). E-rater and IEA are both currently available as web-based applications (E-rater, at http://criterion.ets.org/cwe/student/index.php; IEA, at http://www.knowledge-technologies.com/IEA. html). Because they were built to score print-based essay, both e-rater and IEA focus on the accumulated literacy practices associated with thesis-support forms of writing. In contrast, blogs operate according to the rhetorical logic of the web. Writing in *USA TODAY*, Kathy Kiely defines a blog as "a cross between an online diary and a cybermagazine, aggressively updated to draw readers back" (2003, pp. 1A–2A). In composition studies, many graduate student teaching assistants have been leading the adaptation of blogs as vehicles to get students to write more in first-year college writing courses. Having students keep journals using blogger.com, motime.com, or blogcity.com makes journaling public and makes students see writing as interactive and distributive rather than as simply a one-way dump into the teacher-grader. The writing in blogs is highly associative because of the possibility of linking to other pieces of writing on the web, but it is also very stream of conscious and tends have a different set of features than the writing scored by AES systems or turned in for formal writing assignments.

The difference between writing done for AES systems and writing done for blogs is not simply a graph of the differences between what Peter Elbow (1973, 1981) called high-stakes writing and low-stakes writing. The differences go beyond that, and reflect a piling up of literacy skills in computer-mediated forms of composing. This piling up of literacy practices is dictated by a logic of software as either a tool for correction and feedback or a medium for communication among people. AES systems such as PEG, IEA, and e-rater have been thought of as software tools for judging or improving student writing, whereas blogs are thought of as software media for communicating among students. Understanding the separate uses of software as a tool for correction and as a medium for communication makes it possible to move beyond this dichotomy to think about using both of these information and communication technologies in the same writing course.

Conceptually, this shift requires thinking of teaching and evaluating student compositions as situated activities. As I have argued throughout this book, the works of Eva Baker (1998), Marjorie Goodwin (1990), Paulo Freire (1970), James Dewey (1933), Jacques Lacan (1981), Gunther Kress (2000, 2001, 2003), Pamela Moss (1995, 1998), Lee Cronbach (1988), Brian Huot (2002), and Kathleen Yancey (1992) all resonate, some with more dissonance than others, with this view of learning, teaching, and testing as situated. But discussing AES and blogs drives me to confront a much more difficult and contentious issue: What would a situated assessment look like when the standards-based and discrete skills valued in high-stakes testing environments are integrated with the interactive and multimodal composing techniques promoted by critical and progressive educators through blogs? To answer this question, I review some of the fundamental assumptions and uses of AES and blogs, and then turn to a broader discussion of reflection and description in writing assessment.

AUTOMATIC ESSAY SCORING (AES) SOFTWARE

Epistemologically, AES developers assume that a student's writing skills and subject knowledge can be embedded within a written composition. The job of human readers or software agents is to identify the effectiveness of students' writing skills and their subject knowledge. A secondary goal, once the composition has been scored accurately, could be to provide feedback to the students so that they can improve in both areas. A central idea shared by PEG, e-rater, and IEA is that a composition represents the students' writing ability and subject knowledge, and that there is a true and accurate score associated with that composition. This accurate score could be achieved by having multiple human readers rank the essay, or by having AES software approximate the average score that multiple human readers would give an essay.

To discover this score, AES systems use natural language processing techniques and focus on a variety of essay features. E-rater, for example, concentrates on structure (sentence syntax), organization (discourse features that occur throughout an extended text), and content (prompt-specific vocabulary). Structure includes the way in which a student uses various clauses and verb structures. Organization concentrates on a reading's textual characteristics that are associated with orderly presentation of ideas, including transitional words and phrases and logical connections between sentences and clauses. Using a topical analysis, e-rater also examines an essay's prompt-specific vocabulary. For this vocabulary-based analysis, the assumption is that an essay that receives an outstanding score from human readers offers a model for the subject vocabulary used in an essay that should receive an outstanding score from the software. The software's analysis of these three features allows the computer to assign the essay a score. That is, e-rater makes a value judgment about any given essay. This judgment is intended to model human raters' scoring outcomes for the same essay if not their reading processes (Burstein et al., 1998; Power et al., 2001, p. 5).

Working from a different set of principles, Knowledge Analysis Technology's IEA system focuses on the conceptual content conveyed by a student's written essay. Driven by Latent Semantic Analysis (LSA), IEA examines a work's coherence based on the accumulated semantics of each of its words. Thomas K. Landauer, Darrell Laham, and Peter Foltz (2003) described LSA's semantic-based content scoring this way:

> The basic assumption is that the meaning of a passage is contained in its words, and that all its words contribute to a passage's meaning. If even one word of a passages is changed, its meaning may change. On the other hand, two passages containing quite different words may have nearly the same meaning. All of these properties are obtained by assuming that the meaning of a passage is the sum of the meanings of its words. (p. 88)

In addition to LSA's semantic analysis, IEA scores an essay's mechanics and style based on surface features. The principles behind LSA assume that human judgments about the content knowledge represented in a given text are based on similarities between that text and another text. These judgments, both for humans and for LSA software, are not simply based on a counting up of words or on direct co-occurrences, but rather rely on "a deeper measure of inferred semantic relations based on past contextual experiences" (Foltz, Kintish, & Landauer, 1998, p. 305). In the process of scoring a student essay, IEA integrates its reading based on a text's meaning and coherence with its analysis of stylistic and mechanical elements.

Along with a human reader, e-rater has been used to score the Analytic Writing Assessment segment of the GMAT since February 1999. In addition, e-rater is currently embedded in ETS's Criterion, a web-based essay evaluation system. Using this system, instructors and students can see in real-time their e-rater score and score-relevant feedback. Criterion currently includes model prompts for a variety of exams, including secondary national writing standards, PRAXIS, TOEFL, and GMAT. Registered students can use Criterion for low-stakes practice on these exams. Both as a low-stakes practice tool and as part of a human–computer grading team on the GMAT, e-rater than has been deployed to foster print-based writing competencies. Further, these writing competencies are narrowly defined. They are the writing skills needed to score well on particular, ETS-designed high-stakes exams. Likewise, IEA can be used to judge essays written in the U.S. Army's officer leadership training programs; it can also be used to judge a student's knowledge of a textbook reading. In both of these cases, the software is looking for the writer to reproduce a given set of content knowledge in a classically print-based form. The writer's success is judged by her reproduction of a given bit of content in a well-defined form. Because both the exams and the AES software were created with traditional, thesis-support argumentative or issue related writing as the target genre, it is not surprising that the values associated with Toumlin's thesis-support style of writing are integral both as informing concepts and as practical scoring guidelines. E-rater and IEA are advanced software tools, but with the potential exception of their feedback functions they do not act as communication media.

In all these AES instances, the text that the writer creates is "dead" text, because it is only intended to be read by the software agent. It is not a work that is intended to communicate with another person. In the IEA online sample for a middle school student, the writer is asked to compose an essay about a personal hero, someone who has been inspirational. Although IEA is able to score the submitted essays effectively, these is something cold about this process, even in sample format. When I went to the IEA site to test out the software, I could not get inspired to write an essay that had any deep meaning to it. I knew the writing was only going to be read by a machine, so I kept thinking about how to trick the machine. Literally, I was thinking about the rhetorical problem of how to get a response from my audience. And, ironically, I kept thinking about Elbow's *Writing Without Teachers*, and I kept thinking "Well, I'm certain this is not what he had in mind!"

Still, when I submitted different versions of an essay about "my hero," the IEA scored them as I would have predicted. When I presented a neatly written essay with an opening paragraph, three supporting paragraphs each with a key piece of evidence, and a closing paragraph, I received an outstanding score. When I presented a bulleted list, followed by a paragraph expanding on each of the points from that bulleted list, I received a much lower score. Now the rhetorical structure of my first submission was a traditional, print-based model, and the rhetorical structure of my second submission was much more along the lines of a web page or a blog post. The key elements were stated, not as complete sentences, but merely as free-floating phrases. These were expanded on, but there was no conclusion. Once, you had scrolled down far enough, you could scroll back up and see the main points again, so there was no reason to reproduce them.

Did I stump IEA the way that researchers were invited to try to stump e-rater by ETS? No. I was writing in a different rhetorical structure, and because IEA was not really interested in communication, but rather its work as a scoring tool, its reading reflected that. I was writing for one situation, and the software tool was reading for a different situation.

BLOGS

Blogs are funny. Much of what is written seems almost as if it is written to be *said* rather than to be *read*. Writers seem to gain pleasure from the act of writing as much as they do from the act of someone reading the post. But the public nature of a blog dictates a different dynamic than a private journal. Blogs maintained by journalists and political campaigns can be quite formal and are often well copy-edited works. Personal blogs can run the gamut from formal to informal. Brandon Boyd's post on his White Fluffy Clouds blog captures the spirit of many bloggers; he wrote,

> For those who partake in the findings of this blog please excuse any and all grammatical errors you may come across. Upon closer scrutiny of this work, I felt that inconsistencies like those reflected the human aspects of this project (among other things). Or, maybe I was just too lazy to correct my mistakes. Anyway, I felt that spell checking it after the fact would make a geyser feel more like a sputter. Know-what-I'm-saying?

Even within a subset of blogs, such as campaign blogs, some are tightly structured and do not allow outside users to post comments (i.e., bushchenney04.com), others allow user input from a wide variety of registered users (clark04.com and dean04.com). As blogs become more popular, the residual literacy practices and genre conventions associated with editorial columns and letters in printed newspapers are evident, but blogs are also written beyond print-based literacy practices.

The inherent ability of html to link to other blogs and other Web sites creates a tendency for associative comments instead of claim-support driven structures. For instance, Electablog headlined with this post on February 16, 2004: "Dean's campaign chairman splits . . . (Might have something to do with these comments?" The claim-support structure from print is here in the cause–effect statement: campaign chairman leaves because of these comments. But both the main story and the reason for the main story are accessed through associative links. In fact, to reach the real evidence "these comments?" the reader leaves Electablog and moves to a different Web site. The entire dynamics of reading, and the logic of the "sticky" site (i.e., keep a reader at your site as long as possible), shifts with blogs. Each blog is embedded within a web of other blogs; these are individual journals and group journals, but they are interconnected. A constructivist theory of communication and language such as the one articulated about the intertextuality of novels by Mikhail Bakhtin moves beyond a linear, even beyond a singular recursive, writer–text–reader scheme. Bakhtin (1981) defined the novel's heteroglossia as:

> a process of active, mutual cause-and-effect and interillumination. Words and language began to have a different feel to them; objectively they ceased to be what they had once been. Under these conditions of external and internal interillumination, each given language—even if its linguistic composition (phonetics, vocabulary, morphology, etc.) were to remain absolutely unchanged—is, as it were, reborn, becoming qualitatively a different thing for the consciousness that creates it. (p. 143)

For classroom writing activities, however, what do blogs build? How do they function? And, how does their intertextuality mesh with a view of computers as media through which humans communicate with one another? On a very basic level, a blog can be used as a personal journal, a diary of sorts, and a place to begin reflections on a class that one is taking or teaching. In Spring 2003, I kept a blog for my Teaching Writing with Technology course. I used the interface from blogger.com (see Fig. 8.1). At first, I used one of their existing templates (Fig. 8.2). Later, I modified the html template so that my text appeared in a more customized and personal format (Fig. 8.3). By going to blogskin.com, I could even

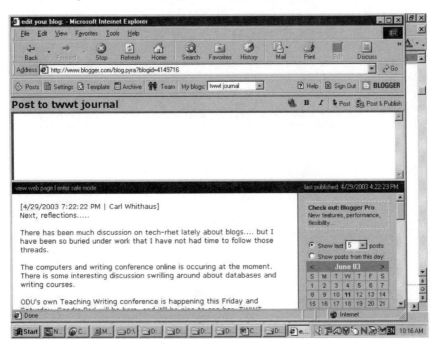

FIG. 8.1.   Blogger screen to enter blog text.

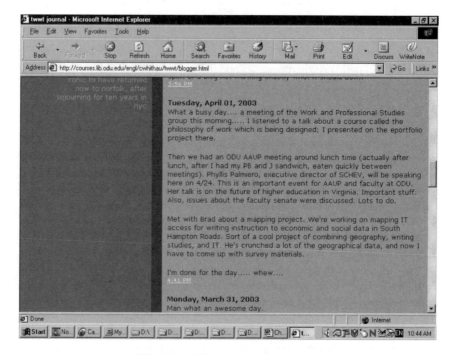

FIG. 8.2.   A blog based on a template.

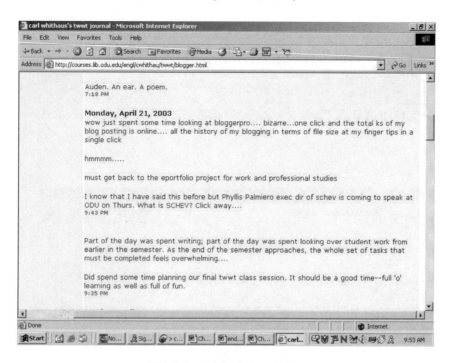

FIG. 8.3.   A fully designed blog.

have created multiple blog "skins" so that different users could have viewed the site based on their inserts, their viewing preferences.

The figures show that the twwt blog was used primarily as a place for reflection, a place for blowing off steam, and just a general repository of thoughts. Student blogs reflected the same sense of the blog as journal:

> Well, it had to happen . . . I have been floating on such a teacher high because all of my computer assignments were working brilliantly . . . until today. My English 12 class was to have their traditional five paragraph essays completed at the beginning of class today. I have seventeen students in my class . . . well . . . five students had their essays partially completed . . . so much for peer editing with technology. It can be so discouraging, but tomorrow is another day. Chaucer here I come. Note to self . . . (and anyone else who is reading) . . . what are the scholars saying about the credibility of WWW sites? How can I guide my students in their web searches? Teaching . . . an endless series of questions.
>
> Once again I am sitting in the computer lab with my Honors 11 students. The good news is that those students who showed up for class this morning actually have their first drafts. Right now they have been divided into writing groups, and their first task is to peer edit using technology. It will be interesting to see how they incorporate technology into this task. They have exchanged email addresses and they are going to send editing suggestions via the internet as attachments. (I'm holding my breath.) I seem to be having good results with this group. It is a dream class . . . 16 students. Thursday, we will tackle collage writing. More reflections later.

The interesting note in the previous posts is that the student in the teaching writing with technology course is making connections between her college course materials and activities outside of the college classroom (i.e., her teaching experiences in high school during the day). The types of writing that happen in a classroom blog would then seem useful not only as reflective for theoretical gains, but also for building connections between a college course and activities outside of that class.

Other student blogs help analyze different online discourses by linking to samples and commenting on these links:

> Okay, now for some fanlistings. What is the purpose of a fanlisting you ask? Check out thefanlistings.com. According to this site, fanlistings are meant to "unite the fans," but it seems to me that they are another method of webpage advertisement.
>
> I have yet to join a fanlisting, I don't exactly have an all-about-me webpage that would necessitate advertisement like this. There seems to be a listing for everything under the sun, and I have come across some very interesting fanlistings:
>
> > Rivalries-Amadeus vs. Salieri—This one interests me because I love Mozart. It just seems weird to have a whole listing for a rivalry.
> >
> > Geek Love—I'd be surprised if this book got too many more fans. But I guess there's at least one fan for everything.

If you check out the Fanlistings site you'll probably find a fanlisting dedicated to some book/movie/era in history you hold dear. I believe you have to have a website to link to in order to join. It's worth looking around at some of the strange things that get so much attention.

The student is writing a descriptive summary of what is on the other sites; she is also putting a spin on that summary and judging the other writer/designer. This meta-discourse encourages students to think not only about communicating with one another but it also allows them a space to reflect on what types of rhetorical and design moves work. Within writing classes, blogs encourage personal journaling, connections between the college course and outside of school activities, and reflections on the effectiveness of various online works.

CLOSING: BRINGING AES AND BLOGS TOGETHER

Given these uses of blogs as writing places where students and teachers reflect on their writing, make connections between college courses and activities outside of their writing class, and employ associative methods of proof and structure rather than the more typical thesis–support–conclusion forms of writing looked for by AES software, what possible connections are there for writing teachers and test developers to consider? How would a high school or college English class use both blogs and AES?

At first, the answer to this question appears difficult, especially if the logic continues of the thinking of computers as either tools for correction or media through which humans communicate with one another. However, stepping back just for a moment reveals that computer technology is already working as both a tool for correction and a medium for communication. For instance, the aforementioned paragraph, which I composed in TextEdit on a Mac, has both instances of blogs underlined with red dots. The software is offering me instruction, correction for my writing. If I was composing on a PC using MSWord and I typed dost, the autocorrect feature would kick in by changing "dost" to "dots." At the point of composition then, word processing software, ranging from the basic freeware that comes installed with an OS to a software package one must purchase, serves a corrective or advisory function. These word processing packages are also serving a communicative function, because ultimately you are reading these sentences. The same process occurs with student compositions. As the students write, word processing software intervenes in their composing processes correcting—sometimes seen and sometimes, as with autocorrect, unseen—their writing. Would the use of blogs and AES in the same writing course be so different?

Yes and no. The word processing software that leads toward a published book or toward an essay that a student turns in provides a single writing environment where correction and software-based feedback precedes communication. With blogs and AES software, the two functions, computer as medium for communication and computer as tool for correction, are separate. It is possible, even preferable as the Brandon Boyd quote makes clear, to leave grammar mistakes in the post. Stylistically, if one employs a bulleted list made of sentence fragments and has links from each of those sentence fragments to other blogs or other Web sites, the blog software does not offer feedback or correctives. Your language is your language. It is translated directly from the writer's fingertips onto the screen. With the AES software, the corrective and feedback functions are delayed. That is, with the web-based versions of e-rater and IEA, writers must wait for the software to evaluate and judge their writing before they receive feedback on it. Unlike MSWord, AES systems are not in the business of real-time feedback; they judge writers' composition (the organization, rhetorical structure, and mechanics) after they have completed their work.

As feedback agents, AES systems offer an interesting twist on blogs. What if an AES system could be designed to look for the effective rhetorical structures found in blog-based writing? Could a software designer create a composition-based blog that also offered feedback and correction? Could these two types of software be integrated? Of course. Anything is possible given time and money. But the very idea sounds preposterous, because composition courses where blogs are used are about communication with other people or the writers' communication with themselves. They are not about correction or feedback or making blogs into venues for high-stakes writing assessment. But why not? What is the pedagogical reasoning for maintaining a space where writing is not evaluated or judged?

Elbow (1997) provided composition studies with an elegant defense of evaluation free writing zones, and Geoff Sirc (2002) argued for just letting writing be. And, surely, their ideas make sense in terms of pedagogy and learning. But, they ignored the institutional realities of writing in the 21st-century academy. Assessment tools will be used on student writing. Do not think of blogs as the great evaluation free zone of writing, but rather ask how assessment systems can be changed so that the types of writing valued in traditional, thesis–support–conclusion assessments and the types of writing utilized in blogs, e-mails, and IMs can both be valued. Are there assessment tools available where multiple samples of student writing, demonstrating a student's varying proficiencies in different genres and media, could be analyzed and displayed?

The answer is yes. Print-based portfolios have long been shown to provide forums where multiple genres of student writing can be displayed. Working through the processes of collection, selection, and reflection, students create portfolios that demonstrate their abilities and provide greater validity across a wider range of writing tasks than prompt-based, single-shot writing exams. In fact, single-shot impromptu writing may be included within a print-based portfolio. Showing how a student composes under timed pressure demonstrates their abilities in one writing environment. It is not unusual to encounter this timed writing situation in college courses both within and outside of English departments. So testing student's ability to write standardized prose and develop an argument according to a thesis–support–conclusion structure is not misguided. It is, however, limited.

Higher order composing skills and proficiencies in visual rhetoric cannot effectively be assessed with a timed, impromptu, single-shot exam. The W-component of the new SAT cuts across a thin slice of a student's composing proficiencies. For the new SAT to be used in a valid fashion, college admissions offices will have to understand that the writing skill measured through 25 minutes of writing and 25 minutes of multiple-choice questions is a very narrow proficiency. In the same way, the proficiencies and content knowledge evaluated by e-rater and IEA are narrow and well-defined. When e-rater or PEG is used to score the PRAXIS, the construct validity is based on the standards of that exam. The question is not whether or not these tools (the SAT W-component or AES software) can effectively evaluate writing. They can! The question is whether or not to accept the narrow scope of writing skills they represent as an accurate indicator of students' composing abilities.

If all anyone wants students to do is to sit down and in 25 minutes write a grammatically correct essay where they make a claim and support it with two or three examples, followed by a summation, then current AES software and the W-component of the new SAT will drive the curriculums perfectly. If, however, the desire is for students to be able to think and compose in multiple media and use multiple modes to do so, then the development of evaluation systems must be encouraged where timed, thesis-driven, print-based writing is one of many composing skills examined. Students need to be provided opportunities to demonstrate their abilities as writers over extended periods of time and working in a variety of genres and media.

Thinking about blogs and AES demonstrates the wide range of composing activities students might be expected to perform in a writing course. Although imagining the synthesis of blogs and AES as a software package does not seem particularly appealing, the possibilities of using both in a single writing course suggests that one writing teacher could help prepare students to write in a variety of different genres. This is nothing new. Writing teachers do this all the time. What is new is arguing for the development of assessment systems that include rather than exclude the multimodal and multimedia forms of composing that students are working on. The conceptual work of writing portfolios as assessment devices must be expanded into the realm of electronic portfolios. Electronic portfolios must be considered not just as a standardized repository for digitized versions of text heavy print-based writing. There needs to be exploration of the possibilities of electronic portfolio assessment systems as containing representations of students' abilities on single-shot, timed, impromptu exams; representations of students' works developed over time through a process of collection, selection, and reflection; and, most important, representations of students' abilities to organize all of this material within a visually appealing design or metaphor.

The development of electronic portfolio systems that include traditional high-stakes tests, samples, and reflective works developed over time, and an overarching visual design to navigate those compositions, will provide opportunities for integrating new and emerging forms of literacy with existing testing methods. Further, these flexible electronic portfolio systems will provide electronic writing environments where secondary and postsecondary students develop useful skills for work and future educational experiences. If flexible electronic portfolio systems are designed to contain samples of high-stakes tests such as the W-component of the SAT and state-mandated writing proficiency exams, then these systems will provide teachers with opportunities to improve student scores on existing exams and to develop the multimodal skills students need to become successful communicators in new and emerging media. By developing teaching techniques and student composing projects that incorporate visual design, argument, and information presentation into students' writing processes, teachers can prepare students at the same time that they help shape the implementation of assessment tools for these new literacy tools and practices.

9

Strings

The written word can no longer be the only, or even primary, vehicle through which students learn to compose. The graphical user interfaces (GUIs) of Macintoshes and Windows machines, as well as the presentation of material on web-browsers pushes a graphics heavy and intensely visual mode of argumentation. The development and publication of composition textbooks such as Lester Faigley, Diana George, Anna Palchik, and Cynthia Selfe's *Picturing Texts* (2004) and Andrea Lunsford and John Ruszkiewicz's *Everything's an Argument* (2003) confirm this shift, and demonstrate its increasing impact on the teaching of college-level composition courses. These textbooks acknowledge that students are already thinking in graphically-intensive ways, and rather than decrying the increasing use of visuals in academic writing (e.g., Halio, 1990), these textbooks incorporate the visual into post-process models of composing. These classroom materials acknowledge that the cognitive processes and tools used to compose (Kress, 2000, 2001, 2003) and to read (Gee, 2003) are becoming increasingly graphics oriented. I have argued throughout this book that not only should English and composition instruction reflect these changes but techniques for assessing student communication skills and proficiencies also need to incorporate these shifting forms. Without this shift in assessment, multimodal and multimedia composing activities and teaching strategies will be perceived as add-ons by students and parents. If it's not on the test, it's not important.

MULTIMODAL AND MULTIMEDIA
COMPOSING THEORIES

Gregory Ulmer, Geoff Sirc, and Jeff Rice incorporated digital, *myhappening-sampler* aesthetics and rhetorics into academic composing processes. Ernest Morrell and Jeffrey M. R. Duncan-Andrade combined rap and information technologies to have students produce both traditional literary analysis essays as well as multimodal works about the themes of an individual's alienation from postmodern society. Research groups (New London), educational organizations (College Board and Bertelsmann Foundation), and testing agencies (ETS) have advocated for the development of multipurpose literacies for students, citizens, and knowledge workers. Still, when the ideas of multimodal literacies hit the English classroom there is a fundamental culture clash—the textual meets the visual.

After acknowledging the impact of information and communication technologies on traditional literacies, there are two ways to move forward.[1] One is to build print-based literacy skills first and then develop multimedia composing skills. The other is to see the acquisition of multimodal composing skills as recursive and informative. Although these two ways of approaching students' acquisition of composing skills could play out over the course of a student's 18 plus years in primary, middle, secondary, and postsecondary education, they can also occur within the space of a single assignment in an English course. In this chapter, I am going to present and discuss three student assignments. The first is a traditional, print-based essay; the second is a revision and a repurposing of that print-based essay into a web-based composition; and, the third is a composition developed with the visual elements of the computer screen in mind from the beginning of the project. Contrasting the finished products and the composing processes involved in producing these works, I argue that when digital elements are added as an afterthought, they are not fully valued by either students or teachers. This finding has implications for the teaching of composition in electronic environments and the development of electronic portfolios, because it suggests that viewing multimedia literacy as a set of skills acquired after print-based literacy skills is detrimental to students' learning.

Teachers know the convention of claim and evidence, particularly as it is formulated for a thesis-driven essay (Toulmin, 1958, 2003). Students construct an opening paragraph that names their topic, argue for a particular take on that topic, and then transition to the body or supporting evidence paragraphs. Each of these paragraphs develops a tidbit or morsel of evidence that was presented in the opening paragraph. Often, in each of these body paragraphs, there are one or two topic sentences that capture the paragraph's main point and offer at least a conceptual link back to the thesis statement from the opening. Finally, there is a point of closure—a summation that says, "Here is what I have covered" or "My argument has been. . . ." This final paragraph will rehearse, or act as a refrain, of the essay's thesis and make explicit the connections between the evidence presented in each body paragraph and the major arc of the argument. Parts of a thesis-based method of organizing a composition prevail, but other aspects shift as composition en-

---

[1]Of course, a third alternative is to follow Birkerts (1994), Malkin (2003), and Bloom (1987) and to reject nontext-based composing and thinking as degenerate hogwash. But, I think in the course of this book that I've shown how this ostrich-head-in-the-sand approach is futile.

counters new and emerging media. Understanding this shift in the abstract is one thing, examining its intimate dimensions through sample work, however, drives home the distinctions in new ways.

A PRINT-BASED, THESIS-DRIVEN ESSAY

Let's dissect a print-based, thesis-driven essay. This essay was composed by a first-year college student on the subject of information technologies in New Jersey schools. The following section moves back and forth between my teacherly and research notes on the essay and the complete text of the student essay. I am attempting to answer the question: "How does the essay work upon a particular reader?" The essay could be scored by e-rater or IEA software. The opening paragraph introduces the subject of advances in communication technology: "Many technological advances have made it easier for humans to accomplish their daily tasks and more importantly have increased communication." The writer then suggests a tension, or a claim, against her original statement: "But as it has brought the world together, it has also divided the different social structures." Although I feel pushed away by a certain abstraction in these two sentences, I am still reading and I recognize the bringing together of these oppositions in the writer's next sentence: "Both the uniting and division of the social structures can be seen on the county level." Finally, she arrives at her thesis: "In this paper I will discuss these unifying and dividing aspects in education in the counties of the state of New Jersey." One could also ask what she means by "social structures" here? It could mean anything. Probably what she means is that technology has increased class divisions with respect to differential access to and use of new technologies. But she does not say that:

> Many technological advances have made it easier for humans to accomplish their daily tasks and more importantly have increased communication. But as it has brought the world together, it has also divided the different social structures. Both the uniting and division of the social structures can be seen on the county level. In this paper I will discuss these unifying and dividing aspects in education in the counties of the state of New Jersey.

One could pause and tease out the Hegelian dialectic that is at work in the opening three sentences. IT technology brings the world together; IT technology creates divisions in social structures; both of these IT-driven impulses may be observed by looking at technology use in education in New Jersey. One could search and find an Aristotelian enthymeme lurking in this paragraph as well. The point, for the purposes here, is to note that this paragraph—although it does sound clumsy and off-putting in some ways—presents a thesis point and mapping sentences that will be explored and supported with evidence in the following paragraphs. Schematically, the following could be the essay's "thesis":

IT brings people together;

IT creates social divisions;

we see both the unifying and the divisive aspects of IT in education in New Jersey.

Consider the next paragraph:

> It is obvious that communication has increased throughout the world because of technology. Communication has gone from sending letters with men on horseback to the most recent form of letter-writing, email. The inventing and further development of the telephone, television, and computer has helped make communication easier and faster. The Internet has made communication almost effortless. The many advances in the sciences, such as space science and medicine have brought the scientists and doctors of the world together. Many other fields such as the arts, music, and engineering have also progressed greatly because of technology. The many sources of media such as the newspapers, magazines, and broadcast news have also helped increase communication and awareness through technology.

The first paragraph in the body of the essay presents general historical knowledge as evidence. When the writer says, "It is obvious that communication has increased throughout the world because of technology," she is making an appeal to general, commonsense knowledge—to what she assumes (correctly in my case) will be her shared experience with the reader. Next, she uses a transition sentence: "Education has been and still is at the core of the advancements in these fields." To move from the general, commonsensical, and historical issues she has talked about to a more focused discussion on "education." It is worth noting that the way that this transition sentence functions is to first introduce the new topic "education" and then to circle back to the subject from the previous paragraph "the advancements in these fields." The reader's mind is introduced to the new subject "education," but is then reminded of the connection with the previous subject, "the advancements in these fields"—both by the entire closing phrase but also by the choice of the word "these." Of course, all of these reflections flash by the teacher's mind in less than half a second, especially if this is just one paper among 27 others. In addition to providing the teacher-reader with assistance by providing a transition sentence, the writer also supports her claim that IT divides as well as unifies; she writes, "Schools are also where one begins to see the separation of social classes":

```
      Education has been and still is at the core of the advance-
      ments in these fields. What is introduced and the method of in-
      troduction in schools is what influences and inspires child to
      study in these fields. Schools are also where one begins to see
      the separation of social classes. Children from different so-
      cial classes only communicate with children from their same
      class, and sometimes children of different social classes are
      even sent to different schools. Have families who can afford to
      send their children to private, non-public schools have caused
      the division between social classes to become even larger? Does
      this lead to children of the higher classes attending better,
      more technologically equipped schools, than children of the
      lower classes?
```

At this point in the essay, she moves toward presenting more concrete evidence in the form of statistics gathered from the New Jersey Department of Education Web site: "Statistics comparing public and non-public school demonstrate that this is not true. The student to computer ratio for public schools is 6.9 to 1 while that of the non-public schools is a higher 10.1 to 1." The apparent authority of these statistics is based on their appeal to logos (reason, statistics, the argument itself, according to Aristotle) and on a certain ethos (the character of the New Jersey Department of Education, which seems, for the student at least, to represent a trustworthy source of information).[2] The weight of statistics within the paragraph almost makes the paragraph unreadable, or at least it is difficult for me to comprehend the meaning of all these statistics arranged the way they are—they shout at me, "Believe me! I have the numbers to prove my claim!" The final sentence of the paragraph ("These statistics show that contrary to logic the public schools are generally more technologically equipped with computer than non-public schools.") returns to the writer's voice, and this sentence, as well as the opening sentence of the paragraph, could be classified as the topic sentences:

```
      Statistics comparing public and non-public school demon-
      strate that this is not true. The student to computer ratio for
      public schools is 6.9 to 1 while that of the non-public schools
      is a higher 10.1 to 1. The student to computer ratio of 10.1 to 1
      of the non-public schools is higher than the average student to
      computer ratio, 7.1 to 1, of the State of New Jersey. Twenty-two
      percent of the computers in New Jersey public schools and
      twenty-seven percent of the New Jersey non-public schools are
      older computers that are not powerful enough to access the
```

---

[2]Although I personally have qualms about the accuracy of the New Jersey Department of Education's study, because it seems very self-serving, I cannot, or would not, question its authority within this student's writing. She has done her homework; she has done as much as one would/could ask a first-year college writer to do.

Internet or to run current software. Furthermore if these low-
end computers are excluded from the analysis, the revised student to computer ratios become 9.0 to 1 for public schools and
14.6 to 1 for non-public schools. Once again the 14.6 to 1 ratio
for non-public schools is higher than the average student to
computer ratio, 9.5 to 1, of the state of New Jersey. While 72%
of public schools and an average number of 3.8 classrooms per
school have access to the internet, only 52% of the non-publics
and an average number of 2.9 classrooms per school do. These
statistics show that contrary to logic the public schools are
generally more technologically equipped with computer than non-
public schools.

The next paragraph presents evidence to suggest that whereas a division between (expensive) private schools and (free) public schools does not affect access
to IT in the ways that would be expected, the wealth of different school districts
does have an effect on access to IT in education. The structure of the essay's fifth
paragraph ("On the other hand, . . .") directly parallels the structure of the essay's
fourth paragraph ("Statistics comparing . . ."). That is, both of these paragraphs
make general claims that relate to the essay's thesis and then present an overwhelming amount of statistics in the middle of the paragraph and then return to
more general claims (topic sentences) at the end of the paragraph: "These statistics can only lead one to believe that a higher amount of money in the county that
is collected from its local families in taxes is set towards funding of the county's
schools. Therefore social class has been affected by the access of technology in
the county's schools." The final "therefore" sentence in this paragraph makes an
explicit conceptual link to the writer's opening contention that social class does
matter when thinking about access to IT in educational settings in New Jersey:

On the other hand, statistics comparing the public schools of
different counties of the state of New Jersey illustrate that
perhaps social class is affected by access to technology. The
five counties with the most favorable student to computer ratio
for public schools are Hunterdon, Warren, Mercer, Cape May, and
Salem with ratios of 4.3 to 1, 4.9 to 1, 5.1 to 1, 5.5 to 1, and 5.7
to 1, respectively. The five counties with the least favorable
student to computer ratio for public schools are Essex, Passaic,
Hudson, Ocean, and Middlesex with rations of 9.4 to 1, 9.0 to 1,
8.0 to 1, 7.8 to 1, and 7.6 to 1 respectively. Hunterdon County,
the county with the most favorable student to computer ratio has
31 school districts with approximately 19,000 pupils. Even
though there is a large amount of pupils the local school bud-
gets for the 1996-97 school year totaled to a high amount of
$181,007,247. These statistics can only lead one to believe that
a higher amount of money in the county that is collected from

```
its local families in taxes is set towards funding of the
county's schools. Therefore social class has been affected by
the access of technology in the county's schools.
```

The next paragraph moves away from statistics as evidence and presents personal experience as evidence: "I attended High Tech High School." (The ethos is no longer the authority of the New Jersey Department of Education, but rather the ethos of the speaking-I, the author drawing on personal experience.) Here the evidence is also clumped together in a list form, but the evidence is now the curriculum at High Tech High School ("desktop publishing, computer animation and design, audio technology, television and video production, radio broadcasting, telecommunications, and even refrigeration") and a list of "media labs" ("computer labs, data processing, telecommunication, network configuration, interactive television center, and media production studio") rather than statistics. Here, the writer contradicts her earlier point based on the New Jersey Department of Education Web site; she suggests that public schools are not great equalizers in terms of the privileges that social class offer: "Growing up in Jersey City and attending Jersey City public grammar schools at an even younger age, I could tell that children from different social classes were not presented with the same opportunities":

```
    I attended High Tech High School, a Hudson County Vocation
School of Technology funded by the county. This school offered
classes such as desktop publishing, computer animation and de-
sign, audio technology, television and video production, radio
broadcasting, telecommunications, and even refrigeration. The
school had many technological facilities such as computer labs,
data processing, telecommunication, network configuration, in-
teractive television center, and media production studio. I now
realize that this high school is not the average Hudson County
high school when it comes to technological facilities and tech-
nological courses. Through personal experience and interaction
with students from other high schools in the county, I learned
that even within our county's schools there was a discrepancy
between the sources of information and education students had
access to. Growing up in Jersey City and attending Jersey City
public grammar schools at an even younger age, I could tell that
children from different social classes were not presented with
the same opportunities.
```

The final two paragraphs mark the summing up of this essay. The final paragraph is particularly interesting because of the ways in which it echoes the implicit questions in the opening paragraph. The first sentence in this paragraph appears as an answer to a question: "Yes, it is clear that technology has increased communication in the world." It also directly parallels the essay's opening sentence: "Many technological advances have made it easier for humans to accomplish their daily tasks and more importantly have increased communication." The next two sentences continue the theme of IT as bringing the world together, and then there is a shift: "Nevertheless, we can see that it has also brought about the division between different social classes." Once again, there is a clear parallel with a sentence from the opening paragraph: "But as it has brought the world together, it has also divided the different social structures." It has taken longer to reach this point in the closing paragraph (four sentences, instead of two), but once again things are at the second part of a dialectic or the second line of a syllogism:

> Within the county the division between social structures in technological, education opportunities was apparent to me as a young child. Today these differences are even more noticeable to me as I look back at my years of education. My experience extends only within the educational school systems of Hudson County. If the division is so evident within a county is not the division within a state, between many different counties, even more evident and obvious?
>
> Yes, it is clear that technology has increased communication in the world. It has brought people of different culture, belief, and languages together. It has helped to progress and develop different areas of study and invention. Nevertheless, we can see that it has also brought about the division between different social classes. With further development and study we can perhaps make the technological inventions we know today flawless means of communication that everyone, despite their social class, can utilize. Our goal is to make technology the means of unifying the world.

The essay ends with a generalized, yet utopian impulse: "With further development and study we can perhaps make the technological inventions we know today flawless means of communication that everyone, despite their social class, can utilize. Our goal is to make technology the means of unifying the world." This student seems to believe strongly in technological progress and the ability to harness technological progress for social good. Her essay feels schematic, but she clearly knows how to structure an essay so that a reader looking for a claim and then supporting evidence will find those elements. Although I lament that the writer's voice is lost except for the utopian sentences at the end of the essay[3] and some of the testimony about High Tech High School, as a teacher-reader, I must acknowledge that she knows the rules of the game—she knows how to write a traditional thesis-driven essay that relies on a formula of claim and then support. I can read this essay, and many others like it, very quickly. I can decide that it meets certain criteria of form without quite moving me as a reader; it does not have what

---

[3]Even her ending utopian impulse may be a learned rhetorical device—go for the big broad sweeping, generalized claim at the end.

Elbow calls voice or POWER. Perhaps it is a B essay in my book, but even that depends on when in the semester the piece is turned in, and what else we have looked at, and what level the students are. . . .

REPURPOSED ESSAY

If this same essay moves into a new media space, particularly a hypertextual space, what happens to the relation between claims and evidence? What happens to the possibility of having the essay scored by e-rater or IEA? The relation between claims and evidence shifts toward an associative "collage" and any software agent that acts as an audience becomes limited by its ability to process only the textual and not the visual elements of the composition. The repurposed revision could not be fully scored by any AES software available today.[4] As a teacher, am I still able to read many of these essays quickly and label them based on a schematic understanding of how large claims and particular pieces of evidence are presented? I know there are still connections between claims and evidence, but how are these claims advanced? The writer still presents facts that suggest other facts "*in such a way as to induce belief in what is suggested on the ground of real relation in the things themselves*" (Dewey, 1998, p. 12, emphasis in original). To continue to paraphrase Dewey's definition of reflective thinking, she is presenting "one thing [that is] the ground, warrant, evidence, for believing in something else" (Dewey, 1998, p. 12). But these connections do not take the familiar form of the print-based, thesis-driven essay. Rather, they shimmer; they are links between one screen and the next, and the form of argument leans toward the fragment, the point rather than the holistic.

Or, there is the *studium*, what Roland Barthes (1981) defined in *Camera Lucida* as the informational content of an image, a word, or a sign that exists on the screen. But it is the *punctum*, the sign's elusive meaning, that draws me as a reader, viewer, or user into the work. The whole is created by my individual join-

---

[4]The most advanced note of AES that I know of comes from Carl Bereiter (2003). He noted that the research team he was working on "is applying the techniques of automatic text evaluation to online discourse. Online discourse is assuming increasing prominence in education as well as in various kinds of knowledge work. . . . Being in digital form to begin with, online discourse provides possibilities for more systematic evaluation than its nondigital predecessors. However, it also presents difficulties. It is more free-form than even the loosest essay assignments; the quantity of text produced by different students can vary greatly; and there are problems of reference of deixis offline. In addition—and this is where the really interesting challenge comes in—online discourse unfolds over time and therefore raises questions about assessing change" (p. ix). Bereiter's analysis of the problems of analyzing online discourse are correct, if understated. He was clearly considering only textual discourse—synchronous and asynchronous discussion forums. The electronic compositions being discussed could have these elements but also have visual elements. Assessment machines may be part of the systems that are developed, but they are clearly a long way away from being able to analyze image, sound, and text at the same time—a thing a human reader/user does quite naturally.

ing of certain fragments together, not into a whole text as defined by the writer but into an experience defined by the interaction of the reader with the text. The writer intends; the writer shapes the images and words and, through constructing links, the writer defines the reader's possibilities for interaction and navigation. Yet, the reader's or user's paradigm is something different—skewed ever so slightly, a door out of square, a paradigm shifting.

English teachers are still heavily trained in the reading and responding to print-based texts. (This is true even when these texts are represented in electronic form, i.e., pdfs.) While some educators have called for approaches that emphasize multiliteracies, a vast amount of the ways of looking at texts, of looking at writing, have been shaped by the dominant, print-based biases of English departments. In short, teachers read and write the way they were taught to. When they encounter new media, particularly when they have students compose new media texts, they expect those works to function within the paradigm of school-influenced, print-based modes of literacy. And the truth of the matter is that these new media compositions often work in other ways. That is, they employ rhetorical structures that they do not know as fluently as they know print-based conventions. The challenge, then, is to slow down and to describe how the students' new media compositions are affecting readers and users. This mode of response will allow teachers to develop responses—a methodology of response—where they will not be as tied to the peculiarities of their own mental habits, which were nurtured in print-based modes of thought and argument. They will not "unconsciously make [our peculiarities] the standard for judging the mental processes of others" (Dewey, 1998, p. 60) as Dewey warns. Description slows down the process of putting a grade on an assignment. It slows down the process of knowing what the value of a student's composition is and delays the judgment of a piece of work.

Figure 9.1 shows a very different opening for the essay that was just read and evaluated. This opening page still gives four sentences, but two of these sentences are not visible immediately upon opening the file. Instead, two sentences and two images grab a reader's attention immediately. In order to read the full paragraph, readers must scroll down using the scroll bar or arrow keys. In addition, the two initial images that are seen are links, and readers are made aware of the possibility of these images as links when—or if—they use the mouse and pass over these images.

The rhetoric of and the expectations for this digital opening then are markedly different than the rhetoric of and expectations for the student's print-based essay. The reader/user must make one of three decisions here that will lead toward physical (or electronic, is there a difference?) interaction with the work. The teacher/reader/user may scroll down to see the entire page, click on the image of the circuitry, or click on the map of New Jersey.

The printed text engaged my mind as a reader, and brought forth mental interactions, and perhaps as a teacher-reader even physical reactions in terms of marking on the paper, but the electronic text demands that I make a move to continue reading. I must start interpreting in order to keep reading.

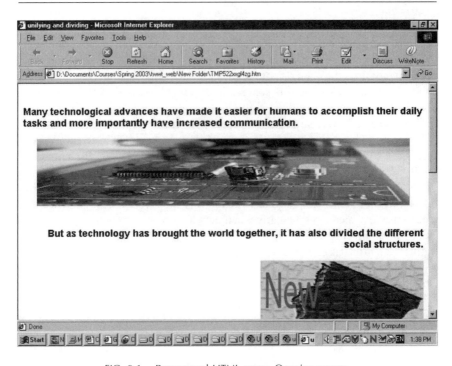

FIG. 9.1.   Repurposed HTML essay: Opening screen.

Say that I scroll down and get an overview of the first page, and then I scroll back up and click on the image of the circuit. (It is the top image on the page, and shouldn't I follow all the links?) Where do I go? What do I encounter? I get another page with the same image that I just clicked on, but also with a second image of a rider from the pony express (Fig. 9.2). What is happening to my connections between claims and evidence? The writer's opening sentence ("Many technological advances have made it easier for humans to accomplish their daily tasks and more importantly have increased communication.") still introduces the general subject of the essay, but it also has a connection—a direct link—to support. The image of the circuit becomes support for the idea of a technological advance, and then clicking on that circuit further develops the suggestion that circuitry is an advance in communication technology by moving readers into the writer's argument. In fact, clicking on this image moves them directly into the writer's appeal to general, commonsense knowledge: "It is obvious that communication has increased throughout the world because of technology." Further, this appeal is then complimented by the image of the pony express rider and the second sentence in size (4) type: "Communication has gone from sending letters with men on horseback to the most recent form of letter-writing, email." The image, as well as the size-4 type sentence, provide further commonsensical evidence based on a shared understanding of American history (i.e., what did the pony express represent?

FIG. 9.2.   Repurposed HTML essay: Second screen.

Some form of advancing communication; what does e-mail represent? Another form of advancing, or speeding up, communication). These layers of argument, or more accurately these layers of claim and evidence, do not exist in the print version of this work.

It is also worth noting that this bypasses the whole question of the opening paragraph's Hegelian dialectic or Aristotelian syllogism. The words are the same, or nearly the same, but my attention is not on the printed words and the familiar structure of arguments in print. My attention is on the graphics, the links, and the possibility of scrolling. I click and I see relationships, particularly relationships between claims and evidence that I did not see before. Was the idea that the pony express represents the increasing speed of communication and e-mail also represents a technological advance in terms of the increasing speed of communication present in the original printed work? Maybe, but I did not notice it; it takes the image to drive home, or to even open up, this possible reading for me. My reading—my experience with the text—is thus different.

After I make a decision about which of the two links to follow, I am suddenly at a chart with data (Fig. 9.3). This chart is easy to read. In the printed version of the essay, I was lost with the words, within the text. The statistics said believe me, but I did not feel compelled to take the time to decipher them—to really understand what the student was saying. Yet, unlike the print version of the essay, I am

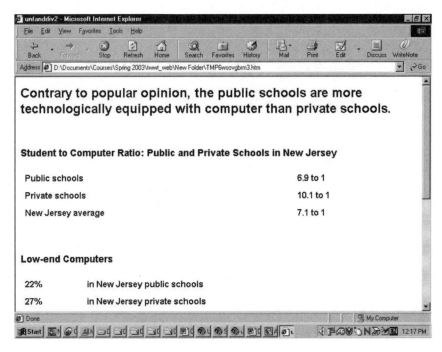

FIG. 9.3.   Repurposed HTML essay: Data chart.

dumbfounded by the transition here. Whereas the student used transitional phrases when moving from paragraph to paragraph, here the transition does not seem to make sense. A click on an image of technology—circuitry, the innards of a computer—leads me to a chart about educational technology in New Jersey. What is the logic? I get this link when it is linked to the chart as a result of clicking on the map, but the content of the chart seems to come from nowhere when the data is produced as the result of looking at an image that contrasts pony express and computer technology. The transition here is off, but I have to admit that I *see* the statistics about access in New Jersey and the differences between public and private school in the electronic essay in ways that I did not in the printed version.

In the printed version of the essay, the statistics were presented as evidence to me, but I could not digest the significance of the numbers in their paragraph form. One could say that the visual rhetoric of the statistics was not effective in the print document, but in the electronic document, the text drops away and the statistics shiver in their own light. I do a little work, but I interpret—I actually read the numbers—and think about the significance of the statistics. I interact with the text. The sentence, "Contrary to popular opinion, the public schools are more technologically equipped with computer than private schools," at the top of the page, and then a repetition with a slight variation of that sentence at the bottom of the page, "The above data shows that contrary to popular opinion, the public schools in New Jersey are more technologically equipped with computer than private schools," guides my interactions and conclusions.

I click further and I get the opposite point of view argued by other statistics (the switch between paragraphs 4 and 5 in the printed version, which were marked by the transition phrase, "On the other hand"), and then I click again, and I am back at the writer's interpretation of the data, and within her personal account of the High Tech High School.

How does this electronic essay work on me as a reader? I know that the relationship, the flow for me as a reader between the claims and evidence, was a different experience. And, as a teacher-reader, I have been trained to judge the ways in which evidence bolsters/supports a claim as an important part of analyzing how well a student is writing. I have also been trained to look at formal qualities of the prose and to look at surface features of the writing. Yet, in this repurposed revision the visual elements of the work—ranging from font size and font selection to the inclusion of graphics and tabular data—become part of the work's meaning and effectiveness. The visuals impact my reading process in a way that is not accounted for in AES systems. How much more extensive would this change be if visuals are incorporated? If teachers use a book such as *Everything's an Argument* or *Picturing Texts* and push the design of their assignments to incorporate visual elements from the moment that the students' composing processes begin, then the visual design of a composition is no longer "eye candy," but is central to invention, analysis, and presentation. These types of multimodal compositions reach back to the artistic composing techniques advocated by Ulmer, Sirc, and Rice, but they also incorporate the scientific as well as the cultural texts created both for workplaces and for play.

SORTIES INTO STRING THEORY AND A WORK AND PROFESSIONAL STUDIES ELECTRONIC PORTFOLIO

Although the electronic essay discussed previously is different than the print essay, the work is fundamentally a repurposing of an already completed composition into another medium. My teacherly reading of the piece is about how effectively the student deals with the new medium and not a reevaluation of the work's content. In his study of electronic portfolios at Ball State University, Rich Rice (2002) pointed out that both teachers and students undervalue the visual and digital components of an electronic portfolio when the works are turned in first as printed essays. Anne Wysocki and Johndan Johnson-Eilola (1999) asked why scholars of composition and communication often return to a literacy metaphor when thinking about students interacting with and composing electronic works. My reading of a composition that attempts to take on string theory provides a glimpse into the different composing techniques and cognitive processes that are involved when multimodel and multimedia elements are incorporated from the beginning of a project. In my reading of this and other multimedia compositions, I find that:

1. The sampling and collage effects that Ulmer (1985, 1989, 2003), Sirc (2002), and Rice (2003) noted become foci of the composing processes and products;
2. The possibility for learning, arguing, and making connections by composing visuals and sounds are apparent; and
3. The arguments (e.g., Bloom, 1987; Birkerts, 1994; and Malkin, 2003) about nontext-based compositions as degenerative and simplistic become irrelevant.

After clicking on either one of the images in Figs. 9.4, 9.5, 9.6, and 9.7, users move to a web page that contains the following sentences:

The idea is that the basic organization of matter as a string becomes a 1-dimensional in space that "sweeps out" to become 2-dimensional "world-sheet."

As a particle the basic organization of matter is a 0-dimensional object that creates a "world-line."

Why is this significant you might ask? F. David Peat in *Superstrings and the Search for the Theory of Everything* provides a less technical take on the subject. Peat writes that the theory of superstrings

proposes that the elementary particles cannot be reduced to featureless points but are essentially one-dimensional objects, strings that rotate and vibrate. Not only does matter find its origins in these one-dimensional objects of incredibly minute size, but the strings themselves are irreducibly linked to an underlying space. Indeed space-time itself must at some level be created out of superstrings. (28)

This page becomes a place where the student works between the more technical scientific prose of Siegel's book and the popular science writing of Peat's work. All the time the student is synthesizing the ideas in these large text chunks. This synthesis emerges when one clicks further into the site.

The student writes that "In the second set of pictures, it's easier to calculate the force and its distribution to other marbles. In the first set of pictures, the string is going to roll across the marbles slightly differently all the time. Prediction and calculation become much more challenging." In Figs. 9.8, 9.9, and 9.10, there is a synthesizing of ideas. The image that he chose becomes the ground or screen through which he reads and interprets and makes sense of a complex prose passage. The images of the string, marbles, and the two line drawings are not add-ons, not illustrations of the textual argument, but rather they are more significant.

FIG. 9.4.   Screen-composed HTML essay: Opening screen.

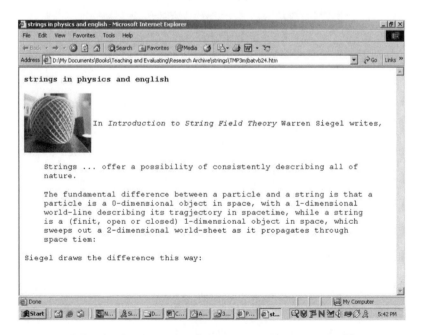

FIG. 9.5.   Screen-composed HTML essay: Opening screen (2).

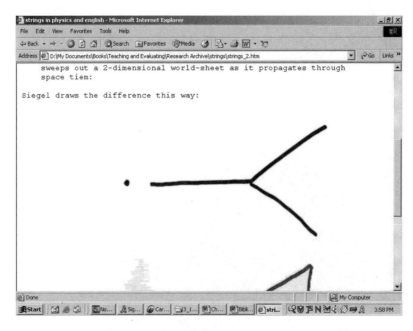

FIG. 9.6. Screen-composed HTML essay: Opening screen (3).

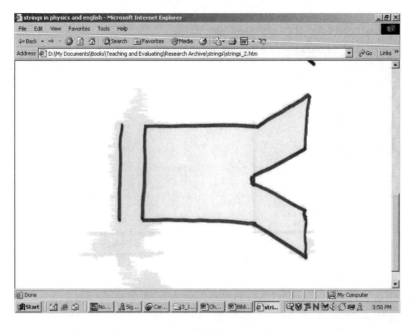

FIG. 9.7. Screen-composed HTML essay: Opening screen (4).

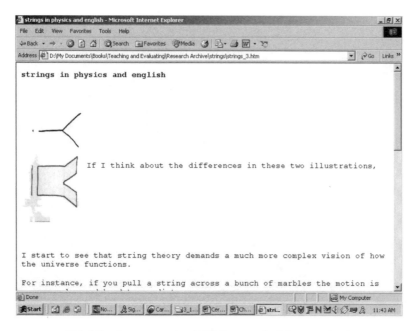

FIG. 9.8. Screen-composed HTML essay: Particles vs. strings.

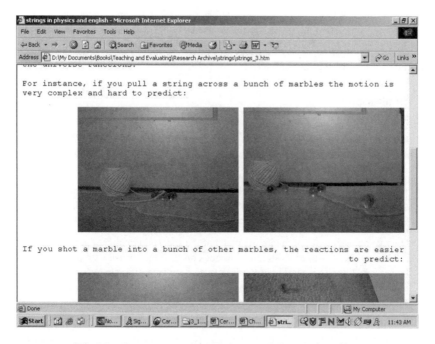

FIG. 9.9. Screen-composed HTML essay: Strings and marbles.

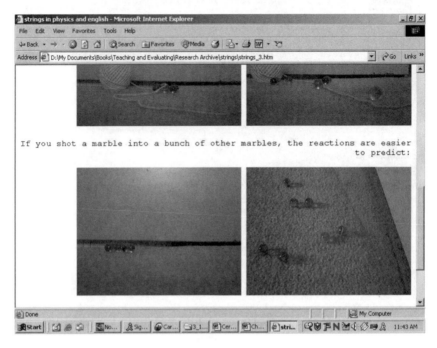

FIG. 9.10.   Screen-composed HTML essay: Strings and marbles (2).

They are prompts for thinking through and composing the writing that follows. Later in the site, the student writes,

{If my shirt was
to unravel...}

Poetry is not often thought about in conjunction with physics. Yet, in *Dark Waves and Light Matter*, Albert Goldbarth has written obliquely about the two:

We almost always think that future eyes—whatever electroluxury or Nuevo-Boschian hovel they review us from—will marvel at our objects (*they had "cans"!*) and maybe customs (*and "vacations"!*) but connect to brains that necessarily function in a sequence and with oversensibility we'd recognize as kindred.

No, can openers will not rewire the paths of the species' circuitry. The electric can opener *is* an easier opener, and our life goes on. But the car *isn't* simply an easier horse; and, after its invention, *different* life goes on, and different eyes are required to be its witness. The shape of the planet and how we understand it—change. (116)

In physics and English, there is something about perspective and time. How you look at something can change the something that you see. But neither Goldbarth nor I would want to slip into relativistic thought. A simple "nothing matters, because everything is subjective" runs away from the complexity of the universe as seen by physicians and poets.

There is a fiber of connection here, but the relationship is tenuous. There is no unity of plot from Aristotle; there is not unity of organization. Or, rather, the unity is created only by the meaning the reader extracts from the juxtaposition of quotations from two science books (one a physics book; one a popular science book about physics), the images of marbles and string, and a quote from a book of essays by a poet. As the reader of this webbed text, I find the juxtaposition meaningful. But I have read the student's summaries of these three sources in his annotated bibliography. I have spoken with him about the connections that he sees emerging—I am a situated and knowledgeable reader. And when I encounter these juxtapositions I know that the quotations, and pictures, and writing represent learning, reading, and an increasing excitement about studying.

Further along the student writes, "Seeing the pictures I took and the essay you pointed me towards, I start 'to get' the math classes I have to take as a pre-med biology major in a different light. I mean I always knew they were important, but here they are something else. . . ." These web pages do not move forward as the writing would in a personal reflective print-based essay. Yet this work, like and unlike the "fuck you" essay that so disturbed Bartholomae, sticks with the reader. These images in particular seem cool and meaningful to me as a teacher and as a reader: They show the student opening up an idea and beginning to understand that idea in relation to his experience.

These summaries, quotations, and pictures do make a strange composition. It does not progress toward proof; it is not really an argument, but an exploration—a thinking through—of a series (a string?) of issues. String theory, reflections on studying. This thinking through occurs with images and quotations. It proceeds as a collage, a process of capturing and then composing thoughts. It is a personal reflection, but it is also engagement with academic discourse. Long quotations become visual evidence that the student has been reading, but they are also valuable as something the writer says—or repeats. Is the repetition here important for learning? Is it a process of internalizing and integrating knowledge from different disciplines? I would argue yes and yes. Repetition is important for learning, but it has to be self-directed. Finding a quotation is an important act. Internalizing the knowledge makes it into the writer's knowledge. Placing cut-ups—quotations and pictures—taken and scanned from books next to each other encourages the writer to think about links, to compose those connections. Here then is one mode of composing to learn: The student provides a visual metaphor that becomes a vehicle to carry on the inquiry and to synthesize knowledge from across disciplines.

Here multimedia composing can yield not only samplers and collages about cultural subjects such as rap music, but also complex nuanced reflections about science. James Britton's (1970) concepts of writing and talking to learn need to be updated to composing to learn, but within that update assessment systems must be moved forward as well. The definitions of standards and achievement must be pushed forward to engage students and to provide them the opportunities for composing complex works that incorporate the multimodal forms of discourse they are already producing.

CLOSING: SITUATIONS

The shocking part of this book should not be my advocacy for teaching multimedia and multimodal forms of discourse. Others (Ulmer, 2003, 1989, 1985; Sirc, 2002, 2000; Rice, 2003; Morrell & Duncan-Andrade, 2002; Gee, 2003, 2001, 1988; Kress, 2003, 2001, 2000; Kress & Van Leeuwen, 2001) already made those pedagogical claims. The shocking part is my argument that teachers and testing experts must develop systems for assessing student proficiency with these new tools and media. During an era of education where high-stakes testing has become the norm, it is too easy for faculty, including high school teachers, college instructors, and university professors, to simply reject any form of outside testing as beyond control: "It's mandated and we must deal with it, and that's all." The danger of this position is that we end up believing that the testing does not reflect student learning and does not improve pedagogy. Yet, there are no suggestions about improvement or changes; composition and rhetoric teachers and researchers are all too happy, as Brian Huot (2003) argues to leave writing assessment to the psychometricians. Large-scale and classroom-based assessment systems for computer-mediated composing skills will have to *situate* their evaluations of student skills rather than excluding contextual variables and efforts at multipurpose testing.

These new evaluation systems will acknowledge that students learn how to become more effective communicators through *interacting* with others. *Describing* what and how the students learn through using multimodal and multimedia skills will replace focusing on deficits judged by outdated print-based standards. Finally, *distributing* a work to multiple readers means that various audiences will read student compositions and judge student skill levels and competencies for particular purposes. A single electronic portfolio will represent students' skills across disciplines because it will contain multiple genres.

Learning about language, writing, and composing requires the development of students' abilities as communicators. This activity is not the same as the development of students' tastes in literature; rather, learning about effective communication requires that students be allowed to make their own judgments about what the effective criteria for a "good" piece of writing or a "good" hypertext is. They also must live with the criteria they create, and apply those criteria. For a long time, teachers have known that tests and assessments drive curriculum. In courses where writing and computer-mediated communication are the media and subjects of inquiry, their interactive and dialogic qualities suggest the need to devise ways of allowing students and curriculum to drive assessment.

Information technologies, such as client–server databases, can help make the management of a distributive evaluation system on a large scale possible. Of course, these systems need to be carefully designed, and the users' needs and wants considered from the earliest stages, as Stuart Blythe (2001) and Michael Salvo (2001) argued. The potential for developing a distributive evaluation that is more than a system of teacher and peer-critique exists, and it is being explored through a variety of electronic portfolio initiatives (Cambridge, Kahn, Tompkins, & Yancy, 2001; Hutchings, 1996). A learning network informed by techniques developed in user-centered design would offer hope for the development of electronic portfolio systems that would move toward fully distributive techniques of evaluation.[5]

Electronic portfolio systems may all too easily become new tools for enforcing norm-referenced, single-digit or letter scores on wider and wider scales. If teachers engage with these new technologies and become involved in their development, then there may be potential for creating engaged, dynamic, and critical assessment systems that are both media for communicating and tools for assessing student compositions. It is possible, although not easy, to "tinker" with writing assessment systems, and try to make them match the complexity of communicating, teaching, and writing, rather than resembling the mind-numbing process of reading the "same" essay written 52 times by 52 different students all hoping to please the "same" imagined, generalized, and ultimately nonexistent reader. If techniques and software tools for writing assessments are developed that honor the impulse behind writing as discovery and communication, the potential will exist to have fuller, more accurate, and more valid interpretations of the multimodal and multimedia compositions students produce. Freire's technique of dialogue applies not only to students, but also to teachers and researchers in composition studies and English, educational measurement and assessment experts, and computational linguists. Teachers need to risk moving beyond their disciplinary comfort zones to analyze how students are composing with new media tools. As they analyze the processes and the multimedia products that students produce, they will find that established methods of evaluating writing—both on the classroom level and in large-scale assessment systems—need to be revised.

Refining the assessment techniques, like having a student revise the draft of a paper, is not a process to be viewed as the result of a failure. It is intrinsic to communication: situations, audiences, and tools for composing change. The skillful writer adapts to the new situation. Likewise, the skillful teacher and the skillful

---

[5]EPAC, an AAHE-sponsored, virtual community of practice on electronic portfolios, was launched by and EDUCAUSE National Learning Infrastructure Initiative (NLII) following AAHE's National Leaders meeting in November 2002. EPAC has the potential to act as a source for the development of distributive techniques, although much of EPAC's "community of practice" seems to be removed from the everyday concerns of writing teachers.

test designer acknowledge change, and reshape their techniques for teaching and evaluating to better address the new situation. Like the student who is about to revise an essay draft, the feedback the audience is providing must be considered (i.e., adjust the teaching of writing to better prepare students for composing activities that include new forms of literacy). Like the student who is about to revise an essay draft, there must be deep revision not just the correction of surface features. Writing assessment is not in the editing stage, rather it is at a stage where deep conceptual shifts need to be made. No individual teacher, no individual assessment expert, no individual educational organization will drive forward these changes. Yet, I have argued throughout this book that in the research literature and in actual classrooms, there is an emergence of situated, descriptive, interactive, and distributive techniques for assessing student compositions. These techniques provide a set of conceptual tools that may signal the end of methods of writing assessment that assume a student's writing skill is merely a container to be filled. Composing is contextual and interactive, the teaching and evaluating of writing needs to become so as well.

References

Alverno College. (2000). *Diagnostic Digital Portfolio*. Retrieved November 21, 2000, from http://ddp.alverno.edu/

Amrein, A. L., & Berliner, D. C. (2002). High-stakes testing, uncertainty, and student learning. *Education Policy Analysis Archives. 10*(18). Retrieved July 29, 2002, from http://epaa.asu.edu/epaa/v0n18/

Baker, E. (1998). *Understanding educational quality: Where technology meets validity*. Princeton, NJ: ETS.

Bakhtin, M. M. (1981). *The dialogic imagination: Four essays* (M. Holquist, Ed., & C. Emerson & M. Holquist, Trans.). Austin, TX: University of Texas Press.

Baldacci, D. (2000). *Wish you well*. New York: Warner Books.

Barrs, M. (1990). "The primary language record": Reflection of issues in evaluation. *Language Arts, 67*(3), 244–253.

Barthes, R. (1981). *Camera lucida: Reflections on photography*. New York: Hill & Wang.

Bartholomae, D. (1993). The tidy house: Basic writing in the American curriculum. *Journal of Basic Writing, 12*(1), 4–21.

Bartholomae, D. (1996). What is composition and (if you how what that is) Why do we teach it? In L. Z. Bloom, D. A. Daiker, & E. M. White (Eds.), *Composition in the twenty-first century: Crisis and change* (pp. 11–28). Carbondale, IL: Southern Illinois University Press.

Bartholomae, D. (1997). The tidy house: Basic writing in the American curriculum. *Journal of Basic Writing, 12*(1), 4–21.

Bartholomae, D., & Petrosky, A. (1986). *Facts, artifacts, and counterfacts: Theory and method for a reading and writing course*. Upper Montclair, NJ: Boynton/Cook.

Bartholomae, D., & Petrosky, A. (1987). *Ways of reading: An anthology for writers*. New York: St. Martin's.

Bateman, D. R., & Zidonis, F. J. (1966). *The effect of a study of transformational grammar on the writing of ninth and tenth graders*. Champaign, IL: National Council of Teachers of English.

Bazerman, C., & Russell, D. R. (2003). *Writing selves, writing societies: Research from activity perspectives*. Fort Collins, CO: WAC Clearinghouse.

Belanoff, P., & Dickson, M. (1991). *Portfolios: Process and product*. Portsmouth, NH: Boynton/Cook.

Bereiter, C. (2003). Foreword. In M. D. Shermis & J. Burstein (Eds.), *Automated Essay Scoring: A cross-disciplinary perspective*. Mahwah, NJ: Lawrence Erlbaum Associates.

Berger, J. (1985). *Ways of seeing*. London: BC and Penguin.

Berland, H. M. (1996). Computer-assisted writing assessment: The politics of science versus the humanities. In W. L. Edward, M. White, & S. Kamusikiri (Eds.), *Assessment of writing: Politics, policies, practices* (pp. 249–256). New York: MLA.

Bertelsman Foundation & AOL Time Warner. (2002). *21st Century Literacy Summit: White paper*. Berlin, Germany.

Birkerts, S. (1994). *The Gutenberg elegies: The fate of reading in an electronic age*. Boston: Faber & Faber.

Bizzell, P. (1992). *Academic discourse and critical consciousness*. Pittsburgh: University of Pittsburgh Press.

Bleich, D. (1988). *The double perspective: Language, literacy, and social relations*. New York: Oxford University Press.

Bleich, D. (1997). What can be done about grading? In L. Allison, L. Bryant, & M. M. Hourigan (Eds.), *Grading in the post-process classroom: From theory to practice* (pp. 15–35). Portsmouth, NH: Boynton/Cook–Heinemann.

Bloom, A. D. (1987). *The closing of the American mind: How higher education has failed democracy and impoverished the souls of today's students*. New York: Simon & Schuster.

Bloom, B. (1956). *Taxonomy of educational objectives; the classification of educational goals*. New York: Longmans, Green.

Blythe, S. (2001). Designing online courses: User-centered practices. *Computers and Composition, 18*(4), 329–346.

Bolter, J. D. (1991). *Writing space: The computer, hypertext, and the history of writing*. Hillsdale, NJ: Lawrence Erlbaum Associates.

Bolter, J. D., & Grusin, R. A. (1999). *Remediation: Understanding new media*. Cambridge, MA: MIT Press.

Bomer, R. (1999). Writing to think critically. *Voices in the Middle, 6*(2), 2–8.

Bomer, R., & Bomer, K. (2001). *For a better world: Reading and writing for social action*. Portsmouth, NH: Heinemann.

Bowers, M. (2003, November 26). Seniors clearing SOL hurdle. *The Virginia-Pilot*, pp. A1, A16–A18.

Braddock, R., Lloyd-Jones, R., & Schoer, L. (1963). *Research in written composition*. Champaign, IL: National Council of Teachers of English.

Brandt, D. (1995). Accumulating literacy: Writing and learning to write in the twentieth century. *College English, 57*(6), 649–668.

Britton, J. N. (1970). *Language and learning*. London: Allen Lane.

Broad, B. (2003). *What we really value: Beyond rubrics in teaching and assessing writing*. Logan, UT: Utah State University Press.

Bromley, H. E., & Apple, M. W. E. (1998). *Education/technology/power: Educational computing as a social practice. SUNY series: Frontiers in education*. New York: State University of New York Press.

Brown, J. S., & Duguid, P. (2002). *The social life of information*. Boston: Harvard Business School Press.

Bruce, B., Michaels, S., & Watson-Gegeo, K. (1984). Reviewing the black history show: How computers can change the writing process (Tech. Rep. No. 320). Urbana, IL: Illinois University Center for the Study of Reading.

Bruce, B., & Rubin, A. (1993). *Electronic quills: A situated evaluation of using computers for writing in classrooms*. Hillsdale, NJ: Lawrence Erlbaum Associates.

Bruffee, K. A. (1973). Collaborative learning: Some practical methods. *College English, 34*(5), 634–643.

Bruffee, K. A. (1984). Collaborative learning and the "conversation of mankind." *College English, 46*(7), 635–653.

Bruffee, K. A. (1993). *Collaborative learning: Higher education, interdependence, and the authority of knowledge*. Baltimore: Johns Hopkins University Press.

Burstein, J., Kukich, K., Braden-Harder, L., Chodorow, M., Hua, S., & Kaplan, B. (1998). *Computer analysis of essay content for automatic score prediction: A prototype automated scoring system for GMAT analytic writing assessment* (RR-98-15). Princeton, NJ: Educational Testing Service.

Burstein, J., Kukich, K., Wolff, S., Lu, C., Chodorow, M., & Braden-Harder, L. (1998). Automated scoring using a hybrid feature identification technique. *Proceedings of the 36th annual meeting of the Association of Computational Linguistics*, Montreal, Canada, 206–210.

Burstein, J., & Marcu, D. (2003). A machine learning approach for identification of thesis and conclusion statements in student essays. *Computer and the Humanities, 37*(4), 455–467.

Burstein, J., Marcu, D., Andreyev, S., & Chodorow, M. (2001). Towards automatic classification of discourse elements in essays. *Proceedings of the 39th annual meeting of the Association for Computational Linguistics*, France, 90–92.

Calvino, I. (1981). *If on a winter's night a traveler*. New York: Harcourt Brace Jovanovich.

Cambridge, B. L., Kahn, S., Tompkins, D. P., & Yancey, K. B. (2001). *Electronic portfolios: Emerging practices in student, faculty, and institutional learning*. Washington, DC: American Association for Higher Education.

Cheney, L. V. (1992). *Telling the truth*. Washington, DC: National Endowment for the Humanities.

Cheney, L. V. (1995). *Telling the truth: Why our culture and our country have stopped making sense, and what we can do about it*. New York: Simon & Schuster.

Cintorino, M. A. (1993). Getting together, getting along, getting to the business of teaching and learning. *English Journal, 82*(1), 23–32.

Cizok, G. J., & Page, B. A. (2003). The concept of reliability in the context of automated essay scoring. In M. D. Shermis & J. Burstein (Eds.), *Automated essay scoring: A cross-disciplinary perspective* (pp. 125–146). Mahwah, NJ: Lawrence Erlbaum Associates.

College Board. (2003). The new SAT: Implemented for the class of 2006. New York: College Board.

Cooper, C. R., & Odell, L. (1977). *Evaluating writing: Describing, measuring, judging*. Urbana, IL: National Council of Teachers of English.

Cooper, M. M., & Selfe, C. L. (1990). Computer conferences and learning: Authority, resistance, and internally persuasive discourse. *College English, 52*(8), 847–869.

Cope, B., Kalantzis, M., & New London Group. (2000). *Multiliteracies: Literacy learning and the design of social futures*. London: Routledge.

Cronbach, L. J. (1988). Five perspectives on validity argument. In H. Wainer (Ed.), *Test validity* (pp. 3–17). Hillsdale, NJ: Lawrence Erlbaum Associates.

Cummins, J., & Sayers, D. (1995). *Brave new schools: Challenging cultural illiteracy through global learning networks*. New York: St. Martin's.

DeLillo, D. (1985). *White noise*. New York: Viking.

Dewey, J. (1933). *How we think, a restatement of the relation of reflective thinking to the educative process*. Boston: Heath.

Dewey, J. (1998). *How we think: A restatement of the relation of reflective thinking to the educative process*. Boston: Houghton Mifflin.

Diagnostic digital portfolio. (2000). Retrieved November 21, 2000, from http://ddp.alverno.edu/

Educational Testing Service. (2002). *Digital transformation: A framework for ICT literacy*. Princeton, NJ: ETS.

Eggers, D. (2001). *A heartbreaking work of staggering genius*. New York: Knopf.

Egnatoff, W. J. (1992). Technology education for democracy. *Canadian Journal of Educational Communication, 21*(3), 195–205.

Elbow, P. (1997). Writing assessment in the 21st century: A utopian view. In L. Z. Bloom, D. A. Daiker, & E. M. White (Eds.), *Composition in the twenty-first century crisis and change* (pp. 83–101). Carbondale, IL: Southern Illinois University Press.

Elbow, P., & Belanoff, P. (1986). Portfolios as a substitute for proficiency examinations. *College Composition and Communication, 37*(3), 336–339.

English standards of learning. (2000). Retrieved January 12, 2002, from http://www.pen.k12.va.us/VDOE/Instruction/solscope/

Faigley, L. (1992). *Fragments of rationality: Postmodernity and the subject of composition.* Pittsburgh: University of Pittsburgh Press.

Faigley, L., George, D., Palchik, A., & Selfe, C. (2004). *Picturing texts.* New York: Norton.

Fairtest. (2003). *The SAT: Questions and answers.* Retrieved July 9, 2003, from http://www.fairtest.org/facts/satfact.htm

Finding proof in the pudding: The viability of reform in higher education. (1997). *Change, 29*(1), 57–60.

Finn, P. J. (1977). Computer-aided description of mature word choices in writing. In C. R. Cooper & L. Odell (Eds.), *Evaluating writing: Describing, measuring, judging.* Urbana, IL: NCTE.

Fish, S. E. (1980). *Is there a text in this class?: The authority of interpretive communities.* Cambridge, MA: Harvard University Press.

Flower, L., & Hayes, J. R. (1980). The cognition of discovery: Defining a rhetorical problem. *College Composition and Communication, 31*(1), 21–32.

Flower, L. S., & Hayes, J. R. (1977). Problem-solving strategies and the writing process. *College English, 39*(4), 449–461.

Flower, L. S., & Hayes, J. R. (1979). *A process model of composition* (Tech. Rep. No. 1). Pittsburgh, PA.

Foltz, P. W., Kintsch, W., & Landauer, T. K. (1998). The measurement of textual coherence with latent semantic analysis. *Discourse Processes, 25*(2–3), 285–307.

Foucault, M. (1979). *Discipline and punish: The birth of the prison* (A. Sheridan, Trans.). New York: Vintage.

Freinet, C., Clandfield, D., & Sivell, J. (1990). *Cooperative learning and social change: Selected writings of Célestin Freinet.* Toronto: Our Schools/Our Selves Education Foundation.

Freire, P. (1970). *Pedagogy of the oppressed.* New York: Herder & Herder.

Freire, P., & Faundez, A. (1989). *Learning to question: A pedagogy of liberation.* New York: Continuum.

Freire, P., & Shor, I. (1987). *A pedagogy for liberation: Dialogues on transforming education.* South Hadley, MA: Macmillan.

Gale, I. F. (1967). *An experimental study of two fifth-grade language-arts programs: An analysis of the writing of children taught linguistic grammars compared to those taught traditional grammar.* Muncie, IN: Ball State University. (Unpublished)

Galinsky, E. (1999). *Ask the children: What America's children really think about working parents.* New York: William Morrow.

Gardner, H. (1983). *Frames of mind: The theory of multiple intelligences.* New York: Basic Books.

Gardner, H. (1991). *The unschooled mind: How children think and how schools should teach.* New York: Basic Books.

Gardner, H. (1999). *Intelligence reframed: Multiple intelligences for the 21st century.* New York: Basic Books.

Gardner, H., & Perkins, D. N. (1989). *Art, mind, and education: Research from Project Zero.* Urbana, IL: University of Illinois Press.

Gardner, J. (2001). *Good work: When excellence and ethics meet.* New York: Basic Books.

Gee, J. P. (1988). Discourse systems and aspirin bottles: On literacy. *Journal of Education, 170*(1), 27–40.

Gee, J. P. (2001). Reading as situated language: A sociocognitive perspective. *Journal of Adolescent & Adult Literacy, 44*(8), 714–725.

Gee, J. P. (2003). *What video games have to teach us about learning and literacy.* New York: Palgrave Macmillan.

Gershenfeld, N. A. (1999). *When things start to think.* New York: Holt.

Gladwell, M. (2000). *The tipping point: How little things can make a big difference.* London: Little Brown.

Goodwin, M. H. (1990). *He-said-she-said: Talk as social organization among Black children.* Bloomington: Indiana University Press.

Greenberg, K. L. (1988). Assessing writing: Theory and practice. *New Directions for Teaching and Learning,* 47–58.

Greenberg, K. L. (1992). Validity and reliability issues in the direct assessment of writing. *WPA: Writing Program Administration, 16*(1–2), 7–22.

Greenberg, K. L. (1993). The politics of basic writing. *Journal of Basic Writing, 12*(1), 64–71.

Gruber, L. C. (1992, March). *Shaping the portfolio course: The uses of direct assessment and the portfolio as a critical thinking tool.* Paper presented at the 43rd annual meeting of the Conference on College Composition and Communication, Cincinnati, OH.

Halio, M. P. (1990). Student writing: Can the machine maim the message? *Academic Computing, 4*(1), 16–19, 45, 52–53.

Hamp-Lyons, L. (2000). Social, professional and individual responsibility in language testing. *System, 28*(4), 579–591.

Hamp-Lyons, L., & Condon, W. (1999). *Assessing the portfolio: Principles for practice, theory, and research.* Cresskill, NJ: Hampton Press.

Hawisher, G. E., & Moran, C. (1993). Electronic mail and the writing instructor. *College English, 55*(6), 627–643.

Hawisher, G. E., & Selfe, C. L. (1999a). *Global literacies and the World Wide Web.* London: Routledge.

Hawisher, G. E., & Selfe, C. L. (1999b). *Passions, pedagogies, and 21st century technologies.* Urbana, IL: National Council of Teachers of English.

Hawk, B. (Ed.). (2002). *Enculturation.* 4.2. Retrieved January 12, 2004, from http://enculturation.gmu.edu/4_2/

Hayasaki, E. (2003). Reading, 'riting, and Rap. *L.A. Times,* January 14, pp. 1, 16, 11.

Hayes, R. L. (n.d.). *First grade cross generational project.* Retrieved June 4, 2003, from http://nsn.bbn.com/community/call_stories/stories_intro.shtml

Herrington, A., & Moran, C. (2001). What happens when machines read our students' writing? *College English, 63*(4), 480–499.

Hillocks, G. (2002). *The testing trap: How state writing assessments control learning.* New York: Teachers College Press.

Hirsch, E. D. J. (2003). The fourth-grade plunge: The cause. The cure. *American Educator, 27*(1), 10–13, 16–22, 28–29.

Holtzman, S. R. (1997). *Digital mosaics: The aesthetics of cyberspace.* New York: Simon & Schuster.

hooks, b. (1994). *Teaching to transgress: Education as the practice of freedom.* New York: Routledge.

hooks, b., & Barlow, J. P. (1995). bell hooks and John Perry Barlow. *Shambhala Sun.* Retrieved August 23, 2004, from http://www.shambhalasun.com/Archives/Features/1995/Sept95/bellhooks.htm

Huot, B. (1996). Toward a new theory of writing assessment. *College Composition and Communication, 47*(4), 549–566.

Huot, B. A. (2002). *(Re)articulating writing assessment for teaching and learning.* Logan, UT: Utah State University Press.

Huot, B., & Yancey, K. B. (1998). Construction, deconstruction, and (over)determination: A Foucaultian analysis of grades. In F. Zak & C. C. Weaver (Eds.), *The theory and practice of grading writing: Problems and possibilities* (pp. 39–52). Albany, NY: SUNY Press.

Hutchings, P. (1996). *Making teaching community property: A menu for peer collaboration and peer review. AAHE Teaching Initiative.* District of Columbia: American Association for Higher Education.

Iannozzi, M. (1997). *Policy perspectives. exemplars. Alverno College.* Philadelphia, PA: Pew Higher Education Roundtable.

Iser, W. (1989). *Prospecting: From reader response to literary anthropology.* Baltimore: Johns Hopkins University Press.

Johns, A. M. (1997). *Text, role, and context: Developing academic literacies.* Cambridge, England: Cambridge University Press.

Joyce, M. (1988). Siren shapes: Exploratory and constructive hypertexts. *Academic Computing, 3*(4), 10–14, 37–42.

Joyce, M. (1995). *Of two minds: Hypertext pedagogy and poetics.* Ann Arbor, MI: University of Michigan Press.

Kahn-Egan, S. (1998). Pedagogy of the pissed: Punk pedagogy in the first-year writing classroom. *College Composition and Communication, 49*(1), 99–103.

Keats, J. (1817). Letter to George and Thomas Keats. December 21. Retrieved August 31, 2004, from http://en.wikipedia.org/wiki/Negative_Capability

Kent, T. (1999). *Post-process theory beyond the writing-process paradigm.* Retrieved May 15, 2003, from http://www.netLibrary.com/urlapi.asp?action=summary&v=1&bookid=45752

Kimball, M. A. (2003). *The Web portfolio guide: Creating electronic portfolios for the Web.* New York: Longman.

King, M. L., & Martin Luther King Jr. Center for Nonviolent Social Change. (1987). *The papers of Dr. Martin Luther King, Jr.: Speeches, sermons, articles, statements, 1954–1968.* Atlanta, GA: Martin Luther King Jr. Center for Nonviolent Social Change.

Kintsch, W. (1998). *Comprehension: A paradigm for cognition.* Cambridge, England: Cambridge University Press.

Kozol, J. (1995). *Amazing grace: The lives of children and the conscience of a nation.* New York: Crown.

Kress, G. (2000). Design and transformation: New theories of meaning. In B. Cope, M. Kalantzis, & N. L. Group (Eds.), *Multiliteracies: Literacy learning and the design of social futures* (pp. 153–161). London: Routledge.

Kress, G. R. (2001). *Multimodal teaching and learning: The rhetorics of the science classroom.* London: Continuum.

Kress, G. R. (2003). *Literacy in the new media age.* London: Routledge.

Kress, G. R., & Van Leeuwen, T. (2001). *Multimodal discourse: The modes and media of contemporary communication.* London: Oxford University Press.

Lacan, J. (1981). The four fundamental concepts of psycho-analysis. (J.-A. Miller, Ed., & Alan Sheridan, Trans). New York: Norton.

Landauer, T. K. (1999). Latent semantic analysis: A theory of the psychology of language and mind. *Discourse Processes, 27*(3), 303–310.

Landauer, T. K., & Dumais, S. T. (1997). A solution to Plato's problem: The latent semantic analysis theory of acquisition, induction, and representation of knowledge. *Psychological Review, 104*(2), 211–240.

Landauer, T. K., Foltz, P. W., & Laham, D. (1998). An introduction to latent semantic analysis. *Discourse Processes, 25*(2–3), 259–284.

Landauer, T. K., Laham, D., & Foltz, P. W. (2003). Automated Scoring and Annotation of Essays with the Intelligent Essay Assessor. In M. D. Shermis & J. Burstein (Eds.), *Automated essay scoring: A cross-disciplinary perspective* (pp. 87–112). Mahwah, NJ: Lawrence Erlbaum Associates.

Landow, G. P. (1989). Hypertext in literary education, criticism, and scholarship. *Computers and the Humanities, 23,* 173–198.

Landow, G. P. (1992). *Hypertext: The convergence of contemporary critical theory and technology.* Baltimore: Johns Hopkins University Press.

Landow, G. P. (1997). *Hypertext 2.0* (Rev., amplified ed.). Baltimore: Johns Hopkins University Press.

Lanham, R. A. (1989). Electronic word: Literary study and the digital revolution. *New Literary History, 20,* 265–290.

Lanham, R. A. (1993). *The electronic word: Democracy, technology, and the arts.* Chicago: University of Chicago Press.

Lannoy, R. (1971). *The speaking tree: A study of Indian culture and society.* London: Oxford University Press.

Lave, J. (1982). *The mature practice of arithmetic problem solving in the daily lives of Americans. Final report.* University of California, Irvine, School of Social Sciences.

Lave, J. (1985). Introduction: Situationally specific practice. *Anthropology and Education Quarterly, 16*(3), 171–176.

Lave, J. (1988). *Cognition in practice: Mind, mathematics, and culture in everyday life.* Cambridge, England: Cambridge University Press.

Lévinas, E. (1969). *Totality and infinity; an essay on exteriority.* Pittsburgh: Duquesne University Press.

Lindemann, E. (1987). *A rhetoric for writing teachers* (2nd ed.). New York: Oxford University Press.

Lunsford, A. A. (2002). *The everyday writer* (2nd ed.). Boston: Bedford/St. Martin's.

Lunsford, A., & Ruszkiewicz, J. (2003). *Everything's an argument.* Boston: Bedford/St. Martin's.

MacDonald, H. (1998). CUNY could be great again. *City Journal, 8*(1), 65–70.

Macrorie, K. (1970a). Percival: The limits of behaviorism. *Media and Method, 6,* 7, 45–46.

Macrorie, K. (1970b). *Uptaught.* New York: Hayden.

Macrorie, K. (1975). Strangling the Engfish. *Media and Methods, 12,* 3, 12, 14, 55.

Malkin, M. (2003, January 17). Hip-hop hogwash in the schools. *Virginia Pilot.*

Marshall, J. D. (1991). *Discussions of literature in middle-track classrooms. Report series 2.17.* Albany, NY: Center for the Learning and Teaching of Literature, SUNY.

Mayo, L. (2001). Using the Internet to teach for social justice. *Kairos: A Journal for Teachers of Writing in Webbed Environments, 6*(2). Retrieved May 12, 2002, from http://english.ttu.edu/kairos/6.2/binder2.html?coverweb/k16/mayo/index.htm.

McGee, T., & Ericsson, P. (2002). The politics of the program: MS WORD as the invisible grammarian. *Computers and Composition, 19*(4), 453–470.

Mehan, H. (1979). "What time is it, Denise?": Asking known information questions in classroom discourse. *Theory into Practice, 18*(4), 285–294.

Morrell, E., & Duncan-Andrade, J. M. R. (2002). Promoting academic literacy with urban youth through engaging hip-hop culture. *English Journal, 91*(6), 88–92.

Moss, P. A. (1995). Themes and variations in validity theory. *Educational Measurement: Issues and Practice, 14*(2), 5–13.

Moss, P. A. (1998). The role of consequences in validity theory. *Educational Measurement: Issues and Practice, 17*(2), 6–12.

Moulthrop, S., & Kaplan, N. (1994). They became what they beheld: The futility of resistance in the space of electronic writing. In C. L. Selfe & S. Hilligoss (Eds.), *Literacy and computers: The complications of teaching and learning with technology* (pp. 220–237). New York: MLA.

Murray, J. H. (1997). *Hamlet on the holodeck: The future of narrative in cyberspace.* New York: The Free Press.

Nas: Tupac better than Shakespeare. (2002). Retrieved December 4, 2003, from http://www.mtvasia.com/news/International/Items/0212/0212012.html

The neglected "R": The need for a writing revolution. (2003). National Commission on Writing in America's Schools and Colleges, College Board.

Nellen, T. (2001). *A view from Pakistani scholars.* Retrieved December 1, 2001, from http://www.tnellen.net/pakistan/

New London Group. (1996). A pedagogy of multiliteracies: Designing social futures. *Harvard Educational Review, 66*(1), 60–93.

Nielsen, J., Schemenaur, P. J., & Fox, J. (1999). *Writing for the Web*. Retrieved July 14, 2002, from http://www.sun.com/980713/webwriting/

No Child Left Behind. (2001). Retrieved July 1, 2003, from http://www.ed.gov/offices/OESE/esea/

Open Source Portfolio Initiative. (2003). Retrieved April 17, 2003, from http://www.theospi.org/

Page, E. B. (1966). Grading essays by computer: Progress report. Educational Testing Services (Ed.), *Proceedings of the Invitational Conference on Testing Problems* (pp. 87–100). October 1966, New York City. Princeton, NJ: Educational Testing Services.

Page, E. B., & Paulus, D. H. (1968). *The analysis of essays by computer. Final report*. University of Connecticut, Storrs.

Page, E. B., Poggio, J. P., Keith, T. Z. (1997). Computer analysis of student essays: Finding trait differences in student profile. ERIC Document Reproduction Service. ED 411 316.

Petraglia, J. (1998). *Reality by design the rhetoric and technology of authenticity in education*. Retrieved May 1, 2000, from http://www.netLibrary.com/urlapi.asp?action=summary&v=1&bookid =24266

Profile. (2000). Retrieved July 29, 2002, from http://www.abrahambeame.lagcc.cuny.edu/beame/

Ragland, E. (1994). Psycholoanalysis and pedagogy: What are mastery and love doing in the classroom? *Pretext: A Journal of Rhetorical Theory, 15*(1–2), 46–79.

Recht, D. R., & Leslie, L. (1988). Effect of prior knowledge on good and poor readers' memory of text. *Journal of Educational Psychology, 80*(1), 16–20.

Reich, R. (2000). *The future of success*. New York: Knopf.

Reynolds, A. (1997, March). *Testimony by Chancellor W. Ann Reynolds, the City University of New York before the City Council Committees on Education and Finance*. Retrieved July 20, 2002, from http://www.cuny.edu/textonly/abtcuny/ff/archive/council.html

Rice, J. (2003). The 1963 hip-hop machine: Hip-hop pedagogy as composition. *College Composition and Communication, 54*(3), 453–471.

Rice, R. A. (2001). Composing the intranet-based electronic portfolio using "common" tools. In B. Cambridge (Ed.), *Electronic portfolios*. Washington, DC: AAHE.

Rice, R. A. (2002). *Teaching and learning first-year composition with digital portfolios*. Unpublished dissertation, Muncie, IN: Ball State University.

Russell, D. R. (1991). *Writing in the academic disciplines, 1870–1990: A curricular history*. Carbondale, IL: Southern Illinois University Press.

Salvo, M. J. (2001). Ethics of engagement: User-centered design and rhetorical methodology. *Technical Communication Quarterly, 10*(3), 273–290.

Selfe, C. L. (1999). *Technology and literacy in the twenty-first century: The importance of paying attention*. Carbondale, IL: Southern Illinois University Press.

Shakespeare in Love METASCORE 82. (1998). Retrieved May 12, 2003, from http://www.metacritic.com/video/titles/shakespeare/

Shapiro, D. (1994). *After a lost original*. Woodstock, NY: Overlook Press.

Shaughnessy, M. P. (1977). *Errors and expectations: A guide for the teacher of basic writing*. New York: Oxford University Press.

Shermis, M. D., & Burstein, J. (2003). *Automated essay scoring: A cross-disciplinary perspective*. Hillsdale, NJ: Lawrence Erlbaum Associates.

Shor, I. (1980). *Critical teaching and everyday life*. Montreal: Black Rose Press.

Shor, I. (1987). *Freire for the classroom: A sourcebook for liberatory teaching*. Boston: Heinemann.

Shor, I. (1992). *Empowering education: Critical teaching for social change*. Chicago: University of Chicago Press.

Shor, I. (1996). *When students have power: Negotiating authority in a critical pedagogy*. Chicago: University of Chicago Press.

Sirc, G. (1993). Writing classroom as A&P parking lot. *Pre-Text: A Journal of Rhetorical Theory, 14*(1–2), 27–70.

Sirc, G. (1995). The twin worlds of electronic conferencing. *Computers and Composition, 12*(3), 265–277.

Sirc, G. (1997). Never mind the tagmemics, where's the Sex Pistols? *College Composition and Communication, 48*(1), 9–29.

Sirc, G. (1998). Never mind the Sex Pistols, where's 2Pac? *College Composition and Communication, 49*(1), 5.

Sirc, G. (2000). Words & music. *Pre-Text: Electra(Lite), 3*(1). Retrieved June 15, 2002, from http://www.utdallas.edu/pretext/PT3.1/sirc.html.

Sirc, G. M. (2002). *English composition as a happening.* Logan, UT: Utah State University Press.

Smith, B. H. (1988). *Contingencies of value: Alternative perspectives for critical theory.* Cambridge, MA: Harvard University Press.

Socrates. (1956). *The great dialogues of Plato* (W. H. D. Rouse, Trans.). New York: Mentor.

Spooner, M., & Yancey, K. (1996). Postings on a genre of email. *College Composition and Communication, 47*(2), 252–278.

Suchman, L. A. (1987). *Plans and situated actions: The problem of human–machine communication.* Cambridge, England: Cambridge University Press.

Swales, J. (1998). *Other floors, other voices: A textography of a small university building.* Hillsdale, NJ: Lawrence Erlbaum Associates.

Syverson, M. A. (1999). *The wealth of reality an ecology of composition.* Carbondale, IL: Southern Illinois University Press.

Tchudi, S. (1983). The write idea: Computer assisted invention. *Focus: Teaching English Language Arts, 9*(3), 10–16.

Texas assessment of academic skills, exit level scoring guide for persuasive writing. (2001). Austin, TX: Texas Education Agency.

Thompson, D. (1990). Electronic bulletin boards: A timeless place for collaborative writing projects. *Computers and Composition, 7*(3), 43–53.

Toulmin, S. E. (1958). *The uses of argument.* Cambridge, England: University Press.

Toulmin, S. E. (2003). *The uses of argument* (updated ed.). New York: Cambridge University Press.

Tufte, E. R. (2003). Power corrupts: Powerpoint corrupts absolutely. *Wired, 11*(9), 118.

Turkel, S. (1997). *Working: People talk about what they do all day and how they feel about what they do.* New York: New Press.

Twenty-first century literacy summit: White paper. (2002). Berlin, Germany: Bertelsmann Foundation and AOL Time Warner Foundation.

Ulmer, G. L. (1985). *Applied grammatology: Post(e)-pedagogy from Jacques Derrida to Joseph Beuys.* Baltimore: Johns Hopkins University Press.

Ulmer, G. L. (1989). *Teletheory: Grammatology in the age of video.* New York: Routledge.

Ulmer, G. L. (2003). *Internet invention: From literacy to electracy.* New York: Longman.

Vassileva, I. (1998). Who am I/who are we in academic writing? A contrastive analysis of authorial presence in English, German, French, Russian, and Bulgarian. *International Journal of Applied Linguistics, 88*(2), 163–190.

Wajcman, J. (2000). Feminist perspective on technology. In A. H. Teich (Ed.), *Technology and the future* (8th ed., pp. 137–149). Boston: Bedford.

Walker, J. R., & Taylor, T. W. (1998). *The Columbia guide to online style.* New York: Columbia University Press.

White, E. M. (1985). *Teaching and assessing writing.* San Francisco: Jossey-Bass.

White, E. M. (1992). *Assigning, responding, evaluating: A writing teacher's guide (including diagnostic tests)* (2nd ed.). New York: St. Martin's.

White, E. M. (1994). *Teaching and assessing writing: Recent advances in understanding, evaluating, and improving student performance* (2nd ed.). San Francisco: Jossey-Bass.

White, R. H. (1964). *The effect of structural linguistics on improving English composition compared to that of the prescriptive grammar or the absence of grammar instruction.* Unpublished dissertation, University of Arizona, Tucson.

Whithaus, C. (1998). Hypertext conceals itself, it announces itself: Rhetoric and collaborative writing in the electronic classroom. *Kairos: A Journal for Teachers of Writing in Webbed Environments, 3*(2).

Whithaus, C. (2002). Think different/think differently: A tale of green squiggly lines, or evaluating student writing in computer-mediated environments. *academic.writing: Special Multi-Journal Issue of Enculturation, Academic.Writing, CCC Online, Kairos, and The Writing Instructor on Electronic Publication*. Retrieved July 7 2003, from http://wac.colostate.edu/aw/articles/whithaus2002/

Wikipedia. (2003). Retrieved July 7, 2003, from http://www.wikipedia.org

Winkelmann, C. L. (1995). Electronic literacy, critical pedagogy, and collaboration: A case for cyborg writing. *Computers and the Humanities, 29*(6), 431–448.

Wohlpart, J. (2004). The use of technology to redesign a humanities class: Strategies for reducing costs and increasing learning. Course Redesign Symposium. Seton Hall University. Retrieved July 18, 2004, from http://technology.shu.edu/webs/tech/mainengine.nsf/resources/PowerPoint/$file/Course+Redesign+Symp+5.5.04+WHOPART.ppt

Wysocki, A., & Johnson-Eilola, J. (1999). Blinded by the letter. In G. E. Hawisher & C. L. Selfe (Eds.), *Passions, pedagogies, and 21st century technologies* (pp. 349–368). Urbana, IL: National Council of Teachers of English.

Yancey, K. B. (1992). *Portfolios in the writing classroom: An introduction*. Urbana, IL: National Council of Teachers of English.

Yancey, K. B., & Huot, B. A. (1997). *Assessing writing across the curriculum: Diverse approaches and practices*. Greenwich, CT: Ablex.

Yancey, K., & Spooner, M. (1996). Postings on the genre of email. *College Composition and Communication, 47*(2), 252–279.

Author Index

163

Subject Index